# The Sling and The Stone

## On War in the 21st Century

# The Sling and The Stone

## On War in the 21st Century

Col Thomas X. Hammes, USMC

*(Published in collaboration with Zenith Press, an imprint of MBI Publishing Company)*

**Manas Publications**
**New Delhi - 110 002 (India)**

**MANAS PUBLICATIONS**

(Publishers-Distributors-Importers-Exporters)

4402/5-A, Ansari Road (Opp. HDFC Bank)
Darya Ganj, New Delhi - 110 002 (India)
**Phones: Off.: 011-23260783, 23265523,**
**Res.: 011-23842660**
**E-mail: manaspublications@gmail.com**
**manaspub6@gmail.com**
**www.manaspublications.in**

Published in collaboration with Zenith Press, an imprint of MBI Publishing Company



**ISBN** 81-7049-282-3 **(10 Digit ISBN)**
978-81-7049-282-5 **(13 Digit ISBN)**

**Rs. 495/-**



*Designed at*

**Manas Publications**

*Printed in India at*
RK Offsets, Delhi
and published by Mrs Suman Lata for
**Manas Publications,** 4402/5-A,
Ansari Road (Opp HDFC Bank),

# Contents

# Introduction

I joined the Marine Corps in June 1975, only a month after the fall of South Vietnam. As I reported to The Basic School, the war that had shaped my high school and college years was finally over. Although the Corps' basic officer training continued to emphasize counter-insurgency tactics, it was clear the country as a whole was tired of dealing with or thinking about counterinsurgency. Then in 1976, Martin Binkin and Jeffrey Record published "Where Does the Marine Corps Go from Here?" which seemed to question not only the need for counterinsurgent forces but for the Corps itself. In fact, the military as a whole was moving out smartly to prepare to fight the Soviets in Europe.

During my first years of service, the Corps shifted focus from small wars to fighting a huge conventional conflict. However, despite the apparent focus on Europe, our defeat in Vietnam remained a major shadow over our forces. Most of the company commanders and all the field grade and general officers who led the Corps during that period had been shaped by their Vietnam experiences. All were frustrated by our defeat and many were striving to understand why. For my part, I too was trying to figure out how the most powerful nation in the world had been defeated by a tiny country with only twenty-two million people and almost no economic power. In almost two hundred years, America had never lost a war—until Vietnam. What had happened?

This was the beginning of my study of what has become known as fourth-generation warfare. Like many military professionals of my generation, I was trying to understand a type of warfare that seemed to change all the rules. In Vietnam, the side with overwhelming wealth, power, and technology had been decisively defeated. We had won the battles but lost the war. One had to wonder what that meant for all traditional concepts of warfare.

For the first ten years of my career, it was very difficult to find material on insurgency. The U.S. armed forces were preparing to fight the Soviet Union in Europe and the Marine Corps was striving to master maneuver warfare concepts. There was plenty of material on big wars but information on small wars could be found only in used bookstores.

Then, in 1986, I was fortunate enough to be offered a fellowship at the Mershon Center for Strategic Studies. I spent the academic year of 1986–87 studying insurgency. This year provided me the opportunity for my first in-depth study of the early practitioners of this new form of war. Mao, Ho, the Sandinistas, the IRA, and the Palestinians shaped my ideas about the future of war. The result was a paper written to clarify my thoughts on insurgency and how a democracy could respond to it. I condensed it to an article for publication in the March 1988 issue of the *Marine Corps Gazette* titled "Insurgency: The Forgotten Threat."

From 1987 to 1990, I got a small taste of the practical aspects of insurgency. I spent those years training insurgents in various locations of the world. This was the tail end of the Cold War and the United States still had vested interests in the outcome of a number of insurgencies. The most intriguing part of that tour was the opportunity to talk to these men. I was particularly impressed with two aspects of the men I met. First was their utter determination to continue the struggle despite the odds. They were not deterred by fear of death. In each case, they were engaged in a struggle with a government force that possessed many times their military power. In each case, they knew the odds and were not deterred. They believed in their cause and were sure that belief was powerful enough to defeat the government. The idea they fought for was central to their resistance. In fact, they were counting on political power generated by that idea to neutralize the overwhelming military power of the government. As I worked with these men, I realized this fact should be obvious to Americans. An idea kept our American revolution alive during seven long years of war.

The second outstanding trait was the remarkable ingenuity they displayed for overcoming problems. Whether the problems were tactical, logistical, doctrinal, or political, they often attacked them from a direction that simply would not occur to a Western-trained soldier. I found insurgents are not impressed with conventional power. They respect it but seek ways around it—and have consistently succeeded in finding those ways. They often used tactics and techniques that were outside the training and experience of the government forces. Despite years of war, they consistently surprised government forces with their ingenuity and determination. Insurgents are living proof why of man is at the top of the food chain. We are the most creative, treacherous, loyal, aggressive, and determined life form to yet evolve. Any nation that assumes it is inherently superior to another is setting itself up for disaster.

This period of practical interaction with insurgents provided a strong verification of much of what I had learned during my year of study at Mershon. The experience also convinced me more than ever that the real threat to American interests were not conventional forces but unconventional ones. Conventional enemies exposed themselves to our military strengths. Insurgents found ways around them. The danger lay in our thinking in conventional terms and seeking to dominate that battlefield at the expense of being prepared to fight on other fields.

Upon completion of this assignment, I went to the Marine Corps Command and Staff College. Just as I arrived, Saddam Hussein invaded Kuwait. The forces we had built to confront the Soviets on the plains of Europe were superbly suited for a high-intensity war in the desert. The amazing success of our forces against the Iraqi military confirmed the U.S. faith in high-technology weapons. Thousands of gun camera clips showing precision weapons flying into the doors and windows of targets vindicated years of research and development. The most highly touted "lesson" of that war was the domination possible if you had the right high-technology equipment. Between trumpeting the lessons of our victory in the Gulf and struggling with the major reduction that followed the war, the services simply ceased to pay any attention to unconventional warfare. Unfortunately, unconventional warfare was not finished with U.S. forces.

This led directly to my next encounter with 4GW. In January 1992, I deployed with Marine Forces Somalia to Mogadishu. After three years of training and learning from insurgents, this was an opportunity to see insurgency from the government side. When I was in Somalia from January to May 1993, allied forces were under U.S. command and succeeded in bringing a modicum of order to what was an exceptionally fragmented tribal society. The level of fragmentation was remarkable, and sadly, marked by the savagery characteristic of conflicts between closely related enemies. The two main warlords, Aideed and Ali Mahdi, were not of different tribes or even different clans. They were members of different sub-clans of the same clan. Despite this close association, they were deadly enemies bent on destroying Mogadishu in an attempt to control it. Essentially, Somali society had descended into chaos.

Operations in Somalia revealed both the complexity inherent in such a conflict and in the techniques that could be used to control it. During the first five months, the U.S.-led U.N. forces took firm control of the country. The key was a unified command where the political, military, and humanitarian organizations coordinated closely and understood the nature of the conflict they were involved in. On the security side, the extensive use of human intelligence sources and aggressive, round-the-clock saturation patrolling allowed us to gain control of Mogadishu. These tactics made use of the strengths of our Marines. They did well as "beat cops" getting to know the neighborhoods they patrolled. They learned who should and should not be there. Their constant presence allowed a semblance of normalcy to return to the streets of Mogadishu and the outlying cities.

Unfortunately, exactly as most had predicted would happen, when the U.N. took over, aggressive patrolling and constant contact with the people that had been the key to U.S. success ceased to be the norm. U.N. forces withdrew into cantonments and counted on their superior conventional power to protect them from the tribal insurgents. They ceded the ground outside the U.N. camps to the Somalis. The outcome was inevitable—defeat and withdrawal. And even with the withdrawal of U.N. forces, the conflict continues today. Somalia is yet another example of the long time lines involved in fourth-generation war.

Upon completion of my tour in Somalia, I attended the National Defence College of Canada. This was an eye-opening experience. Because Canada's forces are small, the Defence College focused on how international society and Canadian society interact. What makes each work? How can each be influenced for the good? Although this may seem an odd course of instruction for a "war" college, the fact that Canada, a country with only thirty million people, is a significant player in many international forums speaks highly of this strategic approach. Less than 10 percent of the course was spent on purely military matters. As a result, I was provided a much broader education than normally given in U.S. war colleges. The college also required a year-long research effort on a subject of the student's choosing —and allowed significant blocks of time for research and writing.

Based on extensive reading and professional discussions, I was convinced that another generation of war was evolving. Further, I thought we could actually trace that evolution. During that year in Canada, U.S. forces were ambushed in Mogadishu and it became clear the United States was leaving Somalia. Once again, a militarily weak force had used fourth-generation warfare to defeat significantly more powerful conventional forces. As the academic year in Canada progressed, I expanded on the research I had done at Mershon and developed my ideas concerning fourth-generation warfare as my required course paper. Subsequently, I shortened the paper for publication in the September 1994 *Marine Corps Gazette* as "The Evolution of War: Into the Fourth Generation." That paper and the subsequent article laid out the basic thesis of this book—warfare evolves from generation to generation. Further, it is genuine evolution. The "revolutions in military affairs" so prominent in our discussion of defense today were not revolutions at all. Rather they were the culmination of practical men seeking practical solutions to tactical and operational problems of their day. As these solutions accumulated, they evolved into the "revolutionary" techniques we discuss so imprecisely. Further investigation showed that the evolution of each generation of war required a preceding evolution in the political, economic, social, and technical structure of the society that uses that type of war. War evolves in consonance with society as a whole.

Over the last ten years, I continued to read about and study the evolution of war. Conflicts around the world seemed to confirm that warfare is indeed evolving. Unfortunately, despite the fact that some of these conflicts involved direct attacks on the United States, our defense establishment chose to ignore them. We preferred to focus on our tactical success in the wars with Iraq and the amazing high-technology weapons we were developing. We did not want to deal with the manpower intensive, low-technology conflicts that were actually taking place around the world. It was much more comfortable to theorize about future high-technology conflicts with "near peer competitors."

Then these low-tech conflicts moved from overseas to the heart of America. I, like most Americans, felt the first visceral impact of 4GW on September 11, 2001. That morning, I was in a staff meeting at the U.S. Marine Corps' Chemical Biological Incident Response Force (CBIRF). The briefing was just getting started when, at 8:45 a.m., one of the Marines in the intelligence section stepped in to inform us CNN was reporting an aircraft had struck the World Trade Center. We immediately shifted our attention to the drama unfolding live on TV. It was particularly poignant because during August CBIRF had conducted a major training exercise with the fire department of New York—which had included a discussion of their response to the 1993 World Trade Center attack. We knew many of our friends would be responding again.

While we monitored the situation, we also alerted the unit. The Chemical Biological Incident Response Force had been formed in 1996 specifically to support first responders during chemical or biological attacks. Since then the unit had expanded its capability to provide assistance in instances of chemical, biological, radiological, nuclear, and high-yield explosive (CBRNE) attacks.

Twenty-one minutes later the second aircraft hit. It was clear to the world this was a terrorist attack. By 9:45 a.m., minutes after the third aircraft hit the Pentagon, CBIRF's immediate response force was ready to roll—we needed only an order to do so. In fact, that order never came. The attack with the third aircraft on the Pentagon raised concerns that these attacks could be part of a much wider pattern. Soon it was obvious New York had all the help it could manage. CBIRF was rightly held in reserve in the event of a weapon of mass destruction attack in the capital region. This time CBIRF was not needed.

Less than a month later, the anthrax letters delivered to Capitol Hill rocketed terrorism back to the front pages. Although CBIRF specializes in the rescue of victims from a contaminated environment, our ability to operate in such an environment resulted in CBIRF being tasked to assist with the cleanup on Capitol Hill. We initially assisted with the biological sampling of the various office buildings, then removed twelve tons of contaminated mail from the P Street postal facility, and finally stripped Senator Daschle's office to the bare walls, ceiling, and floor for the final decontamination effort. The experience of moving through congressional offices, to include the office of the U.S. Senate majority leader, while wearing biological protective clothing and an air purification respirator, was surreal. It was also very thought provoking. The initial shock of the 9/11 attacks followed by the extended restoration efforts on Capitol Hill caused me to reflect on how warfare had changed in the twenty-six years I'd been in the Marine Corps—and why this attack should not have been a surprise.

I became more convinced than ever that we were facing not just a different kind of enemy but a fundamentally different type of warfare. The fourth generation of war had evolved over time as the logical outcome of the political, economic, social, and technological evolution since World War II. It is the type of warfare we face today and will face tomorrow. We do not need to rely on "visions" or gurus predicting the future. We can get a very good glimpse of our future defense needs by studying the recent past. We can trace a logical, coherent evolution from Mao to the events taking place in Iraq, Afghanistan, and Chechnya today. From this study, we can develop a better understanding of what the future holds and build our forces accordingly.

That is what I hope to accomplish with this book. I sought to organize and outline the results of more than twenty-five years of study of the evolution of war. It is the work of a practitioner not an academic—and its intent is to help fellow practitioners understand the threats we face today and those that are evolving. From that understanding, I hope we can learn to fight the low-tech, very human opponents we actually face rather than preparing to fight the high-tech, equipment-intensive enemy visualized by DOD and its colleagues in industry. Although I hope I have written it in a clear, coherent sequence, I can assure the reader that my thought process took many detours in an attempt to reach this point. It is not meant to be a definitive guide to what the fourth generation of war will look like—because like its predecessors, this generation of war will continue to evolve. It is simply meant to help the reader understand how war has evolved from the short, decisive campaigns of blitzkrieg to the decades long struggles of today.

One final caution—fourth-generation war is more than seventy years old and is reaching maturity. While we are only beginning to understand it clearly, history tells us the fifth generation has already begun to evolve.

## CHAPTER 1

# Four Generations of Warfare

On May 1, 2003, President Bush declared the end of major combat in Iraq. While most Americans rejoiced at this announcement, those who study history understood that it simply meant the easy part was over. In the months that followed, peace did not break out, and the troops did not come home. In fact, the Iraqis struck back hard. Instead of peace, each day Americans read about another soldier being killed, a car bomb killing dozens, civilians assassinated, and Iraqi unrest.

People were puzzled and angry. They felt that the war was over, so we should not be losing any more people. The Iraqis should embrace democracy, and the troops should come home. Some pundits described these attacks as unexpected and a new form of resistance. Conversely, others chastised the government for not being prepared for this level of disorder and resistance.

Then in late August, a series of bombs hit a police academy graduation, the Jordanian Embassy, and U.N. Headquarters in Baghdad. The Ayatollah Mohammed Bakr al-Hakim (leader of the Supreme Council for Islamic Revolution in Iraq) was killed by a bomb, and an attempt was made to kill the Baghdad chief of police. Some pointed out that this must be an orchestrated campaign to drive the United States and United Nations out of Iraq.

In rebuttal, pro-administration commentators maintained that the resistance was surprising and was a new type of problem but that we were adjusting. At the time of this writing (March 2004), coalition forces, rocked by large-scale resistance in several cities, struggle to provide security, while politicians struggle to set conditions for transferring authority from the Coalition Provisional Authority to some form of Iraqi government. The fact is that the war has entered a new phase. It has moved into the fourth generation.

Fourth-generation warfare (4GW) uses all available networks—political, economic, social, and military—to convince the enemy's political decision makers that their strategic goals are either unachievable or too costly for the perceived benefit. It is an evolved form of insurgency. Still rooted in the fundamental precept that superior political will, when properly employed, can defeat greater economic and military power, 4GW makes use of society's networks to carry on its fight. Unlike previous generations of warfare, it does not attempt to win by defeating the enemy's military forces. Instead, via the networks, it directly attacks the minds of enemy decision makers to destroy the enemy's political will. Fourth-generation wars are lengthy—measured in decades rather than months or years.

Clearly, 4GW is a very different concept from the short, intense war the administration planned for and celebrated by declaring the end of major combat on May 1, 2003.

At the same time things were degenerating in Iraq, the situation in Afghanistan was also moving into 4GW. Although the Afghans and the Taliban were not attacking U.S. troops directly, they were moving aggressively to defeat the Kharzai government that the United States had promised to support. The Taliban, al-Qaeda, and their supporters—having been decisively defeated in their conventional campaign against U.S. firepower—have gone back to the style of warfare that succeeded against the Soviets.

Over the same fall and winter of 2003–04, al-Qaeda and its affiliates managed a series of high-profile attacks in Saudi Arabia, Turkey, and Spain and were promising a major attack on the United States. Despite the Bush administration's declaration of victory in Iraq and Afghanistan, the overall campaign against terror did not seem to be going well.

As debilitating and regular as these attacks have been, this kind of warfare is not "new" or "surprising" but has been evolving around the world over the last seven decades. The wars in Afghanistan and Iraq have moved from comfortable third-generation warfare* (3GW), America's forte, to fourth-generation warfare, the only type of war America has ever lost. It is much too early to predict the outcome of our occupation of Iraq, or even if anti-coalition forces there are capable of tying the 4GW tactics they are using to an integrated 4GW strategic campaign.

Not only is 4GW the only kind of war America has ever lost, we have done so three times: Vietnam, Lebanon, and Somalia. This form of warfare has also defeated the French in Vietnam and Algeria and the USSR in Afghanistan. It continues to bleed Russia in Chechnya and the United States in Iraq, Afghanistan, and in other countries against the al-Qaeda network. The consistent defeat of major powers by much weaker fourth-generation opponents makes it essential to understand this new form of warfare and adapt accordingly.

There is nothing mysterious about 4GW. Like all wars, it seeks to change the enemy's political position. Like all wars, it uses available weapons systems to achieve that end. Like all wars, it reflects the society it is part of. Like all previous generations of war, it has evolved in consonance with society as a whole. It evolves because practical people solved specific problems related to their fights against much more powerful enemies. Practitioners created it, nurtured it, and have continued its development and growth. Faced with enemies they could not possibly beat using conventional war, they sought a different path.

Mao started this form of war, and each practitioner since has learned from his predecessors or co-combatants in various places in the world. Then, usually through a painful process of trial and error, each has adjusted the

* Third-generation warfare is maneuver warfare. All four generations of warfare are discussed in detail in the next chapter.

lessons to his own fight. Each added his own refinement, and the cumulative result is a new form of war. The anti-coalition forces in Iraq, the Taliban, the Chechnyans, and the al-Qaeda network are simply the latest to use the tactics and techniques that have been developing for decades.

Since World War II, wars have been a mixed bag of conventional and unconventional. The Korean War, the Israeli-Arab Wars of 1956, 1967, and 1973, the Falklands (Maldives) War, the Iran-Iraq War, and the first Gulf War ended with a return to the strategic status quo. Although some territory changed hands and, in some cases, regimes changed, in essence each state came out of the war with largely the same political, economic, and social structure with which it entered. In short, the strategic situation of the participants had not changed significantly.

In sharp contrast, unconventional wars—the Communist revolution in China, the first and second Indochinese Wars, the Algerian War of Independence, the Sandinista struggle in Nicaragua, the Iranian revolution, the Afghan-Soviet War of the 1980s, the first Intifada, and even Chechnya—display a different pattern. Each ended with major changes in the political, economic, and social structure of the territories involved. Although the changes may not have been for the better, they were distinct changes. Even unconventional wars where the insurgents lost (Malaysia, Oman, El Salvador) led to significant changes.

Operation Iraqi Freedom is really two wars. The U.S. started out fighting a high-tech, conventional war. The anti-coalition forces have turned it into a low-tech, 4GW struggle—and the outcome is still very much in doubt.

The message is clear for anyone wishing to shift the political balance of power: only unconventional war works against established powers. Not only does recent history show us that the trend is toward unconventional war, it even shows the strategic, operational, and tactical characteristics future war will take.

By studying these unconventional wars, we can see the evolution of this form of warfare. I use the term "evolution" deliberately. Despite all the talk about the revolution in military affairs, war changes over time. It evolves.

The fact that only unconventional or 4GW has succeeded against superpowers should be a key element in discussing the evolution of war.

Unfortunately, it has been largely absent from the debate within the U.S. Department of Defense (DOD). As the only Goliath left in the world, we should be worried that the world's Davids have found a sling and stone that work. Yet internal DOD debate has largely ignored this striking difference between the outcomes of conventional and unconventional conflicts. In fact, DOD has largely ignored unconventional warfare.

Fortunately, the academic community has engaged in a robust, opinionated debate concerning the future of war. Although most authors agree that warfare is clearly moving to the next era or generation, they strongly disagree about the reasons for the transition and the form it will take. They can agree that warfare is fundamentally changing but have not reached a consensus of what those changes are.

Instead, two principal schools of thought have emerged concerning the future of warfare, best described by J. Arquilla and D. Rondfeldt in their article "Cyberwar Is Coming." They note that there are two primary views of future war. One, cyberwar, envisions a high-technology, short-duration war where technology is vital and essentially machines fight machines. This is the prevalent view in the Department of Defense. It justifies the expensive weapons systems in use today and planned for the future. Unfortunately, it has no basis in history or current events.

In contrast, netwar, also known as fourth-generation war, or 4GW, is the complex, long-term type of conflict that has grown out of Mao's People's War. Its evolution and rise to dominance on the battlefield are the primary subjects of this book.

Before we begin a discussion of how fourth-generation war evolved and why our enemies use it against us, it is important to understand what DOD sees as the future of war and how they plan to prepare for it. The difference between what they envision and the wars we are actually fighting in Iraq, Afghanistan, and worldwide against terror is stark.

With the collapse of the Soviet Union, the Department of Defense struggled to redefine its mission and its force structure in the absence of the single, overwhelmingly dangerous threat the USSR presented. Instead of studying the human and organizational factors that led to the downfall of the Soviet Union, many analysts pointed to the USSR's inability to develop, produce, and finance the high-tech weapons systems necessary to keep up with the United States in our bipolar competition.

The Department of Defense, reinforced by the stunning success of advanced weaponry in the Gulf War, quickly gravitated to a high-tech version of war. After all, it played to the strength the United States had used to defeat both the Soviet Union and Iraq. The result has been more than ten years of "visions" that have consistently guided the Department of Defense toward cyberwar.

The so-called "revolution in military affairs," along with concepts articulated in *Joint Vision 2010, Joint Vision 2020,* DOD's "Transformation Planning Guidance," and "Network-Centric Warfare," show the evolution of official policy within the department. In each of these concepts, technology is seen as the primary driver of change. In particular, these concepts see increased technical capabilities of command and control as the key factor shaping future war.

In its introduction, *Joint Vision 2010** states, "This vision of future warfighting embodies the improved intelligence and command and control available in the Information Age and goes on to develop four operational concepts: dominant maneuver, precision engagement, full-dimension protection, and focused logistics."[1]

The focus of the entire document is on the application of command and control technology, to provide the commander with information dominance to enable the four operational concepts. Unfortunately, although *JV 2010* talks extensively about the four concepts, it spends little time explaining how U.S. forces will achieve the information dominance that is the foundation of the vision.

A cynic might say that the failure to address the issue of information dominance is a bit like the failure to critique the emperor's new clothes.

* Although dated, *JV 2010* was the guiding principle for the development of weapons, organizations, and training during the 1990s. The legacy lives on in the forces we field today.

Everyone knows there is not much there but is reluctant to address the issue. A genuine discussion of "information dominance" requires trying to understand and predict the complicated, increasingly fragmented, all-too-human real world.

Because *JV 2010* clearly prefers technology to people, it is a bit awkward to address the fact that information collection against today's threats requires investment in human skills rather than technology. In fact, a serious discussion of achieving information dominance might reveal its implausibility, as evidenced by our lack of understanding of the situation in Iraq and Afghanistan and our inability to come to grips with the worldwide al-Qaeda network. An honest evaluation of our demonstrated inability to achieve information dominance would invalidate the entire concept of full-spectrum dominance that lies at the heart of *JV 2010*.

The second concept that outlines cyberwar, the revolution in military affairs (RMA), is less clearly defined. Yet, regardless of how it is defined, RMA discussions focus on the technological aspects of warfare—in particular, the military-technical revolution and how to quickly apply that "revolution" to our forces, to assure our continued superiority in combat. The pro-RMA position is simple: technology is the answer. Unfortunately, they never clarify exactly what the question is.

The DOD'S "network-centric warfare" was first articulated by Vice Admiral Arthur Cebrowski and John Garstka in a 1998 article of the same name. At that time, the focus of network-centric warfare was purely technology. Since then, the definition has evolved somewhat and is now expressed as follows:

> [A]n information superiority-enabled concept of operations that generates increased combat power by networking sensors, decision makers, and shooters to achieve shared awareness, increased speed of command, higher tempo of operations, greater lethality, increased survivability, and a degree of self-synchronization. In essence, NCW translates information superiority into combat power by effectively linking knowledgeable entities in the battlespace.[2]

This description of network-centric warfare states that technology is more important than all other factors in driving changes. Technology will provide the information superiority that is at the heart of all DOD concepts. Again, it involves no discussion of our lack of understanding concerning the wars we are currently fighting.

With the publication of *Joint Vision 2020* in 2000, the new chairman of the Joint Chiefs of Staff reiterated most of the material in *JV 2010* but softened the emphasis on technology as the sole driver of future war. Unfortunately, the qualifiers are buried far back in the publication. The introduction to *JV 2020* states unequivocally that technology drives warfare. It focuses on how technology will provide the capability for U.S. forces to execute the four operational concepts described in the earlier version.

In this model, doctrine, organization, training, and education serve only to teach people to take advantage of technology—not to think about, fight, and win wars. Further, it places a premium on DOD's ability to foster innovation—not a characteristic for which DOD is noted.

The latest manifestation of DOD's focus on technology is "Transformation Planning Guidance," issued in April 2003. Evolving out of earlier DOD documents and drawing heavily on them, the DOD's strategy, as outlined in the paper, has three parts:

- a transformed culture through innovative leadership
- transformed processes through risk adjudication, using future operating concepts
- transformed capabilities through force transformation

The document focuses on investment decisions for technology and experimentation. In short, it seeks to transform our military forces into:

> Information age military forces [that] will be less platform-centric and more network-centric. They will be able to distribute forces more widely by increasing information sharing via a secure network that provides actionable information at all levels of command. This,

> in turn, will create conditions for increased speed of command and opportunities for self-coordination across the battlespace.[3]

The document goes on to discuss the types of forces we will field and the types of enemies we will fight. It is interesting that the threats DOD plans to be ready to defeat by the end of the decade have no resemblance to the actual enemies we are fighting today. Although DOD may argue that the types of forces we are fighting today will not exist by 2010, the long timelines of past 4GW wars indicate that not only will they still exist, we will still be fighting them.

Essentially, DOD transformation guidance for the future ignores the success of 4GW in the last five decades. Instead, supposed future enemies will ignore the past and willingly fight America in a high-technology, fast-moving campaign that reinforces all our strengths while avoiding our weaknesses.

Perhaps the most disturbing aspects of these official publications are that they are so inwardly focused and that that focus is not open for discussion. It has already been defined. It is technology. These publications simply disregard any action taken by an intelligent, creative opponent to negate our technology. In fact, they seem to reduce the enemy to a series of inanimate targets to be serviced. He who services the most targets the fastest must win. The wide ranges of other factors that directly affect warfare are not even considered.

Imagine if you made decisions in your personal life using the same model. Let's say you moved to a new home and a new job. You need to get to work. So you ask yourself, "What kind of car should I buy?" You conduct a detailed technical, mechanical, and economic analysis of the various types of cars that could get you to and from work. You feel good about yourself. You are really thinking this one through. Unfortunately, you asked the wrong question. You prematurely limited the research to cars. Although a car may eventually be the right answer, it should not be the only option considered.

The question you should have asked is, "What is the best form of transportation for my new life?" That opens the possibility of mass transit, carpooling, van-pooling, bicycles, and even—heaven forbid—walking. Although this may seem a ridiculous example, it is in effect what these concepts, and by inference the Department of Defense, has done by focusing the discussion on technology. It has already limited the investigation to technology. These concepts all ask, "How do we apply technology to become dominant in future wars?"

These Department of Defense concepts never ask, "What will future war look like?" "How do we recognize it as it develops?" and "How do we respond to it?" These questions would lead to a much broader and more intellectually honest approach than limiting the discussion to the application of technology.

This approach has led us to Iraq and Afghanistan. Our supreme confidence in technology and our willful ignoring of the human aspects of war have led us into a 4GW fight equipped only with the high-technology tools suited for a 3GW battle.

Fortunately, in contrast to the Department of Defense, other authors have taken a much broader approach to the question of why warfare changes.

The Tofflers, in their book *War and Anti-War,* state that society has been driven by three great waves, each defined by the primary source of wealth generation during its era. The way wealth was created largely determines how it was distributed and how society was structured.

The Tofflers describe the first wave as agriculture, coming into existence about 10,000 years ago. The development of agriculture fundamentally changed human society. Freed from the tyranny of a daily struggle for food and with the luxury of remaining in one place, agricultural societies accumulated wealth. Such societies clearly required a different social organization from the nomadic hunter-gatherer societies that preceded them. As a result, specialization became necessary, and a ruling (often priestly) class evolved.

Along with a ruling class came specialization in other areas, not the least of which was warfare. Instead of a tribal system where every person fought, the rise of civilization gave rise to a professional class of warriors. They became experts at the application of violence to protect the wealth that agriculture allowed a society to produce. Often, another duty was to protect the ruling class from the rest of society.

The second wave, according to the Tofflers, was industrial. This represented a major shift in the balance of wealth from land holders to the captains of industry. Clearly, this shift had an impact across the society. Beginning about the middle of the 17th century, industrialization allowed a major increase in wealth while simultaneously providing the ability to mass produce the key weapons of war. Obviously, non-industrial nations could not stand against the wealth and weapons an industrialized nation state could bring to bear.

Now, we are at the beginning of the Information Age. When they wrote their book in 1993, the Tofflers could project only the dramatic changes in society driven by the information revolution. Remember, in 1993, email in a private home was unusual. But they predicted major changes would occur, because information technology is driving another huge shift in the balance of wealth.

The emerging information industries changed not only how wealth was created but even its nature. When an industrial product is sold, its value belongs to the new owner. When an information product such as software is sold, the sale does not decrease the resources available to the original owner. Make a copy of software to a disk and the original disk remains complete.

Similarly, to destroy the source of the wealth, an enemy does not need to seize the plant—merely to pirate and duplicate the idea. In addition, the knowledge that is the key to wealth is not a physical entity that must be protected at a fixed location. Instead, it can be reduced to ones and zeroes and instantaneously sent anywhere in the world. The ownership of expensive, geographically fixed assets forces a corporation to have some loyalty, or at least maintain a good relationship, with the country in which the asset is located. Knowledge requires no fixed address but can easily be moved from location to location if the owner does not like his relationship with the "host" nation. Thus, the nature of wealth and how we protect it has changed.

The Tofflers' model traced warfare to the different forms it took in the different eras. Although this is a useful model, it is too broad for the purpose of studying the evolution of modern warfare. It provides a wonderful theoretical background but does not provide a practical guide for either a military practitioner or a concerned civilian. Unfortunately, many styles and even generations of war can fit into each of these waves. For our purposes, the key point the Tofflers make is that the entire society had to change in order to change the form of warfare in each wave.

In *The Transformation of War,* Martin van Crevald deftly illustrates that the way a society conducts warfare is based in the type of social structure and beliefs it holds dear. He indicates the relative successes of unconventional wars against conventional opponents and highlights the failures of regular militaries to deal with this evolving threat. He points out that insurgents, revolutionaries, and terrorists have been more adept at learning this new style of war than militaries have. He presents a provocative view—particularly his idea that conventional militaries and high-tech weapons are likely to become irrelevant. The diminishing power of the state and the divisions within many states means wealthy citizens will have to turn elsewhere to protect not only their wealth but also their persons.

In a later essay, "Through a Glass Darkly," van Crevald expands on this idea to point out how the last fifty years have led to a fundamental erosion of the state's monopoly on the use of force:

> The roughly three-hundred-year period which was associated primarily with the type of political organization known as the state—first in Europe, and then, with its expansion, in other parts of the globe as well—seems to be coming to an end. If the last fifty years or so provide any guide, future wars will be overwhelmingly of the type known, however inaccurately, as "low intensity."[4]

Van Crevald clearly sees warfare as evolving with the political, social, and economic structures of the time.

Bill Lind, Gary Wilson, and their coauthors, in "The Changing Face of War: Into the Fourth Generation," agree with van Crevald but provide a somewhat more practical guide for those struggling to understand how war is changing today. They see three previous generations of modern war that have evolved over the last few hundred years. In their view, the first generation of warfare reflected the tactics of line and column. The essential requirement was to mass manpower at the point of main effort. It was based partly on technology and partly on the social changes taking place during the French Revolution.

They state that the second generation evolved due to quantitative and qualitative improvement in weapons and relied on massed firepower. In particular, they say that the rifled musket, breechloaders, barbed wire, the machine gun, and indirect fire forced change on the battlefield. This culminated in World War I tactics and the French maxim "artillery conquers, infantry occupies."

Finally, they see the third generation as maneuver. In 1939, the Germans, applying new capabilities presented by reliable tanks, mobile artillery, motorized infantry, effective close air support, and radio communication, restored maneuver to the battlefield and reclaimed the ascendancy of the offense. To these authors, each generation of war grew principally out of the adoption of available technology to military forces. The 1989 article noted that it had been more than seventy years since third-generation warfare started and challenged readers to define what fourth-generation warfare would be.

Although this is not as broad a model as either Toffler's or van Crevald's, it is much more useful for the study of the evolution of modern war. It was one of the first, if not the first, attempt to understand how modern warfare was changing. It evaluated modern eras where the dominant military force was distinctly different from each previous era. In proposing the concept that these differences represent different generations of war, it outlined a useful model. That model will allow us to study why and how the generations evolved and see if we can detect similar evolutionary changes taking place in today's warfare.

From this brief survey, it is clear that numerous authors have seen warfare changing. Those associated with DOD have concentrated on technological changes. Others, primarily historians, have a broader interpretation of the reasons for change. They contend that such change requires changes in all major aspects of society—political, economic, social, and technical—to bring about a generational change in warfare.

This brings us back to the key questions. "What will future war look like?" "How can we recognize it as it develops?" and "How do we respond to it?"

In this volume, I intend to show that a new form of war has, in fact, evolved. It is visible and distinctly different from the forms of war that preceded it. It evolved in conjunction with the political, economic, social, and technological changes that are modifying our world.

Further, I intend to show that, like its predecessors, this new form of war did not arrive on the scene as a fully developed instrument but has evolved over decades and continues to evolve at widely scattered locations. We are not in the midst of a revolution in military affairs but rather an evolution. We can trace that evolution by examining our recent past.

For clarity in terminology and to provide a framework for study, I will adopt the generations laid out by Lind, Wilson, and their compatriots and refer to the new form of warfare as fourth-generation warfare, or 4GW. Like all models, it is not a perfect representation of reality, but it provides a framework to examine how previous generations evolved.

First, we will examine the factors that drove the development of and transition to the first three generations of modern war. Then we will conduct a brief survey of the political, economic, social, and technological changes since third-generation warfare evolved. Next, we will trace the development and evolution of 4GW. In doing so, we can develop a clear view of how this form of warfare has consistently allowed initially weak political movements to defeat powerful Western nations.

Two points are of particular importance as we examine the evolution of 4GW. First is the timeline associated with this form of war. Fourth-generation-warfare struggles are measured in decades rather than months or years. The Communist Chinese fought for twenty-seven years. The Vietnamese fought for thirty years. The Sandinistas fought for eighteen years. The Palestinians have been fighting since 1967. The Afghans took ten years to defeat the Soviets—and the subsequent struggle for power continues today, twenty-five years after the Russian invasion.

The second point is that only 4GW has defeated a superpower. Further, it has defeated both the United States and the USSR—on multiple occasions. It is also the type of war we are fighting in Iraq, Afghanistan, and worldwide against terror.

As we begin our historical examination of shifts in warfare, it is essential to keep in mind that major shifts have occurred across the spectrum of human activity as the world moved from an industrial society to an information one. Every aspect of human life—from the number of political players in the international arena to how an individual communicates and identifies personal loyalties—is completely different from what it was in the first half of the twentieth century. History shows that societal changes of this magnitude cannot occur without a fundamental change in the way we conduct war. It is understandable that we are facing a fourth generation of warfare.

# CHAPTER 2

# The First Two Generations of Modern War

Before exploring the probable form and potential impact of the fourth generation of modern war, we need to understand how the previous generations of war evolved.

### *First-Generation War*

Although Lind and his fellow authors outlined the changes between the generations of modern war, it is essential to understand what caused these generational shifts. The article states that each of the first three generations evolved in response to technical solutions to specific tactical challenges.

Although tactical challenges clearly had an impact, attributing the generational changes in warfare primarily to military factors oversimplifies the problem. In fact, the forces involved could execute those tactics only because of the major political, economic, social, and technical changes that preceded them.

The first generation of war grew not just from the invention of gunpowder but also from the political, economic, and social structures that developed as Europe transitioned from a feudal system to a system of nation-states ruled by monarchs. The transition from the "chivalry" of feudal knights to the armies of Napoleon required centuries. This time was required not only to develop reliable firearms but, more important, to develop the political system, the wealth-generating national economies, the social structures, and the technologies capable of sustaining the mass armies of the Napoleonic era. During this time, the first generation of modern war evolved slowly, in consonance with the societies of western Europe. It peaked with the massive armies of the Napoleonic Wars of the early 19th century.

Politically, warfare of the size and complexity of Napoleonic war required the evolution of the nation-state. Only the resources of a nation-state could raise, train, equip, and sustain the massive armies of the French Revolution. The consolidation of the nation-state's power and the nation's transition from the private domain of a monarch allowed for the mobilization of its wealth, ingenuity, and manpower in support of a war.

The colonization of America provided a major economic stimulus that allowed countries to field larger, more technically advanced armies—the arrival of gold and silver from the New World. Although this led to tremendous inflation, it also vastly increased the coinage in circulation, which stimulated economic growth. Both the population[1] and the gross domestic product (GDP) per person[2] were increasing significantly faster than prior to 1500.

Economically, major advances in agriculture and transportation were essential to generating the wealth and resources required to field and sustain large armies. Improved agriculture and higher-yield crops arriving from America increased farmers' productivity and reduced the labor necessary to achieve these levels of productivity. The combination increased the overall wealth of the nation, provided additional food for major armies, and, by freeing manpower from agriculture, provided an increase in the available manpower for mobilization.

As the wealth and trade of European society increased, so did the transportation network. Although the speed and displacement of ships at sea increased rapidly during this period, the dramatic increases came in the road and inland barge transportation networks across western Europe. Although these changes took place over centuries, they were essential to building the economic base that could both sustain and move much larger armies across Europe. In 1415 at Agincourt, about 31,000 men fought: 6,000 British and 25,000 French. In contrast, by 1815, at Waterloo, more than 200,000 men were present.

Socially, the development of a genuine feeling of patriotism in the mass of men making up the armed forces was essential to enable Napoleonic warfare. The French Revolution brought this feeling to the European continent, and the impact was obvious. Suddenly, warfare did not involve only royalty, a small professional army, and the treasure of a country—it involved the entire population. It was only this sense of patriotism that allowed the poorly trained French infantry to press home costly attacks against opposing armies. It was this enthusiasm that could provide a continuous supply of manpower to support the famous column attacks.

With the early success of the French, the other European powers had to widen the base of their forces, and the concept of nationalism began its transition to the other nations of Europe. This social change carried forward into succeeding generations of war.

Technically, mass production of the reliable, smoothbore musket, development of lightweight artillery, and the advent of rudimentary fast, long-distance communication via visual telegraph all contributed to the evolution of the first generation of modern war. Massed manpower had been the rule in ancient Greece and Rome and had even been a major part of war during the Middle Ages. However, the combination of changes across society provided the much larger armies and massed direct-fire weapons that marked the culmination of the first generation of war at Waterloo.

Clearly, evolution from medieval warfare to the first generation of modern war required significant change in the political, economic, social, and technological structures of the time.

### *Second-Generation War*

Like the first generation of war, the second generation did not grow just from improvements in weaponry. It, too, required changes across the spectrum of human activity. Although the political structure of the nation-state was essentially in place at the end of the Napoleonic Wars, the state's power to tax and enforce taxes increased dramatically during the hundred years between Waterloo and the Miracle of the Marne.

Even more important than an increase in the ability to levy and collect taxes was much vaster wealth to tax. The GDP per person in western Europe almost tripled from 1800 to 1915, while the population increased about fifty percent.[3] The combination of increased GDP per person, major population increases, and significantly better government control massively increased the wealth available to the national governments of Europe.

A great deal of this increase in wealth can be attributed to the rapid industrialization of western Europe and North America. Second-generation war required both the wealth generated by an industrial society and the sheer volume of output that only such a society can produce. Industry had to first design and then mass produce the weapons and the huge quantities of ammunition they consumed.

Even these exceptional production capabilities alone would not allow nations to apply second-generation warfare. The transportation systems also had to mature. In particular, extensive rail systems and their supporting telegraph networks were necessary to move the armies and their mountains of supplies. Although telegraphs were built primarily to support railroads, they proved essential to the national level control and coordination of these greatly enlarged forces. In sum, the economies of all participants had to expand enormously before the massive armies of World War I could be raised, transported, and supported. Further, the European nations had to develop logistically effective general staffs to combine these national assets, mobilize them, transport them, and then hurl them against the nation's enemies.

Finally, second-generation war was not possible without the patriotic enthusiasm that brought millions of men to the colors and held them there through four years of catastrophic losses. In fact, the collapse of Russia's armies can be traced largely to the fact that the Czar and his officers could not generate that kind of patriotism in their ranks. Even in the West, it was a close thing, as evidenced by the French army mutinies of 1917.

All these factors—political, economic, social, and technical—came together to create the stalemate of World War I. Even at the earliest stages of the war, it was obvious that the defense had gained the upper hand. It is clear from numerous diaries and histories that most professional soldiers of 1914 were surprised by the way warfare had changed. The question we need to explore is, should they have been surprised, or should they have been able to anticipate the change by studying recent conflicts?

### *Stalemate Foreshadowed?*

Several key factors normally associated with second-generation war (2GW) drove the supremacy of the defense over the offense: machine guns, magazine-fed rifles, rapid-fire artillery, and barbed wire. The combined effect of these elements took away freedom of movement and forced both sides to rely on firepower—mostly indirect firepower—in tactical engagements.

Just as important to the defense was the extensive use of railroads—first for mobilization, then to swiftly shift reserves behind lines. The ability to shift troops by rail and detrain them close to the fight gave the defense a marked advantage over the offense. The defense's reserves and supplies moved directly to the point they were defending, over well-developed rail and then road networks. In contrast, the offense could move troops only by rail to their pre-offensive assembly areas. The troops then had to move by foot across the horribly chewed-up terrain between the trenches. Even more difficult, the attacker's artillery and logistics had to traverse the same devastated terrain.

The telegraph also played a key role in the stalemate of World War I. It permitted the coordination of armies fighting over a continental land mass. It allowed both sides to communicate the need for reinforcements at critical points and then coordinate the railroad movement of those forces. Combined with the superior mobility on the defense side of the line, it allowed the defense to shift forces to defeat any initial offensive successes.

Unlike the weapons, which could be mass produced for the war, the rail and telegraph networks had to be essentially in place upon commencement of hostilities. Although both sides would lay branch rail lines and send telegraph communications forward to key command posts, the backbones of both systems were in place in 1914. Thus, professional soldiers had ample opportunity to study the utility of rail and communications right up to the start of the war.

In fact, the mobilization plans of both sides not only relied on, but were driven by, railroad timetables and the staffs' ability to control them, using the telegraph. The remarkable thing is that, despite intensive prewar study of the effectiveness of railroads moving troops to distant points, neither side seemed to see how both rail and telegraph favored the defense as it retracted onto its own communications and transportation system while the attacker had to build his as he advanced.

These technologies were the final products of the political, social, and economic changes between Waterloo and 1914. If the thesis of this book is correct, that warfare evolves over time and that the elements of each generation are visible for decades before they "surprise" the world, then each of these elements should have been present in earlier conflicts.

In fact, everything commonly believed to be distinct to World War I was present by 1864 in the U.S. Civil War. In General Grant's final drive south, we see a direct preview of World War I. What starts as a campaign of movement eventually bogged down in trench warfare. Just like their successors in 1914, both sides found it impossible to dislodge an entrenched enemy. Bruce Catton says, "The hard fact was that by 1864 good troops using rifles and standing in well built trenches and provided with sufficient artillery support simply could not be dislodged by any frontal assault whatever."[4]

The net result of three years' experience meant that the firing lines changed from the Napoleonic volley exchanged between standing battalions at point-blank range to individual fire from deep trench lines. The outcome was obvious: the soldier in a trench had only his head exposed, whereas the attacking soldier had his entire body exposed. Firepower could now stop any attacker.

Although troops learned fairly early that the combination of rifled musket fire and rapid-fire artillery could prevent an attacking force from overwhelming a defense, the commanders and staffs were much slower to learn. Throughout the 1863 and 1864 campaigns in the east, both Union and Confederate officers ordered repeated direct frontal attacks on dug-in positions. None succeeded.

Further foreshadowing the First World War was the extensive use both sides made during the Civil War of railroads to shift reserves and sustain forces. They also used the telegraph to coordinate campaigns over the breadth of a continent.

In summary, all the key elements that made defense supreme in World War I were present in late 1864. The outcome was the same as it would be in 1914: the defense had the upper hand. Yet somehow, the professional soldiers of all armies (including ours) missed the lesson. Even more remarkable is the fact that the lessons were repeated in both the Boer War and the Russo-Japanese War—and were still not understood by Western armies.

It is clear that the transition from first to second generation was anything but sudden. It evolved over decades. From the early battles of the U.S. Civil War to the battlefields of South Africa and the trenches of the Far East, war provided repeated, clear examples of the effect that political, economic, social, and technical changes were having on warfare.

# CHAPTER 3

# Transition to Third-Generation Warfare

At 4:45 a.m. on September 1, 1939, the German army invaded Poland. By September 19, they forced the surrender of the last Polish army in the field. Eight days later, they completed mopping up the stubborn Polish resistance in Warsaw. The popular view is that Germany overwhelmed Poland with a massive mechanized attack that quickly overran the outdated Polish army.

In fact, the vast majority of the German army was foot mobile and was supplied by horsedrawn transport. Of the thirty-four German divisions in the attack, only six were Panzer divisions and an additional four were "light" divisions.[1] The other twenty-four were essentially World War I infantry divisions, with horsedrawn wagons carrying all their heavy weapons, artillery, and logistics support.

Further dissipating the impact of massed mechanized formations is the fact that the Army Group South commander parceled out his armor throughout his infantry formations. Only Guderian, commanding Army Group North, massed his two panzer and two light divisions into a hard striking corps. Thus, the German army that overran Poland was not a transformational force but a highly competent army struggling to make use of new weapons and formations. Like all their predecessors, the soldiers were learning as they fought.

One of the most remarkable aspects of the birth and development of blitzkrieg is the action of the German army after its astonishingly rapid victory over Poland. Although most armies would have rested on their laurels, the German army conducted a detailed, even brutal critique of its own performance. It then began an intensive, demanding training program to overcome the deficiencies identified during its review of the Polish campaign.

In contrast to the Germans, who were training furiously in preparation for the inevitable clash, the French army remained inactive, snug in the Maginot Line, lacking the imagination to see how warfare had already changed. Its allies, the British, were desperately trying to expand their small peacetime army to a wartime footing. Lacking time, equipment, and trained personnel, they had no choice but to expand on existing-force structure and doctrine. They, too, had failed to understand what had happened in Poland. Neither army made a concerted effort to understand how Germany had so quickly defeated Poland. "Sitzkrieg" not only described the level of combat over the winter of 1939–40 but also the level of preparation on the Allied side.

Due to the intensive retraining, the force the Germans unleashed on France on May 10, 1940, incorporated the lessons learned from the Polish campaign. The Germans succeeded in making these lessons part of their operational and tactical art. Although still primarily an infantry army, the Germans organized their armored forces into Panzer Corps and used them to shatter the cohesion of the Allied forces. The result was another astonishing victory. Britain was evacuating its forces from Dunkirk only sixteen days after the invasion. France lasted only another month. In contrast to four bloody years of stalemate in World War I, the German's conquered France in weeks. The victory stunned the Western powers. They were certain the Germans had created an entirely new form of warfare.

Third-generation warfare had arrived. Yet, as with previous generations of war, it was not just the militaries' response to specific tactical problems that drove the evolution of this generation of war. The evolution of

3GW required political, economic, social, and technological conditions to be right.*

The political and social atmospheres of the opposing sides were critical to the difference in development. While the politically unified state that permitted 3GW still existed throughout Europe, the social contract between governed and governors had been dramatically altered by the First World War.

In the democracies, people no longer had blind faith in the institutions of government. Virtually every family in Britain and France had lost at least one male relative to the apparently pointless slaughter in the trenches. The Allies had mobilized almost twenty-eight million men and had suffered almost twelve million casualties.[2] The populace of the Allied nations rightly blamed these staggering losses on failures of both their governments and their militaries.

The German people, despite suffering proportionately heavier casualties—six million of eleven million mobilized—did not react in the same fashion at all.[3] They never withdrew support from their armed forces. In fact, the armed forces remained a respected institution in the German government. Over time, the Germans developed the myth of the "stab in the back." They came to believe that their army had not been defeated on the field of battle but, rather, had been betrayed by subversive elements in the civilian sector.

Thus, the political conditions were very different in the interwar period. Hitler was able to use the myth as part of his propaganda and rise to power. Although the Treaty of Versailles was specifically designed to keep Germany from developing a powerful army, Hitler's political will allowed the German army to begin rebuilding years ahead of the Allies. Although the Versailles treaty restricted Germany's technical research to a certain degree, it did not prevent the army from applying the lessons it learned from World War I in building the new army.

* For an in-depth discussion of the key innovations of World War II, see Millett and Murray, *Military Innovation in the Interwar Period.*

Despite Hitler's buildup and the understanding by many British officers that Germany was the primary threat to Britain, the Chamberlain government did not change its official policy until February 1939. Only seven months before the outbreak of hostilities on the mainland, the British army was finally given permission to prepare for that war.

Although no French government adopted the open hostility toward and neglect of its armed forces that the British did, neither did the French prepare for war. Content to focus on the deeply flawed concept of the Maginot Line, they simply failed to prepare their army until it was too late.

Although the political climate varied greatly between the future belligerents, the economic factors were similar. The Great Depression severely limited funds available during the early to mid-thirties. But the impact varied greatly, according to each government's willingness to expend scarce resources on its military forces—and its officers' willingness to test new concepts without the actual equipment they would use.

Hitler willingly spent Germany to the brink of bankruptcy in building up his armed forces. In contrast, the French and British governments severely restricted military spending until just before the outbreak of war. Similarly, the German army worked extensively to develop combined arms tactics—even though it had to use motor cars for tanks, light planes as fighters and dive bombers, and small formations to simulate large ones. The French did little, and the British rejected the experiments they did conduct.

Despite the Great Depression, all three nations, as well as the United States, had the economic base to build the combined-arms forces that made blitzkrieg possible. Although no nation had the technology or industrial capacity at the end of World War I, the rapid technological changes in aviation, armor, motor transport, artillery, and communications meant that the capacity existed in all three nations by 1939. This was essential to the birth of blitzkrieg. Only a society producing sufficient numbers of mechanics, drivers, electricians, and so on, can build, man, and equip a modern armed force.

The French built what were regarded as the best tanks of their days. They were certainly more than a match for the German Mk I, Mk II, and Czech tanks that made up over seventy-five percent of the German tanks in the invasion. Unfortunately, despite some forward-thinking officers, the

French did not concentrate their armored forces but parceled them out among their infantry forces. Their inability to adapt intellectually squandered their technological edge. Only the Germans had the political will and strategic imperative to build a complete combined-arms team to execute the tactics they had developed in World War I.

As discussed in the previous two chapters, the development of a new generation of war is evolutionary rather than revolutionary and should therefore be visible in the decades prior to the appearance of blitzkrieg. In fact, it was.

We can see the thought process behind blitzkrieg developing as early as 1915. In August, Captain Rohr took over the Assault Detachment of the German army. This was in essence a laboratory to refine tactical techniques for breaking through the increasingly sophisticated Allied trench system. Rohr's commander, General Gaede, gave him a simple, mission-type order: "to train his unit according to the lessons that he had learned during his front line service."[4] General Gaede then provided him with a mix of mortars, machine guns, infantry guns, and standard weapons in an innovative way, to restore the offensive capability of the German army. In addition to these close-supporting weapons, Captain Rohr ensured that artillery support was an integral part of his operations.

From this beginning, the Assault Detachment developed the small-unit tactics of infiltration and refined them. In a series of attacks increasing in scale, it worked out the tactics, techniques, and procedures of combined-arms operations at the small-unit level. Based on the Assault Detachment's success, the German army systematically retrained its forces to use assault tactics. These were combined-arms tactics that relied on small-unit initiative to penetrate the enemy's trenches and then move rapidly to exploit those breaches in the enemy lines.

Rather than rigid employment driven by a timeline, the new German tactics emphasized flexibility and reconnaissance pull. No longer would leaders remain in the rear and push forces forward on a predetermined front. Instead, leaders would have to be forward, just behind their lead elements, so that they could lead their units into the gaps those lead elements created.

By 1918, the German army had been retrained to use these tactics in Ludendorff's major offensive. The tactical successes of the new approach allowed the Germans to punch a huge hole in the Allied defenses. Fortunately for the Allies, the Germans had no practical operational or strategic objective. Nor had they solved the problem of pushing fresh troops and supplies across the devastated terrain of no-man's-land. Therefore, the Allies were able to shift reserves faster than the Germans could exploit the gaps they created. Soon, the Allied were able to contain the penetration. This was a last-gasp offensive by the Germans, and the Allied counterattack culminated in the German surrender.

Although the new tactics failed to win World War I, they introduced an entire generation of German officers to the idea of mission-type orders, reconnaissance pull, penetrating a front, and expanding from the penetration. Thus, the intellectual foundation of 3GW was firmly in place in 1918. In addition to the intellectual basis, World War I saw the introduction of tanks, aircraft, long-range artillery, and, on the eastern front, great battles of maneuver.

Not content with a superficial understanding of what had happened in World War I, the German army undertook an intensive historical study of what really happened. They focused on several major issues: the reasons the Schlieffen plan failed, solving the problem of the trenches to restore mobility to the battlefield, the British use of tanks at Somme and Cambrai, the tactical success of the German 1918 offensive and why it failed operationally, and the use of airpower by the Allies against the German 1918 offensive.[5]

It is interesting to note that their studies explored the key components of what would become blitzkrieg. During the interwar period, the Germans continued to study these ideas and to integrate the separate successful tactical and technical innovations into a coherent operational weapon.

So if blitzkrieg was in fact evolutionary, why didn't the British and French militaries learn from World War I and apply those lessons in the interwar period?

The British actually attempted to learn but suffered from the fits and starts of chiefs of staff who exhibited varying tastes for learning. At the end of World War I, the British army did successfully conduct combined-arms mechanized warfare. As Millett and Murray point out:

> It can be seen, therefore, that the BEF (British Expeditionary Force) really conducted two kinds of warfare in the second half of 1918: first, mechanical warfare in July and August; and secondly, traditional or semi-traditional open warfare, from the end of August to the Armistice. Yet the fact that the large scale mechanical attacks did not take place in the last months, while the war was won by means that were familiar to most officers, did strongly influence the way that mechanization and mechanical warfare were debated in the 1920s and 1930s. It is important, however, to note that this debate did not actually start *after* the war, but in fact commenced in late 1917 and early 1918.[6]

In 1918, the British were equal to the Germans in tactical thinking and ahead in the application of technology, in the form of armor. Unfortunately, they did not undertake a detailed study of the lessons of the war until 1932. Even then, they did so only because Lord Milne, a progressive thinker, became chief of the Imperial General Staff (CIGS). However, the report was not finished until the new CIGS, Field Marshal Montgomery-Massingberd, took over.

Montgomery-Massingberd was adamantly against discussing the army's problems in public, so he severely restricted distribution of the report. Unfortunately, he set a trend. Until the outbreak of World War II, all chiefs of the Imperial General Staff after Lord Milne refused to study the lessons of World War I. They tied all armor developments to support of infantry and cavalry, squandering numerous opportunities for Britain to develop true combined-arms tactics.

Further reducing any chance for change was the anti-intellectual bent of the British army. Simply put, unlike the Germans, who saw war as a profession requiring intense study by the best minds in the army, the British seemed to consider the army a pleasant occupation for second sons. The closed-mindedness of the British regimental mess was staggering. Thus, the few innovators who did appear in the interwar period were kept firmly in place by the CIGS, regimental traditions, and their fellow officers.

The French, in contrast to the British, conducted an intensive study of World War I, seeking doctrinal and organizational lessons. Unfortunately, the institutional bias toward "methodical battle" ensured that the study was limited to battles that "proved" that a tightly controlled, centrally directed battle, emphasizing firepower, was the key to victory. Reinforcing the institutional bias was the requirement that "all articles, lectures, and books by serving officers had to receive approval by the high command before publication."[7] The uninspired interwar army leadership, the stifling of discussion, and emphasis on the "methodical battle" ensured that the French army completely missed the evolution that drove blitzkrieg.

It is interesting to note the similarities in the French interwar "discussion" and our current DOD "discussion" of future war. The French general staff defined the discussion and then ensured that all "experiments" and "developments" adhered to the definition. Currently, DOD has defined the future as technology and is driving all experiments and developments in that direction. Much like the French, DOD has not seen the evolution of war taking place in our time but instead insists war is evolving according to its preconceived vision.

Although more compressed than the evolution of first- and second-generation warfare, 3GW also evolved over time. The time frame was shortened for numerous reasons, not the least of which is that the rate of change across society, which had been accelerating during the last few centuries, increased even more in the twentieth century. Further, innovation always accelerates during modern warfare, because the entire society devotes itself to war. With the rise of Hitler, Germany essentially went on a wartime footing—not full mobilization but definitely a level of effort well beyond the peacetime efforts of their past and future enemies.

### *Summary of First Three Generations*

In these first chapters, we traced the evolution of the first three generations of war. A couple of facts leap out. First is that none of them consisted of a sudden transformation—each evolved over time. Each could be seen developing over the conflicts that preceded it.

Second, each new generation required developments across the spectrum of society. Technological change alone has never been sufficient to produce a major change in how man wages war. It requires a complete societal change—political, economic, social, and technological—to create the conditions necessary for major changes in war.

Finally, we can see the logical progression of the three generations. First-generation war focused on the direct destruction of the enemy's close force. Second-generation war relied on firepower but still focused on the destruction of the enemy fighting forces. Both were restricted by the warfighting capabilities of the societies from which they sprang. As society progressed and was able to project power over much longer ranges, third-generation war took advantage of those changes to focus on destruction of the enemy's command and control and logistics as the fastest way to destroy his will to fight.

Each succeeding generation reached deeper into the enemy's territory in an effort to defeat him. If 4GW is a logical progression, it must reach much deeper into the enemy's forces in seeking victory. In subsequent chapters, we will see that 4GW has in fact evolved to focus deeply in the enemy's rear. It focuses on the direct destruction of the enemy's political will to fight.

# CHAPTER 4

# Changes in Society

We have seen that 3GW or maneuver warfare really started in 1915 and came to maturity in 1940. The previous chapters have also shown that major changes in warfare were always preceded by changes in the political, economic, social, and technical segments of society. Given that changes in these areas are apparent precursors to changes in warfare, we have to ask if the changes in society since the evolution of the third generation are sufficient to indicate that it is time for the fourth generation.

We know it took about a hundred years to move from the height of 1GW conflict, as represented by the Napoleonic Wars, to 2GW conflict, as represented by World War I. It required that long for society to develop the industrial, societal, and technical base to support the huge armies during a four-year struggle. We also know that although all the tactical elements of 3GW war were present in World War I, it required the twenty-one years between World War I and World War II for society to develop the base required to generate full-fledged maneuver war (3GW). Therefore, to explore the possibility that 4GW is evolving, the logical period to examine for political, economic, social, and technical changes is the time between the start of World War II and today.

Obviously, a single chapter cannot begin to provide a definitive list of the enormous societal changes since that time. However, this chapter provides an abbreviated listing of some of the key changes. It is designed to stimulate thought concerning the breadth and types of changes in society since the 1940s—and lead the reader to consider how those changes have affected warfare during the same period.

Politically, there have been extensive changes since the end of World War II. The most obvious is the exponential increase in the number of players on the international stage. Prior to the war, the nation-state was the only significant player on the international scene. Immediately after the war, both the political and economic spheres begin changing rapidly, and each added numerous and varied players to the political stage.

The most obvious change in the political scene was the creation and growth of international organizations. The first was the United Nations.. It provided an international forum that had been lacking and was the precursor for numerous other international organizations. While it had little real power, the United Nations was immediately a part of any international political struggle. Initially, one of its prime functions was to provide an appearance of international approval for action taken in defense of both national and international interests, primarily of Western powers. However, as the United Nations expanded to include an ever-increasing number of Third World nations, it became an effective place for those nations to express their disapproval of the actions of Western powers, in particular the United States. Further, the United Nations was only the first of a series of international organizations that now have significant impact on the negotiations and relations between nations. The United Nations alone has given birth to the International Bank for Reconstruction and Development (World Bank), the International Monetary Fund, , and the International Atomic Energy Agency. Each of these international agencies infringes on national sovereignty in one way or another. Nations are no longer free to set their own tariffs, their own interest rates, their own safety standards, their own constructions standards, and so on. These basic elements of national sovereignty were considered integral to a nation-state's power prior to World War II.

Although the enforcement power of these bodies is sharply limited by the nature of the United Nations, we should not underestimate the influence they have through their member nations. Although the United Nations as a whole may not use military force to punish those who transgress, individual states certainly express their disapproval—in the political, economic, social, and even technical realms. A pariah state suffers from reduced contact in all areas. This translates into direct economic harm and may even lead to changed behavior. Although the final causes of South Africa's transition to a majority black government are varied, its status as an outcast in the international community undoubtedly had significant impact.

In a similar vein, subordinate organizations of the United Nations and other independent international organizations, such as the World Trade Organization (WTO), have a major impact on the actions of nations. Membership in the WTO or attempts to join it require nations to yield power concerning labor and trade practices. They must meet international standards that prior to World War II were mostly internal matters. Today, the World Bank can demand that nations comply with their "recommendations" on interest rates, internal distribution of funds, and international borrowing if they wish to continue receiving international funds.

Parallel to the growth of worldwide organizations, we have seen the growth of numerous regional organizations that place real limits on the powers of sovereign nations. Even the United States is not immune to their power: witness the impact of the North American Free Trade Association (NAFTA) on political and economic policies internal to our country. The European Union has an even greater impact on member nations than NAFTA has on its members. Similar regional organizations with varying degrees of power are now present throughout the world.

The second major change in the political structure was the huge increase in the number and diversity of nations. The postwar breakup of the European colonial empires gave birth to dozens of new nations—all theoretically equal partners in the United Nations. As a rough measure of the increase in players, the United Nations had fifty-one members when the Charter was originally signed in 1945. It now has 189 member states.

The proliferation of states and their varying stages of development create a complexity in international relations that did not exist before 1945.

In 1945, the fifty-one nations were mostly political entities of long standing—the majority in the developed world. In contrast, the vast majority of the states that have joined since then are new nations, many artificially created by a colonial power. These nations naturally have different needs, concerns, and motivations than do developed nations of long standing.

The third significant change is the number of stateless actors that influence the international scene. These include both transnational and subnational elements.

On the transnational level, the players are numerous. They range from peaceful transnational movements such as Greenpeace to violent, radical Islamic movements such as al-Qaeda to the business-oriented transnational drug traders. The key element these organizations have in common is that they are not controlled by any nation or group of nations. They are literally free agents on the international scene and will interject themselves into international relations where and when they see fit, to meet their goals. They may seek something simple, such as involvement in elections. They may choose to influence elections through money, volunteering to support a candidate, or official endorsements of a candidate or position.

At the other end of the spectrum, transnational entities may choose to support an insurgent uprising to gain control of a portion of a country. They may simply choose to assassinate key opponents. Today, these transnational organizations employ a variety of techniques and have an impact on national and international events that simply was not present prior to World War II.

On the subnational level, we have numerous nations that lack states. Many of these groups fall either within a single state or straddle various states as a result of the artificial boundaries that evolved from the colonial era. Although these are not powerful organizations, they can play notable roles on the international scene. One only has to consider the impact of the Kurds, the Serbs, the Croats, the Palestinians, or the Irish Republican Army on recent events to see that, although relatively minor players, these subnational organizations can and do have impact.

Perhaps the most powerful and least controlled new international players are the international financial markets. Although there were markets prior to World War II, their impact was small compared to today's markets. Then, market transactions took time, and the various nations could control many of these markets' assets. Today, billions of dollars, pounds, euros, or yen can be moved instantaneously to any of millions of locations. Further, the decision to move those assets is not made in any one place or by any identifiable group of people or organizations. These decisions are made by two networked entities that Thomas Friedman has labeled the "Electronic Herd" and the "Supermarkets":

> The Electronic Herd today consists of two basic groups. One group I call the "short-horn cattle." This includes all those people involved in the buying and selling of stocks, bonds and currencies around the world, and who can and often do move their money around on a very short-term basis. The short-horn cattle are currency traders, major mutual and pension funds, hedge funds, insurance companies, bank trading rooms and individual investors. They include everyone from Merrill Lynch to Credit Suisse to Fuji Bank to the Charles Schwab web site, where anyone with a PC and a modem can trade on line from his living room.
>
> The other group I call the "long-horn cattle." These are the multi-nationals—the General Electrics, the General Motorses, the IBMs, the Intels, the Siemenses—which are increasingly involved in foreign direct investment, building factories around the world or striking international long-term production deals or alliances with overseas factories to make or assemble their products. I call them the long-horn cattle because they have to make longer-term commitments when they invest in a country. But even they now move in and out, like a herd, with surprising speed.[1]

This electronic herd monitors international conditions on an hour-by-hour basis. If they determine that a state is creating conditions hostile to profits, they can punish that state severely via the market. Credit will simply not be available for states that fall into disfavor. Whether political leaders admit it or not, their freedom of action is distinctly limited by the herd.

The second set of key economic players Friedman identifies, the "Supermarkets," are the big stock exchanges in major cities: "According to University of Chicago globalization expert Saskia Sassen, by the end of 1997 twenty-five Supermarkets controlled 83 percent of the world's equities under institutional management and accounted for roughly half of global market capitalization—around $20 trillion."[2]

This is ten times the size of the U.S. government's annual budget—and it moves worldwide based on the independent and essentially uncontrollable decisions of millions of individual decision makers.

Although on the surface the markets seem to be purely economic, their impact is that of a powerful political player. This player can dictate trade policies, influence elections, determine interest rates, place limits on national social policy, decide acceptable banking practices, and drive many other activities of nations.

Even the United States is not immune. Despite the United States' great size and dominant economy, the herd did not hesitate to rush from the market after the numerous revelations concerning CEO corruption and dishonest accounting practices. The sudden outflow of money from the market during July 2002 resurrected strong new regulatory legislation. Before the sudden descent of the Dow-Jones average below 8,000, the administration and Congress had buried the new regulatory laws. The herd responded by driving the Dow down, and Congress acted swiftly to pass the legislation. Clearly, the international markets themselves are now a major player in all political and economic decisions made by rational governments.

The cumulative effect of this proliferation of players on the international scene is a distinct reduction in the power and freedom of action of nations. Although they remain the primary players in international affairs, the wide variety of new players places restrictions on these states that simply did not exist at the beginning of World War II. The multitude of players also provides additional avenues for our enemies to influence U.S. policy.

As great as the political changes have been, economically the shift has been even more distinct. Just prior to World War II, a nation's wealth was frequently measured in terms of tons of coal produced, tons of steel rolled, number of automobiles manufactured—all measures of an industrial power, with an emphasis on mechanical power. In fact, the fundamental sources of wealth in an industrial society were the raw materials and the manufacturing facilities that converted them to finished products. Mass production was the key to efficiency and to meeting customer demand. In a world of durable goods with long service lives, low cost and standardization were critical.

Today, the most rapidly growing sector of the international economy is information. Unlike industrial plants, these wealth-generating assets are easily moved—and are often part of geographically distributed networks in their day-to-day operations. Nations can no longer compel compliance from companies by threatening their physical assets—simply because many of a company's most important assets exist only in cyberspace and can be moved anywhere in the world virtually instantaneously.

Further complicating the allegiance of economic entities is that a fair percentage of wealth today is generated by using knowledge developed in one nation to build factories that exploit resources (people, raw materials, markets) in another—yet all involved know the commitment is not long term. The relationship will continue only as long as it is advantageous economically.

Finally, the stock markets ensure that ownership of any public corporation may well be distributed worldwide, with large and small stockholders having little or no interest in the political needs of the "home" country of the corporation they own.

Warfare is coming to parallel this model. The knowledge of how to conduct an attack is developed in one country, then that knowledge is combined with the raw materials, personnel, and training available in other countries, which can include the target country, to create a weapon in the target country. Both the 9/11 and Madrid attacks were conducted using this approach. Further, "ownership" of the action may belong to contributors who are distributed around the world but provide funding to the terror networks planning the attack.

In the past, it has been possible to at least intercept terrorist weapons at our borders. Now, the modern concept of manufacturing weapons in the target country means there are no materials to intercept. No longer can we as a nation recognize and intercept a weapon before it reaches our shores. Only the knowledge of the attack and the weapons cross our borders—all other materials can be purchased within our borders. Just as some elements of a knowledge-based economy move only knowledge and personnel across international boundaries, so do some practitioners of 4GW.

Socially, prior to World War II, citizens of developed nations dealt almost exclusively with people from within their own country, and often just locally, within their own city or county. Although a limited number of businessmen had regular communication with foreigners, the vast majority of the citizens of even well-developed nations had little or no contact with foreigners. Communication was expensive; travel was time-consuming and very expensive. Only the wealthy few could travel abroad. The middle class relied on local newspapers, national newsmagazines, and radio for their information. Nation-states, like their economies, were hierarchical. Internally, information moved up and down but internationally, information moved only at the top levels of society.

In the undeveloped nations, citizens—or, more commonly, peasants—rarely traveled more than a day's journey from their place of birth. Their view of the world came almost exclusively from oral tradition and family beliefs.

In contrast, today's communications revolution has completely changed how people get information. In the same way governments, businesses, and trade associations are becoming networks rather than hierarchies, so are relations between people of different states. Citizens of today's developed nations have virtually unlimited access to the people and ideas of other cultures. With the advent of cheap communications and transportation, international connections have multiplied exponentially. For the first time in history, it is easy for average residents of one state to develop strong interests and common bonds with those of other states.

For instance, a member of Greenpeace in the American northwest may have more in common with another Greenpeace member in Germany than with the logger who lives next door. Using email, web sites, and inexpensive long distance, they may communicate more often with each other than with their neighbors.

This has major implications for all government, but particularly for democracies. Although this free association may seem powerless, it was a purely volunteer effort by the International Committee to Ban Land Mines, organized primarily over the Internet, that drove the treaty to ban land mines. Another purely volunteer effort created Linux as an alternate operating system to Microsoft. A volunteer effort organized over the Internet built the coalition of anti-globalization activists that shut down the WTO meeting in Seattle during the summer of 2001.

The same technology that enables Greenpeace and the International Committee to Ban Land Mines also facilitates organizations such as the Islamic fundamentalist groups. Even more challenging from a security point of view is that the people do not have to go out to establish these networks. They do not have to be in the same country or even be on line at the same time. The old police technique of tracking illegal activity by watching certain places and certain people does not work when communication is carried out on line. Although police agencies around the world are beginning to track some activity in cyberspace, the sheer volume makes it daunting. In a later chapter, we will explore how much of the new technology favors the terrorist rather than the government.

In short, citizens of developed nations are no longer limited to living in a hierarchical nation-state. They can now live in a networked international community.

At the other end of the spectrum, citizens of even the poorest nations have access to television and magazines that portray the riches of the developed world. Although a generation ago the most they could hope to see was the next village, now they can see Park Avenue. This creates a much greater sense of relative deprivation and unrest in those nations. Along with the Internet, it also eliminates the government's monopoly on information. No longer can any state assume its citizens will believe only what the government tells them.

This unrest, combined with the artificial nature of the boundaries of many states, has resulted in the severe breakdown of order within many of these postcolonial "nations." Often it has led to the effective, if not the official, dissolution of many of these creations of the colonial powers. The result has been the reversion to much earlier social organizations—tribal, clan, or gang. The result is a major change in whom we might fight and how they see a fight. In the last hundred years or so, Western nations have become accustomed to fighting disciplined, uniformed soldiers of another nation. Now we are faced with fighting warrior or clan societies. The difference between a soldier and a warrior is essential.

Soldiers are disciplined members of a specific profession. As such, they are under the control of a political entity and do not have specific financial or social benefits from continuing to fight. Although there is increased prestige and opportunity for promotion during war, most professional soldiers will at least pay lip service to a preference for peace.

In contrast, a warrior society thrives on and exists for war. Often, the young warrior has everything to lose (except his life) if he stops fighting. Consider the young clansman in Somalia. As a member of a fighting clan, he has prestige and income. They combine to give him access to money, food, property, and women. If he puts his weapons down, he loses that prestige and the income—and with them everything else. Although the risk of death from fighting is always present, it is actually less than the risk of death from starvation if he stops fighting.

Unfortunately, most of these warrior societies' mechanisms for keeping violence to a manageable level are based on traditional systems. For instance, in Somalia, clan elders would meet and determine fines imposed on an individual or family who killed another during a camel raid. However, the advent of powerful new weapons has escalated the killing beyond the control of the old social systems. The young warriors have learned new techniques to employ the new weapons. Like all human organizations, they have adapted.

This creates a major problem for Western soldiers facing such a warrior society. These societies have learned that pushing women and children to the front, even in close combat, will often neutralize the superior firepower of Western soldiers. Sometimes the women and children are armed, sometimes not. Further, women and children at the front shows that the entire society has mobilized against a perceived threat to its livelihood, territory, or customs. Even when the confrontation does not include weapons, warrior societies have learned that Western soldiers have trouble dealing with large numbers of women and children—and have added them as a tactical tool when it creates an advantage.

In sum, there has been an enormous social change from what Western forces faced at the beginning of World War II. The societies of rich nations have fragmented and are beginning to align by interests rather than nationality. Many poor nations have failed completely, with their populations breaking up into the tribes or clans that preceded the nation-state imposed by the colonial powers. Unfortunately, the tribal organizations were never designed to deal with the challenges inherent in a failed nation. Thus, many of the poor face little hope. In short, social changes since World War II have been extensive and wide-ranging.

The cumulative changes in political, economic, and social arenas since World War II are clear and distinct. The changes in the technical area are overwhelming. Frankly, they are much too extensive, and too familiar to the reader, to explore in depth here. Still, consider the following examples. In 1940, the first computer had not even been developed. The first satellite was almost twenty years away. Television did not exist. Commercial aviation was in its infancy—transpacific flights took days. The total capacity of all transoceanic cable and phone lines was less than one of today's fiber optic cables.

Further, as technology continues to evolve, it is just as rapidly reordering every aspect of our lives. The entirely new fields of complexity and network theory are changing how we see the world. Our understanding of biology is increasing at an ever faster pace. In each of these areas, the world has leapt ahead since World War II.

It is intuitively obvious to any observer that almost unimaginable change has occurred in the last sixty years. Although not all sectors of a society evolve at the same rate, all are moving in the same direction. As we evolved into the industrial era, governments, business, and social organizations moved to a hierarchical structure that was often national in scale. In the same way, as we move into the Information Age, all sectors of society are becoming networked on an international scale. What is less obvious is that the rate of change has been accelerating—and not just over the last sixty years but over recorded history.

Consider world population alone. It took from year 1 until 1800 to grow from three hundred million to one billion. Yet the population doubled in only the next 150 years, reaching two billion by 1950. Then it tripled in a mere fifty years, reaching six billion by 2000.

It took more than 1,700 years for the first democracy to evolve after Rome became an empire, yet the next 200 years saw democracy spread around the world.

It took almost a hundred years from the invention of the steam locomotive for it to become a central element of national economies. It took less than twenty-five years for the personal computer to do the same. It took less than five years for instant messaging to penetrate most societies.

In warfare, change is also accelerating. It took hundreds of years from the development of the musket and cannon for first-generation warfare to evolve. Second-generation warfare evolved and peaked in the hundred years between Waterloo and Verdun. Third-generation warfare came to maturity in less than twenty-five years. Clearly, third-generation warfare cannot be the leading edge of war more than sixty years later. The next few chapters will outline how fourth-generation warfare has evolved and has dominated war since World War II.

# CHAPTER 5

# Mao and the Birth of Fourth-Generation War

Fourth-generation war actually made its first appearance before World War II. However, much like the fighting in the U.S. Civil War, the Boer War, and the Russo-Japanese War, it took place far from the European centers of power and was therefore largely ignored. Just as the pre–World War I professional militaries missed the obvious precursors to the disasters of World War I, Western professional militaries completely missed the evolution of 4GW. And like their predecessors, they were doomed to suffer their own disasters in Asia and Africa.

Its first practitioner to both write about and successfully execute a concept of 4GW, Mao Tse-Tung, was a product of the intense turmoil that characterized China in the early twentieth century. Mao was nineteen when the last emperor of the Qing Dynasty abdicated in 1912. Thus he grew up under the collapsing imperial system. He had seen China humiliated by the West, raped by its warlords, and failed by its emperor and his court. During Mao's youth, China was a peripheral player at best—more a source of conflict among other nations than a center of power in its own right.

The abdication of the emperor ended 290 years of Manchu rule. Even more remarkably, it ended a 2,000 year tradition of rule by an emperor. His abdication was not voluntary. He had been forced out by revolutionaries who hoped to bring China into the twentieth century. In his place, Yuan Shikai, a leading Qing general in alliance with the revolutionaries, became president of the new republic.

Unfortunately for China, he rapidly assumed the role of dictator, going so far as to declare that he would make himself emperor on January 1, 1916.[1] Not unexpectedly, his declaration resulted in widespread protest, the fragmentation of the revolutionaries into competing factions, and continued fighting as Yuan Shikai attempted to consolidate power. His attempt to seize power ended when he died suddenly in June 1916.

The next twelve years saw China torn by civil war, as the various warlords each tried to achieve dominance. It took until 1928 for the Nationalist Party to seize control of China and declare itself the legitimate government, with Generalissimo Jiang Jieshi (Chiang Kai-Shek) at its head. Initially allied with the Communists, the Nationalists turned on the Communist Party once Jiang felt he was winning. Jiang knew that the biggest single threat to his rule was the Communists. From 1927 to 1933, his Nationalists did their best to destroy the Communists, to consolidate his hold on power.

It was against this background that Mao came to power in the Communist Party. Mao had been a member of the party since its first meeting in Shanghai in 1921. By the time of the Nationalist Anti-Bandit Campaigns (1927–33), he was a seasoned organizer and planner. More important, he got things done. One of the most impressive and important things Mao achieved was to completely rewrite the Communists' strategic approach: first, against the Nationalists, then against the Japanese, and finally against the Nationalists again. His vision would guide the party to its complete victory in 1949.

In understanding the evolution of 4GW, it is essential to remember that the Communist insurgency in China did not use the strategy of People's War at the beginning. At its founding in 1921, the Chinese Communist Party subscribed to the Soviet concept of an insurgency based on the urban workers of the nation. The party leadership, advised by Soviet liaison officers, clung to the Marxist-Leninist view that revolution must be based in the urban proletariat. This was a matter of dogma and therefore not subject to discussion, despite the huge differences between the political, social, economic, and religious systems of the two nations.

Unlike most of the Marxist leaders, Mao, as the son of a prosperous peasant, had spent most of his life in the countryside. He did not believe that the urban proletariat had sufficient power to conquer the warlords and control all of China. During 1926 and 1927, Mao, in his continuing study of what worked and what didn't, developed a new revolutionary concept. He stated that the revolution in China must be based on the strength of the peasants.[2] He recognized that in China's social structure, the industrial workers simply did not represent a force strong enough to ensure success. In contrast, the hundreds of millions of peasants, if properly organized, could be that force.

Mao did not develop these theories in an academic setting. He lived his theory. During this period, he was an active army commander who constantly sought ways to increase the effectiveness of his forces. He understood the key facts. First, he must avoid direct confrontation with superior warlord and government forces. Second, he needed the peasants on his side to win. He developed a strategic approach around those two precepts:

This was summed up in a pithy folk rhyme, which conveyed the essence of the Red Army's future strategy. In its final form, drawn up by Mao and Zhu,* and popularized throughout the army in May, it contained sixteen characters:

> Di jin, wo tui, [When the] enemy advances, we withdraw,
> Di jiu, wo roa, [When the] enemy rests, we harass,
> Di pi, wo da, [When the] enemy tires, we attack,
> Di tui, wo jui, [When the] enemy withdraws, we pursue.

* Zhu De—co-commander of the Zhu-Mao Army in 1928. This army consisted of about eight thousand men.

Meanwhile the guidelines for the army's treatment of civilians, which Mao had first issued at Sanwan in September 1927, were expanded into what became known as the "Six Main Points for Attention." Solders were urged to replace straw bedding and wooden bed-boards after staying at peasant homes overnight; to return whatever they borrowed; to pay for anything they damaged; to be courteous; to be fair in business dealings; and to treat prisoners humanely.[3]

Mao's thoughts on revolution were clearly evolving. He did not see revolution as a spasm created by an urban proletariat that overthrows the government. He saw it as a political struggle where he must pay attention to maintaining the goodwill of the people. Further, he understood that maintaining the goodwill of the peasants was not simply a propaganda slogan but essential to his army's survival. He knew that only the peasants could provide an unbeatable intelligence network, a constant source of manpower, and resources in the form of food and labor. This was the entire thrust of the six main points.

Mao was taking active steps to keep the peasants on his side. In China, simply being the lesser of two evils helped. Showing conscious, consistent concern for the welfare of the peasants was a powerful weapon against the warlords and government. The people responded by supporting Mao's armies. They not only provided manpower and intelligence for the armies but raised and manned local resistance groups that took their direction from the Communists. As the French and Americans were to discover in Vietnam, these local forces tied down major government forces and ensured that the local population remained loyal to the Communists. At the same time, the local forces provided essential intelligence, logistics, and even combat support to the regular guerrilla formations.

Although Mao stressed good behavior toward the peasants, this did not mean he was above taking what he needed from the merchants. Yet even when dealing with these "enemies of the people," he ensured that his soldiers couched his demands as requests and either paid cash or gave a credit slip to the person from whom the supplies were taken.

As Mao's thoughts evolved, he put them forward to the Central Committee with the intention of shifting the strategic approach of the entire revolution. Through a series of political maneuvers which, in their ebb and flow, matched his stated strategic approach, Mao convinced the Central Committee to at least acknowledge the power of the peasants. Although the communiqué from the Central Committee did not give unqualified support to Mao's position, it did recognize it as the correct path, while leaving other options open.

However, the issue was not settled. As with any group threatened by an attack on its core beliefs, the Marxists, who still believed the revolution must be based on the urban proletariat, fought back. In fairness, a great deal of the difference in opinion was based on a difference in experience. The proletariat branch of the party had survived by fighting a mobile war, keeping their army together and moving from place to place. They were convinced they could act as a catalyst for the urban uprising. Based on their combat experience, they disputed Mao's heretical deviation from Marxist-Leninist thought and resisted its implementation.

This faction of the party worked constantly to overcome the shift to Mao's strategy. Yet on December 8, 1929, they suffered another setback. The Central Committee issued a directive to combine the urban and peasant approaches much more closely. They directed the Red Army to expand from a mobile force by enlisting peasant self-defense units:

> The previous tactics of avoiding the capture of major cities must be changed. So long as there is a possibility of victory, and so long as the masses can be aroused, attacks should be launched against them and they should be occupied. Rapidly taking possession of major cities would have the greatest political significance. This strategy if coordinated with the workers', peasants', and soldiers' struggle throughout the entire country, will promote the greatest revolutionary tide.[4]

Although the continued emphasis on the cities shows that the directive was not an unqualified shift to Maoist tactics, Mao was pleased to see his thoughts woven into the Central Committee's strategic approach. In the highly conservative clique that was the Communist Party, it was a major victory to have his "heretical" thoughts included as part of the official strategy. More telling than the inclusion of his thoughts in Communist doctrine was the great face he gained when he was promoted to army group commander and placed in charge of the Fourth, Fifth, and Sixth armies.

Although anathema to the Marxist-Leninist traditionalists, Mao's views were decisively reinforced by the abject failure of the Soviet-ordered 1930 offensive against the cities. All elements that adhered to the urban-proletariat line of urban uprisings and attacks were defeated with heavy casualties. This offensive exposed the urban cadres to Nationalist firepower and led to heavy casualties among those who enthusiastically executed the offensive against the cities.

In contrast, Mao proceeded much more cautiously with his armies. He chose to encircle his target city rather than occupy it. Thus, when the other Communist armies were defeated, he withdrew in good order. Although technically defeated, because he, too, had failed to seize his target city, the minor losses suffered by forces using his tactics stood in sharp contrast to the catastrophic casualties suffered by the Marxist-Leninist faction. In fact, Mao could point to some limited success from his efforts.

While Mao's prestige grew markedly, the failure of the offensive against the cities greatly weakened the Communists as a whole. The Nationalists saw an opportunity and stepped up their efforts to finish the job and destroy the Communists completely. Generalissimo Jiang Jieshi initiated a series of Anti-Bandit Campaigns. (Like all counterinsurgents, Jiang wanted to reduce the legitimacy of the insurgents by labeling them bandits.) Mao, using his tactics and basing his forces in the countryside, easily defeated the first two campaigns. The tactics of his "Sixteen Characters" proved more than the very conventional Nationalist forces could handle. He drew the Nationalists deep into Red Army territory, then attacked.

The contrast of his success and the urban proletariat's defeats finally settled the doctrinal argument in Mao's favor and greatly increased his prestige in the Communist Party. He was becoming the first among equals. Mao used this new prestige to radically alter the Marxist-Leninist theory of revolution. He abandoned the Soviet theory, based on a sudden revolution of the urban, industrial proletariat, and adopted his own theory, based on protracted war conducted by rural peasants.[5] Although this decision alienated the traditionalists and split the Communist Party, history proves it was correct.

Thus, 4GW began evolving in the same way its predecessors had. Faced with specific tactical and operational problems, practical fighters developed effective solutions. The development of 4GW parallels Mao's growing understanding of the capabilities and limitations inherent in his strategic, operational, and tactical circumstances. Given warfare's Darwinian nature, those who clung to the impractical Marxist-Leninist approach were eliminated. Their deaths served as pointed lessons for the survivors smart enough to understand.

As Mao was reorganizing the Communist Party based on his new principles, Generalissimo Jiang Jieshi decided that despite the Japanese invasion of Manchuria, his most dangerous enemy continued to be the Communists. Minimizing his efforts against the Japanese, he expanded his Anti-Bandit Campaign with the specific goal of wiping out the Reds.

Although initially repulsed by the Communists, the Nationalists achieved success when they adopted the rail, wire, and blockhouse techniques the British used against the Boers in South Africa. By building railroads, the Nationalists cut the countryside up into more manageable pieces. The railroad lines were protected by blockhouses that allowed the Nationalists to greatly reduce the Communists' ability to move from one sector to another. In addition, the railroads allowed for rapid reinforcement of any blockhouse under significant attack. Slowly but surely, the Nationalists were strangling the Communists by cutting them off from their source of strength, the peasants. The Communists were being beaten.

Recognizing that they were dealing with an entirely new situation, the Communists made the tough and fateful decision to abandon their home area in the south and commence the Long March to reestablish their forces in Yenan. The Long March itself is one of the epic tales of human endurance and determination. In a little more than a year, the Communists marched nearly 5,000 miles while fighting more than 200 battles. Despite constant combat, hunger, and deprivation, the Communists averaged fifteen miles a day over difficult terrain, across mountain ranges, over swollen rivers, and through desolate plains. Of the 86,000 who started the march, fewer than 5,000 completed it.

The Long March had the immediate effect of consolidating Mao's authority in the Communist Party and providing an incredibly tough and intensely loyal cadre he came to draw on in the future. From this point forward, Mao had a firm grip on power within the Communist Party. Although he fought off several subsequent challenges to his authority, using various and often brutal tactics, he never again gave up control of the party.

In addition to providing a safe place to consolidate his power, Yenan gave Mao time to reflect on what he had learned. While in Yenan, he wrote his famous *Yui Chi Chan* [*Guerrilla Warfare*]. As remarkable as this slender volume is, Mao never claimed to have created a new form of warfare—he knew that guerrillas had been around for centuries. He was simply a practitioner of war laying out what he thought would be a war-winning strategy.

Although this book ostensibly discusses the anti-Japanese war, Mao was looking beyond the war with Japan to the inevitable struggle with the Nationalists. Although not claiming to have created a new method of war, he did provide a strategic concept that moved guerrilla warfare from a subordinate effort to support a conventional army to a war-winning approach.

As the first practitioner to define insurgency, Mao, like Clausewitz, understood that war is fundamentally a political undertaking. However, he went much further than Clausewitz in his definition, stating, "The problem of political mobilization of the army and the people is indeed of the utmost importance . . . political mobilization is the most fundamental condition for winning the war."[6] He further emphasized the primacy of political efforts when he stated, "Our job is not merely to recite our political program to the people. . . . [We must] transform the political mobilization for the war into a regular movement. This is a matter of the first magnitude on which the victory primarily depends."[7]

After firmly establishing the overriding political nature of insurgency, Mao outlined his famous three phases for the successful conduct of insurgency. Boiled down to their essence the three phases are:

> **Phase I:** The insurgents concentrate primarily on building political strength. Military action is limited to selected, politically motivated assassinations. Any other military action must have a propaganda purpose to cement the population's support of the insurgents.
>
> **Phase II:** The insurgents gain strength and consolidate control of base areas. They begin to actively administer some portions of the contested area. And, because Mao had no outside sponsor providing weapons, they conducted military operations both to capture arms and to wear down government forces.
>
> **Phase III:** The insurgents commit regular forces (which have been carefully husbanded up to this point) in a final offensive against the government. This phase can succeed only if the "correlation of forces" has been shifted to the insurgents during the early phases.

Although apparently simple, these three phases show a sophisticated understanding of the powerful political, economic, and social elements that constitute the "base" of military power. Mao knew that insurgents could not match the government's conventional military forces initially. Therefore, he conceived the careful buildup of political, social, and economic power during phases I and II. His goal was nothing less than to change the "correlation of forces" between the government and the insurgents. Only after that shift would the insurgents be ready to move to phase III, final destruction of the government by conventional forces.

Thus Mao developed, tested, and used two critical concepts in his victorious effort to overthrow the Nationalist Chinese government. The first was that political power was the essential force in an armed conflict. The second was that political power could be used to change the correlation of forces so that insurgent conventional forces could conduct the final offensive to overthrow the government.

Mao's practical solutions to the problems the Chinese Revolution faced resulted in the evolution of a new form of war, which became known as "People's War." His emphasis on building a firm political base among the masses of people and using that political power to slowly wear down an enemy's superior military power was an innovation of the first order. It was not the first time this approach had been used. However, it was the first time it had been clearly articulated and then disseminated as a form of warfare capable of defeating much more powerful enemies.

Mao also thought beyond the boundaries of China. He expanded his ideas to state that to maximize political power, insurgents must project it beyond their borders. Through propaganda, they must attack their enemy by undermining the political will of that enemy's people, allies, and sponsors. The insurgents must further mobilize neutral political opinion to pressure the enemy's major allies into withdrawing support. The final task of the insurgent propagandist was to generate material and economic support for the movement from friendly and neutral countries.

Mao understood the international aspect of his struggle. Although he did not receive major weapons shipments or direct support from outside sources, he was keenly aware that international opinion could significantly reduce support to his Nationalist foes. In discussing his plan to defeat the Japanese (and later the Nationalist Chinese, whom Mao always knew he would have to fight), he stated, "It is not enough for China to rely on her strength alone and she cannot win without utilizing the aid of international forces and the change within the enemy country, her international propaganda and diplomacy will become more important . . .[8]

Mao counted heavily on political maneuvering to change the "correlation of forces" both internal and external to China. He had also developed long-term, effective strategic, operational, and tactical approaches to achieve that shift in forces. Generations before Westerners began to discuss the power of networks, Mao strove to develop both internal and external networks to support his revolution.

Internally, the networks provided a way to move information to his followers and a way to keep those followers under close observation for security reasons. The party tried to ensure that each party member was a member of one of numerous party groups, such as the Young Communist League, Young Workers, and Young Students. If each party member was a member of several groups, he was caught in a thick web of both support and control.

Thus, long before networks became essential elements of the wider world, Mao was employing them in his political and security organizations.

Internationally, Mao built networks to neutralize, as much as feasible, support for the Nationalists. Although these networks could not stop support, they had an impact—and Mao always took advantage of any edge in his struggle.

Although Mao employed every technique he could devise to shift the correlation of forces, he knew that the final destruction of the Nationalist government would depend on a maneuver campaign by conventional forces: "The concept that guerrilla warfare is an end in itself and that guerrilla activities can be divorced from those of the regular forces is incorrect."[9]

Mao's People's War was a major evolution away from the Western concept of campaigns fought purely by regular forces. However, he did not move completely away from the concept that only regular forces, by destroying the enemy's armies, can win a war. While reversing Clausewitz's relative value concerning political as opposed to military power, Mao still saw the application of military power as the final step in the revolution.

Even with this caveat, Mao is the father of a new strategic approach to war. His three phases served as an outline for successful insurgencies, whether urban or rurally based. He recognized that war is essentially unpredictable and he therefore built great flexibility into the model. Based on his own successes and failures, stretching over decades as a commander, he knew that the phases could not be rigidly separated but merged into each other. An insurgency may be in late phase II in some parts of the country while still in early phase I in others.

Conversely, if government counterinsurgency actions become successful, the insurgents may revert to phase I. In fact, if the insurgents are organizing properly, the covert organizations essential in phase I remain intact and underground, ready to resume functioning until the final victory of phase III.

People's War was correctly hailed as a new form of war. Mao was the first to envision political power as the key to insurgency. He saw it as a long-term struggle that would ebb and flow before leading to final victory. He also understood that networked, interlocked, mass organizations were the key to political power. Long before we conceived of our "modern," wired, interconnected society, Mao had established an entire insurgency based on that principle. Using mission-type orders for most day-to-day operations, he reserved all major strategic decisions to himself—and also used the network to ensure that none of his subordinates could accumulate enough power to depose him.

Mao's real genius lay in learning from his mistakes, then taking those lessons and organizing them into a coherent, articulate strategy for seizing power. His was the fundamental work upon which the fourth generation of war would be built.

CHAPTER 6

# The Vietnamese Modification

Necessity being the mother of invention, Ho Chi Minh and Vo Nguyen Giap developed and employed the next major modification of Communist insurgency doctrine. The first Communist insurgents faced with defeating a powerful outside government, they developed an interesting twist on the concept of People's War. While maintaining the Maoist model of a three-phase insurgency based on the peasants, they refined the model to include an aggressive attack on the national will of their principal enemy—first France, then the United States. Ho and Giap developed the ability to take the political war to their distant enemy's homeland and destroy his will to continue the struggle.

For purposes of this study, it is vital to understand how nations as sophisticated and powerful as France and the United States could completely misunderstand the type of conflict in which they were engaged. It is clear that much as the generals of World War I did not understand that warfare had changed, first the French and then the U.S. political and military leaders missed the changes.

To illustrate how completely the United States missed the type of war we were fighting, consider Col. Harry Summers' *On Strategy: A Critical*

*Analysis of the Vietnam War.* Published in 1982, it was widely acclaimed in political, military, and academic circles as a clear, accurate strategic assessment of the U.S.-Vietnamese War. In it, Summers used Clausewitzean logic to argue that the proper role for the United States in Vietnam was to act as a screen between the North Vietnamese regulars and South Vietnam. He believed that the true threat to South Vietnam was not from insurgency but from a conventional invasion. The insurgent activity simply served to distract our attention from the real threat—the North Vietnamese Army. Colonel Summers backs this argument by pointing out that it was, in fact, the North Vietnamese Army that finally invaded and destroyed the South.

He states:

> It is indicative of our strategic failure in Vietnam that almost a decade after our involvement the true nature of the Vietnam War is still in question. There are still those who would attempt to fit it into the revolutionary war mold and who blame our defeat on our failure to implement counterinsurgency doctrine. This point of view requires an acceptance of the North Vietnamese contention that the . . . North Vietnamese regular forces were an extension of the guerrilla effort, a point of view not borne out by the facts.[1]

Colonel Summers was joined in this viewpoint by a number of other senior U.S. officers. Admiral U. S. Sharp, CINPACFLT 1964–68, contended that the Vietnam War was essentially a conventional war and was subject to solution by application of conventional military force. Sharp stated, "We could have forced Hanoi to give up its efforts to take over South Vietnam. But authority to use air power to this end was simply not forthcoming."[2]

Agreeing with this conclusion, General R. G. Davis stated, "[F]rom the beginning, it was known that the real enemy would be those 14 NVA regular divisions plus the Viet Cong main force regiments and battalions."[3]

In his otherwise outstanding article comparing Vietnam to El Salvador, Lieutenant Colonel Hayden also subscribed to this theory. He wrote:

> [I]n Vietnam in 1968, following the Tet offensive . . . a combined civil-military campaign plan for nation building ultimately defeated the insurgents by 1970 and forced the North Vietnamese to conventional military tactics in 1972. It was not a barefoot guerrilla who kicked in the Saigon Presidential Palace gate in April 1975, but a North Vietnamese T-54 tank. It took a major North Vietnamese conventional military offensive to do what a revolutionary insurgency could not do in South Vietnam.[4]

The common theme that comes out in all these writings and that has many proponents even today is, *South Vietnam was not defeated by an insurgency but rather by the conventional forces of a "foreign" nation.*

Although the statement that we had destroyed most of the insurgents in South Vietnam is accurate, the interpretation that South Vietnam fell to a conventional, foreign invasion is not. Even more significant, the idea that concentrating on the North Vietnamese conventional power would have won the war is a gross oversimplification of the conflict—a fundamental misunderstanding of the nature of the war.

Yet the idea that Vietnam fell to an invasion has great appeal, precisely because it simplifies the situation. It moves us out of the complex realm of insurgency and 4GW into the relatively orderly and easy-to-understand realm of conventional war. Unfortunately, if we are seduced by this idea, we fail to see the nature of the war we fought and therefore cannot learn from it. We will not see the significant contribution the Vietnamese made to 4GW.

### *Reality*

Although the conventional foreign-invasion theory sounds convincing to an American reader, its fundamental flaw is that it reflects an American point of view. Viewing these events from an American point of view helps us understand what we did, but it obscures what the Vietnamese Communists were doing and therefore what was really happening on the ground.

In contrast, the study of the war from a Viet point of view, using Mao's model of a three-phased insurgency, clearly shows that the Second Indochina War was an insurgency brought to its planned conclusion. In the last chapter, we briefly explored how Mao developed People's War. We can now explore how Ho Chi Minh and his followers modified that three-phased approach to succeed in Vietnam.

In his address to the Second National Congress of the Viet-Nam Worker's Party, Ho summarized the Viet Minh revolution to date: "Our Party and Government foresaw that our Resistance War has three stages. In the first stage . . . all we did was to preserve and increase our main forces. In the second stage, we have actively contended with the enemy and prepared for the general counteroffensive. The third stage is the general counteroffensive."[5]

Clearly, Ho is using Mao's three-phased model Not only did he openly declare he was using Mao's model, he did so in February 1951. In his address, the war he was discussing was the First Indochina War, between the French and the Viets. The speech was made three years before the decisive conventional campaign of Dien Bien Phu. Even this early, Ho saw exactly how he could defeat a militarily superior enemy.

Despite Ho's stating exactly what his strategic approach would be, the majority of the French officers either never understood the concept or simply did not believe it could work. Those who did understand utterly failed to develop a strategy to counter it. After floundering tactically from 1945 to 1953, the French appointed General Navarre on May 28, 1953, to command the French Union Forces in Indochina.

At the time, the French effort was stalled—and, as in all insurgencies, if the government is not succeeding, the insurgents are getting stronger. Navarre had to do something. There was never an official published program known as the "Navarre Plan." However, according to various public statements made at the time of its inception, the practical meaning and purpose of the plan becomes clear. According to Navarre's own chief of cabinet, Colonel Revol, the Navarre Plan was designed to break "'the organized body of communist aggression by the end of the 1955 fighting season, leaving the task of mopping up the smaller guerrilla groups to the national armies of Cambodia, Laos, and Viet-Nam."[6]

General Navarre did not understand the Maoist tactic of retreating before pressure to ensure survival of the insurgent's forces. Nor did he understand that the guerrillas were not a peripheral supporting element of the insurgents, but that during phase II, the guerrillas' forces are at the heart of the insurgent's strategy.

In October 1953, General Giap, commander of the Vietnamese People's Army, showed that he was using Mao's admonition:

> Di jin, wo tui, [When the] enemy advances,we withdraw,
> Di jiu, wo roa, [When the] enemy rests, we harass,
> Di pi, wo da, [When the] enemy tires, we attack,
> Di tui, wo jui, [When the] enemy withdraws, we pursue.

Where Navarre massed forces, Giap withdrew. Where Navarre held fast, Giap harassed and bled the French garrisons. Where Navarre economized forces, Giap attacked. Where French forces tried to withdraw from the highlands, Giap pursued ruthlessly—wiping out most of the detachments.

By October, it became clear that the French forces were destroying neither the Communist main force nor the guerrilla forces. Therefore, Navarre initiated an offensive in the south, with the stated objective of seizing a major Communist base, Phu Nho Quan. He seemed to believe that Giap would be forced to defend this asset and the forces located there. As Bernard Fall, French author and expert on the Indochina conflict, points out, "Contrary to the hopes of the French, communist General Giap did not let himself be goaded to commit the mass of his elite forces for the sake of saving one division. When Phu Nho Quan had become useless, the VPA forces around it merely melted again into the rice paddies and hills, and the French entered a deserted city."[7]

After seizing the base area, the French could see no strategic value in retaining it, so they returned to garrison. The battered but still effective Vietnam People's Army (VPA) regiments immediately moved back into the contested space. Frustrated at their inability to come to grips with the VPA (and still erroneously thinking that they could beat an insurgent via the "big battle"), Navarre decided to take the fight to ground of the Communists' choosing. He struck deep into Communist territory with an airborne assault on Dien Bien Phu on November 20, 1953. Giap responded by attacking French outposts in the four corners of Indochina. Navarre spread his already thin forces even thinner by moving forces to the threatened areas. As Fall observed:

> Giap thus had fully succeeded in making Navarre progressively throw his painfully gathered mobile reserve into the four corners of Indochina in pursuit of a "single-battle decision" that was definitely not part of the pattern of the war fought in Indochina. Yet in his New Year's message to his troops, Navarre stated: "Having lost all hope of winning a decisive battle in the Red River Delta, the Viet-Minh disperses its forces.... However, in that type of warfare, we have the advantage of being able to concentrate our forces rapidly at any essential point. . . . A campaign begun under such conditions can but turn in our favor."[8]

Once potential French reinforcements were scattered, Giap hit Dien Bien Phu hard. By May 15, 1954, Dien Bien Phu had fallen. By July 21, a cease-fire had been negotiated in Geneva, and hostilities had ceased. The French people were exhausted. Unable to see any successful conclusion to the war and concerned with the rising conflict in Algeria, they simply wanted out. The French conceded control of the northern half of Vietnam to the Viet Minh.

Although jubilant at their victory, the Viet Minh obviously felt they had been cheated of what they had won on the battlefield. They were not content with leaving half the country in control of another government, even if it was nominally Vietnamese. After biding their time to see if the promised 1956 elections would be held, the Communists continued the struggle. During this period, Ho also ruthlessly put down unrest in North Vietnam. The peasants, angered at the failure to keep the promises made during the fighting, attempted to organize. Ho crushed them.

After securing his rear area, Ho restated his faith in the Maoist theory he espoused as the basis for the struggle for complete unification. While addressing the Third National Congress of the Viet-Nam Workers Party in 1960, he said, "Over the past nine years, our Party, implementing the line of the Second Congress, led our people's bitter, difficult and heroic War of Resistance . . ."[9] He proudly stated that the liberated areas now serve as the "firm base of the struggle for national reunification. . . . Our nation is one, our country is one. Our people will undoubtedly overcome all difficulties and achieve national reunification and bring the north and south together."[10]

Ho repeatedly stated that he would follow Mao's model right through phase III. Even so, we don't have to take his word for it. We can compare what happened in the military and political arenas from the mid-1950s to 1975 with Mao's three-phase model.

During the late 1950s, different parts of Vietnam were in different phases of the insurgency. This didn't worry Ho, because Mao had said this would be the case in virtually all insurgencies. Unless the government collapses, as did Batista's, insurgents lack the strength to simultaneously execute phase III throughout the country. Instead, they must progressively take over sections of the country. For example, regular Communist forces occupied North Vietnam, the Iron Triangle, and portions of the Central Highlands, which therefore represented territory at the successful conclusion of phase III. These areas served as the secure bases Mao declared were necessary to prosecute phases I and II.

Other provinces were heavily contested, and administration in these areas passed back and forth between insurgents and the government. Often, it was literally a matter of night and day. The government withdrew inside compounds at night, and the insurgents ruled until morning. In keeping with Mao's writings, the insurgents fought when conditions favored them, governed when they could, and withdrew when faced with superior forces. These areas fulfilled Mao's description of contested areas in phase II of his model.

Finally, in the government strongholds, insurgent activity was limited to covert political organization and assassinations, clearly phase I activities. In these areas, in keeping with Mao's writings, insurgents focused on building the political base that would sustain the guerrillas when they moved to phase II. Just as important, they sunk those roots deep, so that the organization could survive any government actions. Therefore, despite early U.S.

financial and advisory assistance to the South Vietnamese government, the insurgents were making accelerating gains during the late 1950s.

In the early sixties, greater U.S. assistance and Diem's consolidation of power initially resulted in numerous Communist reverses. Unfortunately, after these early successes, Diem became more and more remote from his own people. His government became more and more corrupt and dictatorial and his tactics more and more brutal. His treatment of dissenters ensured that no one could come forward to try to correct the problems that were driving people away. As a result, the insurgents regained the initiative in the countryside. The Communists' obvious progress and Diem's alienation from his own people led to his overthrow and execution in 1963.

In the turmoil following Diem's death, the Communists pushed hard nationwide. Using constant military pressure, international propaganda, and organized political agitation, they exploited divisions in the government and changed the "correlation of forces" strongly in their favor. Therefore, in keeping with Mao's model, they moved to dramatically expand their phase III areas in early 1965. They committed major conventional forces, in an attempt to seize the highlands and cut South Vietnam in half. However, they ran smack into the newly deployed U.S. combat forces and were badly mauled.

The entry of major U.S. combat forces suddenly and dramatically shifted the correlation of forces back in favor of the South Vietnamese government. Unable to stand up to U.S. forces in conventional combat, the Vietnamese were forced to abandon phase III in most of the south and return to phase II. In areas of American concentration, they were even forced to drop back to phase I.

Mao had anticipated this possibility. He had said, "[T]he strategic counter-offensive of the third phase will not in the initial phase assume a uniform and even pace throughout the country, but will rise in one locality and fall in another . . . China's task will be to take advantage of this international situation in order to attain her complete liberation and establish an independent democratic state . . . ."[11]

Mao knew that enemy successes could force an insurgent to regress to an earlier phase. However, he was convinced that as long as the insurgents remained active and followed his theory, they would eventually win.

With the entrance of U.S. combat forces into the war, the Communists were forced back to phase II operations until the "correlation of forces" once again shifted in their favor. Aware of his military and economic inferiority, Ho sought to use international political maneuvering in conjunction with guerrilla warfare to bring about this change. He foresaw that the long-term course of the war was subject to change, based on the international political situation: "It is possible to examine the general situation in order to divide it into big stages, but it is not possible to cut off completely one stage from the other like cutting bread. The length of each stage depends on . . . [t]he changes between the enemy forces and ours, and also on the changes in the international situation whether the general offensive will come early or late."[12]

Besides being closely attuned to the international political situation's influence on the war, Ho envisioned a long war of attrition, leading to ultimate victory. As he explained to Bernard Fall in 1962, "Sir, you have studied us for ten years, you have written about the Indochina War. It took us eight years of bitter fighting to defeat you French in Indochina. . . . The Americans are stronger than the French. It might perhaps take ten years but our heroic compatriots in the South will defeat them in the end. We shall marshal public opinion about this unjust war against the South Vietnamese."[13]

He openly explained how he expected to beat the U.S.–South Vietnamese alliance. He planned a war of attrition, accompanied by intensive national and international propaganda to weaken American resolve. After accurately explaining what he planned, Ho then proceeded to execute that plan.

Much as he had done against the French, he spread American forces out by engaging them throughout South Vietnam. Again, as he had against the French and Mao had against the Japanese, he instructed his commanders to choose the time and place of all engagements. That way, he could control the tempo and attrition of his forces as well as those of the Allies.

The attrition from 1965 to 1968 convinced the north that the time had come to shift to phase III, the conventional fight. We do not have access to North Vietnamese records, so we do not know if they really thought the South Vietnamese civilians would rise up or if Tet was a desperate measure because the north felt they were losing. Whichever is the truth, the long period of attrition and optimistic predictions by General Westmoreland, followed by the massive shock of Tet 68, did indeed change the correlation of forces.

Although Tet drastically changed the balance of military forces in favor of the U.S.–South Vietnamese, it even more decisively changed the political climate in favor of the Communists. Although Tet resulted in crippling casualties among the insurgent infrastructure, it did little or no damage to the "base areas" of the revolution in North Vietnam, Cambodia, Laos, and portions of South Vietnam. In contrast, the U.S. tactical victory could not reduce the terminal strategic damage caused to the political will of the United States.

There has been a great deal of discussion about this apparent dichotomy between the battlefield results and the strategic outcome. Yet if you look at it from a 4GW point of view, it is the natural outcome. Remember that the struggle is primarily political, so it matches the political strength of one opponent against the political strength of the other. Our leaders had expended their political capital both domestically and internationally by repeatedly underestimating the Communists and promising early victory. In contrast, the combination of the iron control of a dictator and the repeated statements to his people that the struggle could take decades kept Ho's political capital high domestically.

Internationally, Ho turned up his propaganda. To sway Westerners who were already leaning to the left, Ho portrayed the Viet Cong as a small group of freedom fighters trying to overthrow a corrupt regime. He emphasized the destruction wrought against Vietnamese civilians and villages by American firepower and large-scale operations.

To undercut the support of the center and the right of the United States, Ho focused on a different message. For them, he emphasized that the corrupt southern regime was happy to let American soldiers die for it as long as key members of the regime could get rich. And of course, the South Vietnamese government helped his campaign by living up to many of his slurs.

In contrast, even post-Tet, the United States simply stuck to its pre-Tet statement that it was winning and that the South Vietnamese were a democratic government. We seemed to feel that the destruction of the cadre and the improving security situation in the south should speak for themselves. Unfortunately, the U.S. government's poor credibility made Americans reluctant to accept the same line they had been hearing since 1965.

The result was the steady shift of American public opinion against the war—and ever-increasing international pressure to terminate our involvement.

From 1968 to 1972, the security situation in the south actually continued to improve. Although the exact reasons for the improvement are multiple, a major factor had to be the devastating casualties the insurgent cadres took during Tet-68. Throughout the south, key leaders of the Viet Cong cadre had revealed themselves to participate in what they believed was the final offensive—and took massive casualties as a result. The combination of the attrition among the leaders and the fact that the people did not rise up to support the revolution meant that the Viet Cong never recovered in the south. Yet despite the continuing success of the Allied forces, we witnessed the irreversible erosion of U.S. political support for the war during this period.

The Vietnamese achieved this remarkable coup by maintaining minimal military activity while aggressively pushing their international propaganda (which included the "negotiations" in Paris). They moved back into phase II of a Maoist insurgency. Maintaining a low level of military pressure and husbanding their strength, the Communists concentrated their effect on the international political arena to prepare the scene for another move to phase III.

With the erosion of American will, President Johnson's abdication, and the election of President Nixon on a "peace with honor" platform, America shifted its strategic approach to Vietnamization. Under this plan, American combat forces would be withdrawn from the country and the Vietnamese would assume responsibility for their own defense, backed by U.S. firepower and logistics support.

The North Vietnamese were not able to rebuild their network in the south, despite sending large numbers of North Vietnamese to do so. Frustrated in these efforts, they could see that the withdrawal of U.S. forces presented different opportunities. The withdrawal, combined with the

South Vietnamese concentration on pacification in the countryside, led the North Vietnamese to once again attempt to move to phase III.

Seeing the dispersion of the south's military forces and the withdrawal of virtually all U.S. ground combat forces but misreading the international political situation, the Communists prematurely kicked off a major conventional offensive: the 1972 Easter offensive. Once again, the Communists suffered enormous casualties, but this time to their regular forces. Once again, the South Vietnamese people rallied to the government and drew encouragement from their ability to stand against the north. The survival of the South Vietnamese government should have strongly encouraged the United States. Instead, once again this campaign resulted in a further decline in U.S. support for the war.

The combination of continued conflict, corruption in the South Vietnamese government, and the domestic political problems of the Nixon administration completed the destruction of the American people's support for the war. "Vietnamization" continued at breakneck pace and, in 1975, we abandoned the southerners to the tender mercies of their Communist countrymen.

Trained to rely on heavy firepower that is integral to the American way of war, the now penniless South Vietnamese Army was overwhelmed when the North Vietnamese attacked during the spring offensive in 1975. President Ford, as an unelected president serving in the wake of a disgraced president, could not even convince Congress to provide funds and emergency resupply for the South Vietnamese. Although the south had won the pacification war, the Army of the Republic of Vietnam (ARVN)—out of ammunition, spare parts, and hope—was helpless to withstand the conventional forces of the north. The collapse was swift and sudden, if not predictable.

The final phase III offensive—the spring offensive of 1975—brought a Communist victory in the Second Indochina War just as the campaign culminating in Dien Bien Phu represented the decisive phase III success of the First Indochina War. For the third time in as many decades, Mao's approach to war had triumphed.

History shows that the guerrilla war was not a separate war we "won." Rather, it represented phases I and II of a classic Maoist insurgency.

Although we devastated the insurgent infrastructure, the local guerrillas, and the guerrilla main force units, they fulfilled their role in the insurgency. Through their sacrifice, they changed the correlation of forces and set the stage for the final, successful phase III invasion by the conventional forces of the north. The activities of phases I and II were not a separate war but part of the continuum of the insurgency.

This brief review of the Maoist theory, Ho's public statements, and the course of the Second Indochina War should make it clear that Vietnam was an insurgency that showed some marked and clever evolution from Mao's original model. The Vietnamese used 4GW to defeat two powerful overseas enemies without ever placing a soldier on their soil.

In 1951, Ho publicly stated how he was going to beat the French and then did so. In 1962, Ho explained to Bernard Fall exactly how he was going to beat the Americans and then did so. In both cases, he stated he was going to employ Mao's People's War. Despite all this proof, some Americans continue to argue that the troops who seized the presidential palace on April 30, 1975, were "foreign troops." Therefore, we won the "insurgency" but lost the war by failing to deal with the conventional forces that were the real enemy.

For purposes of this study, it is essential that we destroy that myth. If we do not understand that the Vietnamese won using a variation of Mao's People's War, we cannot see it as a logical progression in 4GW. In fact, the following brief look at Vietnamese history will show that South Vietnam was not invaded by a "foreign" army but fell to the phase III efforts of a Vietnamese insurgency.

### *The Foreign Invasion*

The first and most basic problem with the concept of a foreign troops destroying South Vietnam is that it looks at the problem purely from a Western point of view. The Vietnamese Communists, north and south, certainly did not think of themselves as foreigners. They saw Vietnam as a single nation that had evolved over more than 2,000 years. Much of that time, the Vietnamese had endured incredible hardships fighting to eject Chinese invaders.

In addition to resisting the Chinese, the Vietnamese constantly strove to subjugate neighboring peoples. Throughout the last thousand years, they slowly displaced a variety of peoples (primarily the Chans and the Khmers) eventually expanding to fill the area we now know as Vietnam. Vietnamese thought of their country as a single entity—and continued to do so even after the French conquered it and divided it into thirds for ease of administration during the 19th century.

In contrast to this long historic tradition, the Western concept of a North and South Vietnam was born in the Geneva Accords of 1954. These accords further stated that separation was to be temporary, with free elections and unification by 1956. After the accords, Ho himself said, "At present what are the revolutionary tasks of our Party? On the national level, we have not yet completed the task of a national people's democratic revolution. As for the north alone, since the restoration of peace (1954), it has been liberated completely. . . . In the south, we are carrying on the task . . . and are struggling for national unity."[14]

Thus the concept that South Vietnam, an artificial entity with a short history, fell to an invasion of foreign troops is absurd from a Vietnamese point of view. Clearly, despite the continuing denials of some Americans, this was a classic insurgency.

Once we accept the fact that we were defeated by an insurgency, the key question is, "Did the Vietnamese develop any strategic, operational, or tactical innovations that advanced 4GW?" The clearest proof they did is that from Tet until 1975, the insurgents consistently lost on the battlefield, yet they won the war. Strategically, they shifted the focus from the battlefield to the political arena. The Paris peace talks provided a venue to present their arguments to the world. They could appear to be negotiating but in reality remain as intransigent and focused on victory as ever.

Operationally, they tied their tactical actions to wearing down the political will of the United States. They did not seek major battles or victories but steady attrition, at their own pace, that would result in changing the correlation of forces in their favor. Tactically, they controlled the tempo, frequency, and location of most engagements. They maximized their advantages while minimizing American firepower. They even turned that firepower against America by ensuring that they fought as often as possible in areas where American supporting arms killed civilians. They did not try to "hold" the field at the end of the day. Thus, by Western standards, they were consistently losing the battles. This would have mattered in 3GW but is irrelevant in 4GW.

### *Defeat and the Press*

The puzzling dichotomy between apparent battlefield success and long-term strategic failure led many Americans to blame the press for the fact that the Vietnamese could lose so consistently yet still win the propaganda battle. It is essential to examine that charge to see whether "the press," as an independent entity, caused our defeat—or if it was a combination of U.S. failure to get our message out and Vietnamese success in disseminating theirs. In other words, was the shift in opinion the result of independent outside forces or the actions of the governments involved?

Essentially the "it was the press' fault" argument states, "The United States won great military victories throughout the war, and particularly during Tet 68. It was the press that turned these victories into a political defeat." Unfortunately, this theme does not recognize that war has changed. It still subscribes to the Clausewitzean idea that destroying the enemy's army is the key to winning a war. This theme argues that Tet 68 should have been a victory in itself and a serious strategic setback for the Communists. Further, the continued U.S. and Army of the Republic of Vietnam successes against the Viet Cong and NVA should have sealed our victory rather than seen the erosion of support. Instead, according to this view, the Communists actually gained strength because of inaccurate reporting by the U.S. and international press. According to this thesis, the inaccurate reporting heavily contributed to the destruction of America's will to fight.

This statement shows a fundamental misunderstanding of the evolving 4GW tactics and techniques. All military actions have value only if they contribute to the political goal of the government. The comparative body count and control of a specific geographic area is not significant. The only issue is whether the action affects the political strengths of the combatants.

The Communists clearly did not expect the devastating defeat of Tet and probably did not foresee its powerful political fallout. Yet, unlike the United States, they were quick to capitalize on it. Worldwide, they hammered home Ho's recurring theme:

> The truth is President Johnson wants neither peace nor peace negotiations. As a matter of fact, at the very moment when he talks a lot about peace discussion, the U.S. imperialists are further expanding their war of aggression in South Viet-Nam, massively sending there tens of thousands of U.S. troops and extending "escalation" in North Viet-Nam. The peoples of the world have clearly seen this. That is precisely the reason why the progressive American people are actively opposing the U.S. war of aggression in Viet-Nam.[15]

Given insurgency's political nature, Ho understood that the U.S. center of gravity was our political will. He used the impact of Tet to attack that center of gravity. He turned the battlefield defeat into a major strategic victory in his effort to change the correlation of forces in preparation for the conventional battles of phase III. In contrast, the U.S. government did not seem to understand that the perception of what happened in Tet was more important than what really happened. Even worse, the government had squandered its credibility with the press and, through them, with the U.S. public. According to John Laurence, a young CBS reporter at the time:

> Bad information was in the military reporting system. . . . Each stage of the reporting system was vulnerable to inaccuracy. At times, lies were deliberate. Body counts were exaggerated. Civilian dead, wounded and captured became enemy dead, wounded and captured. The numbers of weapons and supplies captured and destroyed were inflated. Territory swept was misreported. Details of combat were adjusted to look more favorable to the U.S. side. Successful enemy ambushes were not reported. Casualties from friendly fire were listed as combat dead and injured. Mistakes of all kinds were unreported. Cover-ups were commonplace.[16]

Laurence is not talking about the late sixties and early seventies in Vietnam. He is talking about his perception as a young reporter in 1965 and 1966. By the end of his first tour in Vietnam, he had completely lost faith in official government statements. By 1966, the official Military Assistance Command Vietnam (MACV) news conference was derisively referred to as the "Five O'Clock Follies." The government's credibility continued to decline from that point.

Further eroding the government's credibility was the fact that General Westmoreland flew home just before Tet to reassure the American people that we were winning, that "there is a light at the end of the tunnel." He completed this cheerleading tour of the United States only a month and a half before Tet.

The embarrassment of being surprised and the disastrous erosion of the government's credibility prevented it from convincing the American people that Tet was really a U.S. victory. Further, the government was never able to recover its credibility with the people or the media. In reality, the press did not turn the tactical success of Tet into a strategic defeat. The inability of U.S. decision makers to understand its political ramifications and deal with those ramifications did.

Understanding how Ho made such good use of the highly inaccurate press reports on Tet is critical to understanding one of the most powerful tools of 4GW. We know the media will continue to play a critical role in all forms of war and, just as with initial military reports, initial press reports are apt not to be accurate.

Even more problematic is the huge increase in the number and types of reporters who will cover any event. Much of that coverage will be unedited, live footage, with narration provided by an anchor who probably has no military experience and, as in a domestic crisis, will simply keep talking to fill airtime.

Because 4GW is essentially political—and we will rarely see the measure of control we had in Desert Storm—the rapid dissemination of accurate, credible information can make or break the counterinsurgents' effort. We must go beyond "disgust" with inaccuracy of the past and try to understand how the press relates to the future conduct of war.

### *Summary*

The thrust of this entire discussion has been to illustrate that key U.S. decision makers never fully understood the nature of the Vietnam War. Like Colonel Summers, they saw the struggle in Clausewitzean terms and felt they could wear down the Vietnamese through sheer attrition. Because they could not conceive of the idea that we could lose until much too late, we never even focused the government on the war. The fact that we had no one above the level of colonel in Washington working on Vietnam full time shows that we considered this a less than serious war. Unfortunately, the phrase "limited war" summed up our level of commitment.

In contrast, the Communists understood the nature of the war they were conducting. They knew the key to victory was the will of the American people. Knowing this, they developed a strategy to attack that will. They dictated the tempo, timing, number of engagements, terms of engagement, areas of operations, and final outcome. The question remains, how did this come about?

Given the enormous gulf between the culture, histories, and political organizations of the antagonists, it is understandable that neither side began with a good understanding of the other. Yet, despite having started with major misconceptions about the United States and its relationship with its South Vietnamese ally, the Communists proved flexible enough to analyze the situation in light of new information, learn from their mistakes, and reorient their efforts toward our weak point: our national will.

Like the Communists, the United States and South Vietnam started without a clear picture of what was necessary for victory. However, we never changed. We clearly misunderstood the Communists and struck at the periphery of their strength: their regular combat forces. Not understanding Mao's insurgency, despite the wide availability of books that articulated it and Ho's public endorsement of it, we focused on the North Vietnamese conventional forces. We consistently sought "big battles" against those forces. As a result, we virtually ignored the key battle for political credibility and strength essential in this new form of warfare. We were fighting an entirely different war than the Vietnamese.

Despite the initial groping by both sides, the Communists had a clear understanding of the nature of the war they were fighting. They had a guide and stuck to it. Even when they misinterpreted the situation and attempted to move to phase III prematurely, not once but twice, they maintained their strategic focus and dropped back to phase II. The result was an insurgency that developed mostly as described by Mao. Making use of their secure base area in North Vietnam, "protracted war," and continual political propaganda, the Communists changed the "correlation of forces" between the warring factions and destroyed the political will of the United States.

Against both the French and the Americans, the Vietnamese successfully exploited the natural divisiveness of a democracy to erode support for the war. The effectiveness of the North Vietnamese attacks was reinforced by the failure of Western leaders to comprehend what was happening. In both cases, Ho's successful campaign against outside "aggression" cleared the way for the military victory that constitutes phase III of the Maoist model.

In contrast, our strategic decision makers could not escape their inherent prejudices in their views of war. As Shy and Collier put it, "American strategy severely challenged Ho and Giap, but in the end it failed to defeat them, in large part because it never grasped the kind of war being fought nor the particular Vietnamese conditions that gave the war its revolutionary character."[17]

Even today, many Americans point to the apparent sudden willingness of the Vietnamese to negotiate after the Christmas bombing offensive as proof that we could have won the war with proper application of conventional forces. This makes sense only if you view negotiation in a Western European sense as a way to end a conflict. In contrast, Mao and the North Vietnamese saw negotiation as simply another tool in the conflict. Mao stated openly that:

> Revolutions rarely compromise; compromises are made only to further the strategic design. Negotiation, then, is undertaken for the dual purpose of gaining time to buttress a position (military, political, social, economic) and to wear down, frustrate and harass the opponent. Few, if any essential concessions are to be expected from

> the revolutionary side, whose aim is only to create conditions that will preserve the unity of the strategic line and guarantee the development of a "victorious situation."[18]

First France, then the United States, saw superior military power neutralized by the superior political agility of the Vietnamese. The result was a successful execution of a classic insurgency, right down to the final conventional battles—and the continued evolution of the fourth generation.

Although the Vietnamese strategy was developed only after a long series of mistakes and at great cost, Ho's determined adherence to People's War and his eventual understanding of the strategic situation allowed him to focus his efforts on the real enemy. In doing so, he provided yet another step forward in insurgent theory. He showed insurgents how to defeat the political will of outside sponsor states and refined the concept of "changing the correlation of forces."

Although this entire chapter may seem an exercise in semantics, its purpose is to stimulate the reader to consider the nature of the war itself. Like most Westerners, we are more comfortable with the European concept of war, with its clearly defined use of force and relatively clear delineation of the responsibilities of the military. Unfortunately, political, demographic, and religious trends since World War II indicate that future wars will be complex, confusing, and nasty 4GW struggles rather than the simpler conflicts of earlier generations.

During the thirty years of conflict, the Vietnamese Communists refined and improved on Mao's doctrine. They showed insurgents how to use a wide variety of information channels to directly attack the will of external powers. These great powers, the United States and France, thought they were protected by oceans from direct enemy action—and found out too late that they had misunderstood the nature of the war they were fighting.

# CHAPTER 7

# The Sandinista Refinement

With the success of the Vietnamese, insurgents worldwide took heart. If a small Third World nation like Vietnam could defeat the United States, anything was possible. This led to increased efforts by insurgents in widely separated areas of the world. And like all efforts to adopt new forms of warfare, some were successful and others were not.

In Nicaragua, the Sandinistas, through evolutionary steps, further increased the emphasis on political development driving the battlefield outcome. They refined the Maoist doctrine by making political strategy itself the endgame. In the Sandinista strategy, political maneuvering would not be the precursor to a conventional invasion—it would serve as the invasion itself, by destroying external support for the Nicaraguan National Guard. However, like previous innovations, it took time, mistakes, and numerous false paths before the Sandinistas found the solution to seizing power.

The movement started in 1961, when Thomas Borge and Carlos Fonseca founded the Sandinista Front for National Liberation (FSLN). Although this is the accepted date for the start of the movement, they did not publish a clear manifesto concerning their doctrine at that time—most likely because they had not yet developed one. However, they did state that they were Marxist-Leninists who subscribed to the "foco" theory of insurgency.* With Castro's success in Cuba and Che Guevera's popularity, this was a logical choice for a Latin American insurgent at the time.

In June 1963, they felt ready to attempt an armed revolution based on that theory. In keeping with the "foco" theory, Borge led approximately sixty guerrillas into Nicaragua, in an attempt to start the revolution. By October, the effort had failed. The simplistic "foco" approach never had a chance of building the organization necessary to overcome the Somoza security apparatus. The few survivors retreated across the border into Honduras and were arrested. Not perceived to be a genuine threat, they served varying times in Honduran prisons and were released.

Upon release, the Sandinistas spent the next few years struggling simply to survive while they figured out a new approach. Learning from the mistakes they made and from the failure of similar movements throughout Latin America, they abandoned the "foco" theory. In its place, the FSLN experimented with different approaches to establishing a popular uprising against Somoza.

First, they flirted unsuccessfully with an urban revolution. This, too, failed—in the same way it failed in other nations. The entire theory of forming guerrilla forces in the cities played to the strengths of the dictator's security forces.

After failing in direct attempts at urban warfare, they attempted to organize urban labor but could not organize the labor unions into Communist fronts. Refusing to give up, the Sandinistas agreed to try a Maoist

* The "foco" theory of insurgencies states that by creating a small focus group of armed guerrillas, an insurgent group will be able to stimulate a spontaneous uprising of the mass of the people and rapidly overthrow the government. Che Guevera proposed this theory, based on his experiences with Castro in the Cuban Revolution. He did not understand that their success was based on the unique conditions of Cuba, which included a pending collapse of the Batista regime. Che paid for his mistaken theory when he tried to apply it in very different conditions in Bolivia and was killed by government forces in October 1967.

People's War. After two years of preparation, they selected the area around Pancasan mountain to build the base area for their insurgency.

In keeping with Mao's concept, they planned to focus on political organization of the peasant population and avoid fighting the National Guard. Led by Borge and Fonseca, the FSLN returned to the mountains in 1966 to establish a peasant support network. However, they were unsuccessful in generating peasant support. As middle-class, college-educated, urban Communists they failed to inspire Catholic peasants. They were making little or no progress—and frankly did not seem to understand the peasants' inherent distrust of outsiders.

In May 1967, the Nicaraguan National Guard discovered their presence and rapidly moved to destroy them. Twenty-five of the thirty-five Sandinista cadres were killed during the National Guard's campaign. The surviving Sandinistas were forced to flee, first to the cities and then to Cuba. Finally, they fled to Costa Rica, where they were reduced to financing their organization by robbing banks. After the National Guard's campaign, Anastasio Somoza announced that the Sandinistas had been destroyed.[1]

One unexpected benefit accrued from this failed effort in the mountains: the Sandinistas captured the admiration of a number of Latin American students attending Patrice Lumumba Friendship of the Peoples University in the Soviet Union. Nikita Khrushchev had established this university in an attempt to capture and influence the next generation of leadership in the Third World. To attract future leaders to the Communist cause, Khrushchev provided scholarships to promising young Socialists or Communists from all over the world.

Throughout this period, a significant number of Latin American students were enrolled. Because the purpose of the university was to encourage revolution, the faculty naturally provided full reporting on the "heroic" activities of the Sandinistas. As the Latin American students either graduated or dropped out, they returned home and gravitated to the Sandinista cause.

Despite their limited success and even more limited political organization, the Sandinista leadership resolved to continue a People's War. Unfortunately for them, they lacked the clarity of Mao or Ho. The one "intellectual" Sandinista, Fonseca, produced a concept based on Marxism. However, other than promising to redistribute large land holdings to peasants, it did not provide a coherent message for a rural insurgency.

This is a major deviation from both Mao and Ho. Each of them had carefully thought-out political agendas that were central to their plans to unify the peasants behind them. Although neither intended to keep the political promises he made, both had an extensive agenda to present to the people as part of phase I political organization—and they would repeat that theme throughout their struggles. A coherent, applicable message is central to 4GW.

However, neither this lack of a message nor the lack of organization kept the Sandinistas from attempting yet again to establish a peasant-based uprising in the northern mountains. In a variation of tactics, they also began to organize an urban insurgency at the same time. Although the main cadres returned to the mountains, urban organizations would be formed to mobilize students, rob banks, instigate labor disputes, and so on. Like all successful insurgents, the Sandinistas kept trying new approaches until they found something that worked.

Although they did have limited success in the cities, the Sandinistas once again failed utterly to gain the support of the peasants. In addition to being college-educated outsiders, most of the Sandinistas were also "light-skinned"[2] urban dwellers who stood out among the much darker mountain peasants. Unable to convert the peasants to their cause, the Sandinistas were easily tracked through the National Guard's network of peasant informants. As a result, the National Guard was able to kill many Sandinista leaders and easily defeat their second attempt to organize the peasants.

And once again, defeat brought unexpected benefits for the Sandinistas. During 1971, a small group of university students from affluent Nicaraguan families began to seek alternatives to Somoza's regime. They went to a spiritual retreat run by a Catholic priest. Although supposedly discussing religious issues, they turned the discussion to political issues. Over the course of the next year, they applied Marxist thought to the political situation in Nicaragua.

During 1972, they were joined by a Sandinista *commandante* for several days of intense discussion. Then in early 1973, they abandoned the retreat and went underground with the Sandinista movement.[3] They provided new blood, political camouflage, and extensive new contacts for the badly battered Sandinistas. This was the Sandinistas' first expansion of the personal networks so vital to an insurgency.

The Sandinistas got a second major break on December 23, 1972. Nicaragua's capital city, Managua, was virtually destroyed by a massive earthquake. More than eighty percent of the buildings were damaged or destroyed, and about ten thousand people were killed. International aid poured into the country—and was promptly siphoned off into the personal accounts of corrupt members of the Somoza government. The abysmal failure of the government to help the people purely because they were enriching themselves created an issue the Sandinistas could use.

The combination of another setback in the mountains and the rising anger among the people at Somoza's corruption created a sense of urgency among the Sandinistas. The FSLN debated whether to adopt the rural struggle or use a mass urban revolution. The urgency of the debate was enhanced by the feeling that a people's revolt was coming. Conditions in Somoza's Nicaragua were rapidly approaching those of Batista's Cuba in 1959.

In the aftermath of the earthquake, Somoza's cronies were squeezing into areas of the economy that had traditionally belonged to aristocratic families not associated with Somoza. These new incursions alienated those powerful segments of Nicaraguan society. The Sandinistas felt that the combination of the corruption and the competition among the elite would inevitably lead to revolt. Yet as far as most of the country was concerned, the Sandinistas had been destroyed. They clearly had a huge challenge to overcome. They had to prove their continued existence and take the lead in the building resistance to Somoza.

On December 27, 1974, the Sandinistas executed a daring raid on a holiday party and took hostages. Although they narrowly missed capturing the American ambassador, they did get Somoza's foreign minister and many members of his cabinet. Their successful escape to Cuba with $1 million in ransom spectacularly announced that they were not destroyed and resulted in numerous new recruits. It also triggered an internal struggle in the FSLN among those who sought a Maoist protracted-war strategy, those who sought a Marxist proletarian approach, and the *terceristas,* or third-way advocates.

The Maoists went back to the northern mountains and were again easily defeated by the National Guard. Their leader, the intellectual Fonseca, was killed in an ambush on November 8, 1976. Once again, Somoza was convinced he had destroyed the Sandinistas. The urban movement also failed. However, the *terceristas* survived, largely because their key leaders remained outside the country throughout the struggle. From this vantage point, they had the benefit of learning from the mistakes the other factions of the party made while not suffering the casualties that are an inevitable part of such mistakes.

In January 1977, the Sandinistas got another major break. Jimmy Carter was sworn in as president of the United States. Although the Carter administration made no immediate major changes in policy in Central America, the Nicaraguans perceived that Somoza had lost one of the major pillars of his family strength—the unqualified support of the United States. As Shirley Christian points out, "In many countries, even some others in Latin America, Washington's attitude would have meant little, but in Nicaragua the key to power over public policy was to give the appearance of having the support of the United States, whether the U.S. government was consciously giving this support or not."[4]

Like all insurgents, and all warriors for that matter, the Sandinistas learned by trial and error and a series of painful defeats. But finally, they were developing an approach, the "third way," that would lead to victory. At this critical juncture, Humberto Ortega took stock of what their failures had taught them. He recognized that his college-educated, urban colleagues could never earn the trust of the peasants. The Maoist concept of a "peasant revolution" could not work, given the current organization and personnel of the Sandinistas. If he planned to use a Maoist approach, it would require a great deal of time to recruit and train people who could win the confidence of the peasants.

Then, examining the earlier Sandinista attempts to use the "foco" theory and incite urban insurgencies, he understood that the prime weakness of both was their failure to develop a political base. Unlike their problem with the peasants, the Sandinistas' inability to create a political base in the cities probably had more to do with their lack of a clear political agenda. His people were city dwellers, so they could blend in and be easily accepted in the cities. Ortega also recognized that the tremendous population shift to the cities made an effort in the urban areas essential to success. Further, he understood that things were happening quickly in Nicaragua. If the movement went back to the mountains to develop a Maoist insurgency, it would be irrelevant to the coming revolution.

Ortega understood one other key aspect of the strategic situation. The greatest threat to the Sandinistas was the democratic reform movement. If it succeeded while the Sandinistas were still getting established in the mountains, the cause of the insurgency would be neutralized. The formation of a moderate, reformist government would present the Sandinistas with a much greater problem than the repressive Somoza regime.

Ortega's bold solution was to create a third way. He formed a broad-front, urban-based coalition whose strength rested in the middle-class businessmen, entrepreneurs, unemployed students, and urban poor of the shantytowns. On May 4, 1977, he published a new FSLN strategy pape called the "General Political Military Platform of Struggle for the Sandinista Front for National Liberation." Written primarily by Humberto Ortega, it contained the basic insurrectional strategy, including (1) development of a program without leftist rhetoric; (2) creation of a broad anti-Somoza front with non-Marxist opposition groups; (3) creation of mass organizations to support the FSLN; (4) agitation to bring about the radicalization of the moderate opposition; (5) action to undermine the integrity of the National Guard; and (6) unification of the three FSLN factions under a joint leadership.[5]

His emphasis on concealing the FSLN's leftist doctrine combined with active propaganda for a moderate coalition allowed him to convince a wide range of Somoza's opponents to join the coalition. Even without these efforts, Somoza's opponents were driven toward the coalition simply because they no longer had any other outlet for their opposition to his regime. Somoza had driven even legitimate opposition into the shadows.

Taking advantage of the alienation of the business class, the Sandinistas used their extensive network of contacts—often even family members—to encourage key business leaders to join this apparently moderate opposition. This was where the recruitment of the upper-class students from the religious retreat proved critical. Given the small size of Nicaragua's elite business community, many of these young adults knew and were even related to key members of the elite. The Sandinistas exploited those connections to push their agenda forward. They were so successful that a group of twelve prominent citizens actually signed a proclamation of opposition to the regime and published it. They became known as *Los Doce* (The Twelve).

Ortega's success in forming this coalition co-opted most of the opposition factions. By forming the coalition front, the Sandinistas positioned themselves to block any compromise brokered by outside agencies such as the United States. The last thing they wanted was a compromise that could defuse the coming revolution. The Sandinistas' real innovation was that, despite the appearance of a broad front, Ortega ensured that the key elements of power, namely all of the coalition's military and security elements, remained firmly in the hands of the Communist leaders.

Thus, his third way created a broad base of support with a wide range of allies while maintaining firm control of the revolution. Once the coalition took power, the other members of the coalition found that Sandinistas held all the key positions in the new police and military organizations. The moderates realized too late that this arrangement gave the Sandinistas effective control of the country.

With this broad front as a power base, the Sandinistas continued working for the uprising they felt sure was coming. During this period, the FSLN conducted a number of attacks on the National Guard, to keep the movement in the eyes of the people while solidifying the party's control of the front's military arm. At the same time, they moved quietly but effectively to take over all the key security billets.

Much more important to the revolution was the work the Sandinistas did to further undermine support for the Somoza regime in the international community. They showed true strategic vision and operational finesse in orchestrating this campaign while simultaneously consolidating their control on the "popular front" that was opposing the regime.

This was made easier by the fact that the Carter administration regarded the Nicaraguan "problem" as essentially a human rights issue. Other than identifying it as such, the administration seemed incapable of putting together a coherent strategic policy concerning Nicaragua. The Nicaraguans were expecting the United States to provide its "normal" unilateral solution to their problems. Instead, the administration tried to work through the international community, encouraging Somoza to let an international commission referee between him and the opposition. Somoza was not interested—and the Sandinistas worked hard to ensure that the coalition refused to join such negotiations.

The Sandinista attack against U.S. support was based on showing the Sandinistas as a democratic and popular opposition to the corrupt and brutal Somoza regime. The presence of the moderate members of the coalition was essential to this deception. Once they had the moderate and respected leaders in the coalition, the Sandinistas ensured that these were the key spokespeople who met international visitors. There was no talk of a Marxist paradise or the spread of Communism. The spokesperson focused on the theme of a moderate, thoughtful opposition trying to remove a hated dictator without plunging the nation into chaos. To spread this message, they used a number of paths. The most effective were the Western media, the priests who supported "liberation theology," and peace groups in the United States—particularly mainline Protestant churches.

The Western media were invited to Nicaragua to visit with the Sandinistas and report on the atrocities committed by the National Guard. The Sandinistas could count on the Guard committing atrocities virtually every time they operated against the guerrillas. In addition, the media were encouraged to interview members of the coalition, to reassure themselves that the Sandinistas were not Communist but simply moderates who sought a representative government after the overthrow of Somoza.

The media were encouraged to speak to the young priests who were leading the liberation theology movement. Liberation theology had developed because clergy could see the abuses of the Somoza regime. These priests felt they could no longer follow the bishops, because the official church gave support to the Somoza regime. Given the tremendous prestige local priests held in the very religious Nicaraguan society, they were key elements in the coalition's efforts in the countryside. They also proved highly credible spokesmen for the coalition, both to international visitors and their own parishioners.

Another piece of the Sandinista strategy was the effort to use mainline Protestant churches to carry the coalition (Sandinista) message to the U.S. Congress. During this period, they invited numerous members of U.S. congregations to visit Nicaragua and witness for themselves the brutality of the government and the moderate approach of the coalition. They knew that upon their return, these concerned Americans would serve as catalysts in their communities to push for a cutoff of aid to the Somoza regime. Reinforcing the Sandinistas' effort was the fact that the Somoza regime was becoming more and more brutal—and therefore provided plenty of material for the Sandinistas to show their American guests.

Finally, the Sandinistas, representing the coalition, maintained offices in Washington and New York to ensure that their message was transmitted directly to executive and legislative branch personnel as well as to the United Nations and other international organizations. They understood that a multitude of new players were on the international scene and made major efforts to influence them to support their revolution.

As Ortega predicted, widespread turbulence began. It was genuine grassroots resistance to the abuses of the Somoza regime. Well positioned to control the actions of the coalition, the Sandinistas did not immediately grasp that the uprisings were the ones they had been waiting for. Although surprised by the first few uprisings, the Sandinistas quickly understood their significance and formed a flying column to immediately move to any uprising and attempt to sustain it against government forces. Thus they continued to consolidate their hold on all security and military elements of the coalition while raising the profile of key Sandinistas in the eyes of the Nicaraguan people.

With increasing disorder and failed brutal attempts to put down the uprisings, internal and international pressure on the Somoza regime to compromise increased. In November 1978, the International Monetary Fund refused to guarantee $20 million in new loans to the Somoza regime. Other international organizations and banks followed suit. The Sandinistas' efforts to use international bodies to influence the action worked.

Still Somoza would not compromise. Reinforcing his stubbornness, the FSLN leadership ensured, through various selective operations, that no compromise amenable to the government could be proposed. Ortega's actions, combined with Somoza's obstinacy, ensured that the revolution would play itself out.

In April 1979, the Sandinistas started their final, three-pronged offensive. First, a general strike was called to tie up the cities. Second, popular uprisings were initiated in six major cities. Third, rural columns struck in the north and west. The combination of attacks, their wide dispersion, and the obvious withdrawal of American support simply overwhelmed the National Guard.

The insurgents, possessing only minimal military strength, had relied almost entirely on their political strength to achieve final victory. They never conducted large-scale military operations and certainly never conducted the phase III conventional operations characteristic of a Maoist insurgency. According to Monimbo, a Sandinista leader, "[I]t was that the [*sic*] guerrillas who provided support for the masses so they could defeat the enemy by means of insurrection."[6] This is a critical variation on Mao's concept that the people provide support to the guerrillas so that the guerrillas can defeat the government. The Sandinistas moved 4GW yet another step forward.

In his survey of Latin American insurgencies, Col. John Waghelstein, a Special Forces officer who both trained and fought insurgents over a thirty-year career, quoted a Sandinista leader on why the revolution was successful:

> An armed element is still a key requirement for revolution wherein the cadres are educated and "blooded." We earn our leadership positions in the new order by paying our dues in Sierra. The mass appeal of a broad-front political organization is also a must

> in which disaffected non-Marxists and non-Marxist-Leninists are brought into the movement. This ensures not only better and wider internal support but outside support that does not have Cuban, Eastern Bloc or Soviet taint can also be obtained.
>
> Because of the superior unity and discipline of the Party, the real power will not be shared with those who provide essentially window dressing for the revolution.
>
> The Church, by now heavily infiltrated with Liberation Theologists, gives us guerrillas the moral high ground we've never enjoyed before.[7]

This honest appraisal shows how the Sandinistas advanced the art of war. Notice he never claims that guerrilla military success was essential to victory. Rather he states that, like all insurgents before them, the leaders learned their trade by fighting. So although the Sandinistas consistently failed in their efforts to instigate a rural insurgency, the rural efforts provided a crucible to toughen the leaders who would lead the guerrilla elements of the insurgency.

The Sandinista leader is clear that the broad-front political organization was essential, both to attract people to the movement and to ensure external support from non–Communist bloc countries. He states that the party (the FSLN) was the real power behind the coalition at all times—and had no intention of ever sharing power with the moderate coalition members. The moderates were simply window dressing.

Finally, he states that the Sandinistas used the priests and philosophy of liberation theology to provide unassailable moral high ground for the insurgency.

Col. John Waghelstein summed up the Sandinista strategic approach as follows:

> • bringing the mass appeal of broad-front political organization into the movement to ensure not only better and wider internal support but outside support that did not have Cuban, Eastern Bloc or Soviet taint.

- using the church, through liberation theology, to give the guerrillas the moral high ground.
- *not* losing sight of the U.S. attention level.
- controlling or influencing U.S. and world opinion through the media. Guerrilla chiefs actually wrote editorials for the *New York Times.*
- targeting the U.S. Congress through public opinion and orchestrating the propaganda campaign to minimize the U.S. response.
- establishing front groups outside the country to function as public affairs/information offices to generate support for the movement and to pressure the United States into a less responsive mode.
- orchestrating and financing guest speakers to U.S. academic, civic and church groups. These groups, in turn, will write letters to U.S. congressmen who hold key committee positions overseeing security assistance operations.[8]

Thus insurgency theory took another step forward. Although still using Mao's basic elements, the Sandinistas changed the mix to take the best elements of People's War, liberation theology, and urban insurgency to advance the concepts of fourth-generation warfare. The Sandinistas' unique contribution was to eliminate the requirement for the final conventional military offensive. Their political efforts so severely changed the "correlation of forces" that the government collapsed, and they occupied the vacuum.

# CHAPTER 8

# The Intifada: Civilians versus an Army

Tuesday, December 8, 1987, started like any other day in the occupied territories. No one envisioned a simple truck accident igniting a conflict that would change the balance of power between the Israelis and the Palestinians. Traffic accidents, even fatal ones, are common in the occupied territories.

At first, this one didn't seem much different. An Israeli truck hit a car filled with Palestinian laborers, killing four and injuring others. This was a serious accident but not notably worse than many before it. For some reason, this accident exploded into a riot. Riots are also not uncommon in the territories and, at first, this one didn't seem any different. But it was. This one was the first explosion of the sustained anger and defiance that became the Intifada. It served as the spark that ignited years of accumulated Palestinian frustration and rage.

Throughout the Israeli-occupied area of the Gaza Strip where the accident happened, Palestinians spontaneously took to the streets. When the Israelis sent an army patrol to disperse them, the rioters responded by turning on the patrol and driving it back into its compound. The rioters even surrounded one Israeli army compound to volley stones and Molotov cocktails into the position. Shots fired in the air, the normal Israeli technique for dispersing unruly crowds, had no effect. So the Israelis waited. Typically, such disturbances broke up at nightfall.

This one continued till almost midnight—openly defying the Israeli authorities. Even more unusual, it continued and spread the following morning. The disturbances continued all day. Each Israeli patrol that ventured out was driven back by crowds, rocks, and Molotov cocktails. Again it continued after dark—and into the third day.

By now, it was clear to the people of Gaza that this was a new type of riot, a new type of resistance. However, it caught the Israeli intelligence services completely by surprise. They had misread the buildup of tension prior to the outbreak and continued to misread it long after the violence had exceeded all previous Palestinian mass resistance.

After two full days of rioting, the Israeli minister of defense decided to continue on his trip to the United States, because he felt the situation was not serious. He clearly did not understand the gravity of the situation. Even more amazing, the Israeli Defense Force (IDF) would not send its first reinforcements to the Gaza Strip until December 18, the eleventh day of the riots.

Yassir Arafat's Palestinian Authority, the official representatives of the Palestine Liberation Organization (PLO) still located in Tunisia, was just as surprised. Initially, they could not grasp what was going on. Even as the riots continued, the top leadership misread the situation and did not put together a coherent plan to seize the opportunity.

Not until December 19 did the PLO first take advantage of the ground-level eruption of resistance, and only after the rioting and resistance had spread throughout the occupied territories, moving from the Gaza Strip to the West Bank. Most of the occupied territories had to erupt in civil disobedience before the PLO, still headquartered in Tunisia, sensed that something new was happening.

Even then, the only action taken was by two little-known members of the PLO living in the occupied territories, Mohammed and Majid Labani. These brothers recognized the potential of bringing the disturbances to Jerusalem. They recruited and positioned activists throughout

Jerusalem and then, at 9:20 a.m. on the nineteenth, initiated citywide riots that overwhelmed the 150 policemen who were the only Israeli security force in the city. The Israelis were caught completely off balance. Even as late as the nineteenth, eleven days into the riots, the Israelis did not understand the magnitude of the discontent, nor how it would manifest itself.

Only two days later, on December 21, the Israeli Arabs declared a "Peace Day" strike. They blocked roads in numerous areas in Israel proper and, when Israeli security forces tried to clear them, pelted the Israelis with rocks and Molotov cocktails. This was yet another surprise for both the Israeli and PLO leadership—it was the first time the Israeli Arabs had joined the Palestinians in any significant numbers. Given that there are 790,000 Israeli Arabs in an Israeli population of six million, it was a major escalation.

In contrast to the initiative shown by junior Palestinian leaders inside Israel, it was two more weeks, after the turn of the new year, before the uncomprehending and disorganized offices of Arafat printed their first pamphlets exhorting the Palestinians to greater efforts. Even this late, the PLO was following, not leading, the Intifada. They began desperately trying to put a positive spin on it by the patently false claim that Arafat himself had conceived of and initiated the uprisings. Yet it is clear from the sequence of events that Arafat's instructions consistently lagged behind what was happening in the streets.

One of the first actions taken by the PLO was to order their units to conduct armed attacks on the Israelis. But by the time this order went out, the street Palestinians had already figured out that the one thing the Israelis seemed incapable of controlling was unarmed attacks by mobs using only slingshots, bottles, and rocks. The Palestinians in the street also figured out that more Palestinians were being wounded by the unstable and volatile Molotov cocktails than Israelis. So they simply ignored the orders from Arafat to resort to weapons and took away any weapons that students or activists brought to the streets. It was several more weeks before the PLO figured it out and, belatedly, published pamphlets stating that no one was to use weapons—once again claiming it was Arafat's idea.

In early January, the disturbances began to lose intensity. To maintain the effort, the various Palestinian organizations—Fatah, Popular Front, Democratic Front, and the Communist Party—all called for strikes. Yet even here, the old-line external organizations lagged behind the new leadership inside the occupied territories. The new leadership not only called for strikes but established a Unified National Command to publish the handbills that would sustain the Intifada over the coming months.

In fact, by the end of January, the leading PLO official responsible for the occupied territories, Mahmoud Abbas, was convinced that the effort would exhaust itself soon.[1] He was not alone. The Israeli government also misread the relative lull in resistance that took place in late January. They, too, felt that the worst was over and that life was returning to normal in the occupied territories.

What the leadership of the two "official" sides failed to understand was that this was a genuine revolt by the people of the territories. The lull was in fact the young local leadership modifying the tactics from simple confrontation in the alleys to better-organized and larger confrontations in major cities.

Further, they were expanding the base of the revolt to include the relatively well-to-do Palestinian business class. These affluent Palestinians, caught between the arson threats of the Palestinian youth and persecution by the Israeli authorities, opted to side with the Palestinians. They knew that taking either side could result in bankruptcy. If they sided with the Israelis, the Palestinians would boycott their businesses and probably much worse. If they sided with the Palestinians, the Israelis would shut their shops down or, conversely, force them to stay open, to provoke a reaction from the Palestinians. Most of these businessmen made the logical choice and sided with the Palestinians. If they had to go bankrupt, they were better off having friends in the community when it happened. By this time, it was clear to everyone but the authorities that it was a genuine popular uprising. Everyone had to choose a side.

Three obvious questions arise at this point. What was the cause of this tremendous burst of resistance on the part of the Palestinians? How did the Israeli and PLO leadership miss it so completely? How did it organize itself to sustain action for more than four years—and eventually defeat the Israelis?

The uprising required two major elements: first, a deeply discontented population, and second, an organization that could focus the anger of that discontent. The discontent certainly existed, but to see how the combination of factors came together, it is important to understand how the Palestinians came to feel the frustration of the powerless.

The initial displacement of Palestinians came about as a result of the Israeli-Arab Wars of 1948. With the British withdrawal from the Palestine Mandate and U.N. resolution 181, the Israelis declared their independence. Immediately, the surrounding Arab nations swore to destroy the Zionist state. They rejected all attempts at mediation or offers by Israel to negotiate. Instead, they went to war—and lost.

Not only did the Israelis win, they actually increased the size of the territory they had been granted by the United Nations. Yet despite the increased size of the territory, the new Jewish state did not have a significant Palestinian minority. The Palestinians had fled their homes before the Israelis took over the territory, for a number of reasons.

One of the most important was that the Arab governments encouraged them to do so, because they did not want the Palestinians to be in the way of the soon-to-be "victorious" Arab armies. These governments assured the Palestinians that their departure would be brief and that as soon as the Arab armies crushed the Israelis, the Palestinians could return to their homes. Many Palestinians believed the Arab broadcasts and fled their homes, confident they would soon return.

Others fled out of fear of Israeli retaliations or atrocities. Although there were few Jewish atrocities, the Arab rumor mill inflated them and struck fear into the hearts of many. This added to the refugee flow.

A single chapter cannot explore all the reasons for the Palestinians becoming refugees. For our purposes, we need only know that most of them left the territory that was to become Israel proper.

Thus, from 1948 to 1967, the Palestinians were scattered to various Arab nations. They could not organize as a body, simply because it was against the interests of those Arab nations to allow them to do so. In fact, the Arab nations preferred to keep them in a refugee status and made full use of their extensive police powers to keep them in the camps. The Arab national leaders wanted to exploit the refugee issues against the Israelis, not help the Palestinians start a new life.

In addition, attention to the plight of the Palestinians proved an effective way to deflect criticism from their own people about the corruption of the Arab regimes. It was to the benefit of the Arab dictators to ensure that the Palestinians remained refugees. Further, the destabilizing effect of large numbers of refugees on Jordan did not escape the notice of other Arab dictators.

The few Palestinians left in Israel were agrarian, isolated, and fragmented along religious lines (Muslim/Christian). Their society was poorly suited for resistance. Moreover, they did not face a classic, fading colonial power but a small, tightly knit, homogenous Jewish society that had the support and sympathy of much of the rest of the world.

Given their situation, the Palestinians could not develop classic insurgent popular organizations. The Palestinians inside Israel were too few to create mass organizations essential for a popular uprising. The Palestinians living outside Israel were not even in the territory they wanted to win back and were being heavily suppressed by the "host" Arab governments.

Because the Arab governments feared unrest in their own countries, they limited Palestinian activities to conducting minor raids into Israel. The Arab governments were adamantly opposed to letting the Palestinians organize. It was not until 1965, when Yassir Arafat founded the Fatah, that the Palestinians had an audible voice. Even this voice was external to Israel. Under these circumstances, the Palestinians could not develop a coherent 4GW strategy.

The Israeli triumph in the 1967 war actually improved the political situation of the Palestinians. Israel became, in essence, a classic colonial power in the West Bank and Sinai Peninsula (particularly the Gaza Strip). While Arafat still controlled the PLO from outside the territories, a significant internal resistance movement began to take shape in the territories.

The Israeli occupation gave birth to two separate entities. First is the well-known armed underground. It sought violent action, and some elements took orders from the PLO. This was the most visible face of the Palestinian resistance and the one the Israelis were most successful in countering. It was not a genuine insurgency but simply terrorists operating without political mobilization. Although they killed many Israelis and kept the population on edge, these armed activists could not be a decisive force in a 4GW struggle.

The second group, although much less visible, would in the long term be a much greater problem for the Israelis. These were the local service institutions that grew to fill the gaps in the services provided by the Israelis as the occupying power.

Upon occupation, the Israelis had to set up a government of sorts for the occupied territories. Unfortunately, they made no conscious effort to genuinely incorporate the large Palestinian population into their society. Instead, they provided a minimalist government to keep the territories quiet. This left the Palestinians without many of the services normally provided by government. As a result, they organized to provide labor, educational, medical, and social services.

The Israelis allowed these service organizations and, to a limited degree, even encouraged them, because they reduced the Israeli cost of running the occupied territories. What the Israelis did not recognize was that these organizations provided both a base for mass organization and a training ground for Palestinian leaders. Gaining experience through running these organizations, a generation of local leaders emerged within the occupied territories.

As early as 1982, the new Palestinian leadership exerted its influence in the Shabiba refugee camp. Inside the camp, the Youth Council for Social Activity organized the camp residents to clean up the camp. They provided trash and sewer services, established sports leagues, provided medical care, drove out the pimps and thieves, and expelled suspected Israeli collaborators. In essence, they formed a local government and began to take care of their people.

They took control to the point of keeping Israeli patrols out of the camp. In 1987, when the Israeli army sent a battalion into the camp to make arrests, the battalion was stopped cold by mass protest and actually driven out of the camp. The Israeli security services did not seem to understand the significance of this action nor the potential for widespread civil disobedience.

By early 1987, only the Palestinian small businessmen and landowning elite avoided helping the Palestinian service organizations. Instead, they cooperated with the Israelis to protect their property. Yet they, too, would soon be coerced into joining the Palestinian resistance.

As stated earlier, Israel's act of occupying the territories in 1967 dramatically improved the Palestinians' political position. They now had a large number of Palestinians inside Israeli territory—which, for the first time, provided sufficient population for a mass movement. Second, the Israelis had become a classical colonial or occupying power. This gave the Palestinians a focus to organize against while simultaneously eroding Israel's position in the eyes of the world.

By the mid-1980s, the local Palestinian service organizations were functioning well and were ready to play their role when the Intifada literally exploded onto the political landscape. The service organizations "concentrated on out administering, not outfighting the enemy. The aim . . . is not simply to inflict military losses on the enemy but to destroy the legitimacy of its (the Israeli) government and to establish a rival regime. . . ."[2]

Thus, by the mid-eighties, the factors normally associated with 4GW were in place. The people felt a common identity, they had an enemy to focus against, they had mass organizations, and they had effective local leadership. From these factors grew the types of resistance we have seen at the beginning of most insurgencies: general strikes, riots, singlehanded attacks by young men who become icons of resistance, and the normal confusion of an occupying army that finds itself thrust from the deceptively simple-appearing task of occupation to the tricky and volatile task of pacification.

According to Schiff and Ya'ari:

> So it was that the raw materials of anger and frustration built up to a critical mass. The litany of Palestinian fears and grievances that had festered for an entire generation went on and on. The difference at the end of 1987 was a new sense of self-confidence nourished by the latest round of riots, the single-handed

> attack on the army camp, the derring-do of the Islamic Jihad, and the clout of the youngsters of Balata—all made even more pronounced by the signs of confusion and capitulation on the part of the IDF. Together with the latest moves suggesting Israel's intent to strip the Palestinians of the last of their assets and resources, these events seemed to confirm the belief that having reached a nadir, the residents of the territories had no other choice but to take their fate into their own hands. They had new models of heroism; they had begun to conquer their fear of the army; and most important they had very few illusions about the future awaiting them if they did not cast off the chains of their own anxiety and act. If they continued to hope that a solution would come from without, soon it would be too late. And the mass demonstrations of October and November had proven at least one thing; those who took to the street enjoyed the support of countless others who were convinced of the Koranic dictum that the Jihad had turned into a battle cry: "Allah helps only those who help themselves."[3]

The cauldron had been coming to a boil over a period of years. How did the Israeli and external Palestinian leadership miss the signs so completely?

Apparently the Israelis had become complacent. They had sustained the occupation for twenty years without major eruptions of Palestinian anger. They seem to have deluded themselves into believing that the Palestinians felt themselves better off under Israeli rule than under Arab rule. Just as important, the Israelis had become used to the benefits of being a colonial power: cheap labor, reduced costs of providing services to second-class citizens, and the confidence that came from defeating every major Arab army in three major wars.

Unfortunately, this confidence seemed to allow them to completely overlook their pending defeat in southern Lebanon. Despite a twenty-year struggle in southern Lebanon, they had not been able to defeat the guerrilla resistance. Even with the assistance of the Lebanese Christian militia, they could not crush this 4GW enemy. However, despite the continued disturbances, they had convinced themselves they had defeated the Palestinians in south Lebanon using their conventional forces. In 1987, the Israelis could not see that defeat was looming for their forces there.

On the other side, the external PLO leadership in Tunisia missed the Palestinian frustration that erupted into the Intifada simply because they were external. All reporting came from elements inside the territories that were supported by payments from the PLO and Fatah rather than by their work among the people. Afraid of losing their jobs, they were careful to report what Arafat wanted to hear rather than reality. The combination of physical distance, institutional bias, personal prejudices, and distorted reporting ensured that the PLO did not grasp what was going on in the territories.

The local Palestinian leadership quickly understood that this uprising was different from any that had preceded it. Because they understood the difference, they could take advantage of the spontaneous eruption of rage. Galvanized by the widespread popular uprising, the local Palestinian leaders were the first to understand and react to what was really happening in the occupied territories. This is not surprising, given that the local leadership was just that: local. They lived among the people. They met with them every day as they went about their legitimate business of providing essential services in the occupied territories. Also, unlike both the Israeli leaders and the overseas Palestinians, the local Palestinian leaders were genuinely concerned for the welfare of the people.

The first step they took was to simply continue providing the medical and social services they had before the Intifada started. These services sustained the civil disobedience in the street. The medical organizations provided medical care to wounded Palestinians, who were afraid to go to the hospitals because the Israeli security forces were arresting those involved in the disturbances. The women's groups collected donations, distributed food and money, helped organize blood drives, and greatly enlarged the role of Palestinian women in the resistance. The agricultural unions, which previously had focused on improving the lot of the day labor employed by the Israelis, now worked hard to improve the food supply of the occupied territories by providing encouragement, advice, and supplies for local Palestinians to cultivate any empty plots.

Because they already had a leading role in the day-to-day lives of the Palestinian people, the local leaders could easily transition to providing tactical guidance in the form of simple directives, such as not to use weapons and to abandon the Molotov cocktails. These were both highly practical instructions.

First, they knew they could not match the Israelis in a conflict based on the use of weapons. It simply gave the Israelis license to use lethal force. Second, the use of weapons would eliminate the strongest weapons the Palestinians had: the image of young Palestinians armed only with rocks and bottles facing heavily armed Israeli troops.

The decision to not use Molotov cocktails was even more practical. Through their medical services, they determined that the highly volatile weapons were killing and injuring far more Palestinians than Israelis. In addition to this practical reason for dropping the Molotov cocktails from the arsenal, the local leadership quickly understood that they undermined the international image of teenagers with rocks fighting a well-equipped, powerful Israeli army. The visceral human fear of fire made any Israeli use of force against people throwing fire bombs seem much more reasonable than firing on teenagers armed only with rocks. At the beginning of the Intifada, as in most chaotic situations, local leaders focused first on understanding and getting some degree of control in their own area. They then reached out to adjacent areas and tried to coordinate their activities for the benefit of all. Finally, they tried to organize some form of crisis-wide leadership.

The Palestinian support organizations displayed all the characteristics of a self-organizing network in action. While the Israeli and external Palestinian leadership struggled to move information through hierarchical command channels to try to figure out what was going on, the locals were organizing. By the end of December, they put together the Unified National Command (UNC), which was composed of relatively unknown but very savvy local leaders. It was actually started by Mohammed Labadi, a bookshop owner, and his driver.[4] The goal of the UNC was to sustain the territory-wide revolt.

Their initial step was to produce handbills. Although these handbills were later to become famous and a critical part of the revolt, the first few issues were put together quickly by a few dedicated and astute local leaders. They managed to draft, print, and distribute tens of thousands of handbills, with distribution of each taking place on the same night throughout the territories. They may not have understood the effect their first handbills would have, but they immediately recognized their impact. These handbills articulated the Palestinian anger, put forth their demands for cessation of the hostilities, and provided direction on how they should resist the Israelis:

> All roads must be closed to the occupation forces. . . . Its cowardly soldiers must be prevented from entering refugee camps and large population centers by barricades and burning tires. . . . Stones must land on the heads of the occupying soldiers and those who collaborate with them. Palestinian flags are to be flown from minarets, churches, rooftops, and electricity poles everywhere. . . . We must set the ground burning under the feet of the occupiers. Let the whole world know that the volcanic uprising that has ignited the Palestinian people will not cease until the achievement of independence in a Palestinian state whose capital is Jerusalem![5]

Although initially using almost classical leftist prose, the handbills provided a source of information and a series of ideas for the Palestinians to rally around. Of particular importance, the handbills focused on 4GW techniques and tactics. They exhorted the Palestinians to use rocks instead of rifles and to ensure that their symbols (the flags) were present everywhere. Further, they emphasized what they believed to be achievable political goals.

One of the critical early decisions the UNC made was to not reveal their identities. This served two purposes. First, it enhanced the mystique of the UNC. Because the leaders were not prominent people but mid-level locals, they were concerned that the Palestinians would not respond once they found out that they were, in essence, being led by their neighbors. The fact that the UNC leadership was "unknown" enhanced their prestige. In the minds of the people, they were a hidden hand guiding the revolution. They provided a focus and reassurance that the suffering and disruption of the Intifada would lead to some concrete improvements in the lives of the Palestinians.

Anonymity also gave the leadership a seeming invulnerability to the Israeli security forces. They knew that the Israelis would imprison any leaders they identified—and in fact, the Israelis did so. Repeatedly, they captured the entire UNC. But because the UNC names had never been published, new leaders simply stepped forward and kept producing the handbills. As long as the handbills were produced, the Palestinian people did not know that the leadership had been captured. With this simple deception, the Palestinian leadership neutralized the police power of Israel and sustained the UNC much longer than would have been possible with any other method.

In addition to providing national leadership in the form of the handbills, the Palestinians continued to organize at the local level. Like the UNC, local leaders remained mostly anonymous. There are no clear records on how many local committees existed, but it must have been in the hundreds. By the spring of 1988, they had organized local Palestinian leadership in every village in the occupied territories. Like the UNC leadership, the local leaders were often arrested and confined—only to be replaced by other low-level activists determined to see the Intifada continue. In effect, they created a web-like organization, a network that was not subject to decapitation, as a hierarchical organization would be. The networked nature of the leadership made it virtually impossible to destroy. This is a definitive characteristic of a 4GW organization.

The ability of the UNC and local committees to continually reconstruct themselves after Israeli roundups was essential to the effectiveness of the Intifada. The first UNC handbills were produced in early January. By late January, the UNC was producing its sixth handbill—and was suddenly rounded up. The Israelis would conduct five roundups but never interrupted the flow of the handbills, which continued to be produced at seven-to-ten-day intervals.

Clearly, command of the Intifada developed from the bottom up. First, the local leadership simply continued to provide services, although under much more difficult conditions. Next, they matured and networked, providing tactical guidance. Then the UNC evolved from these local elements. Finally, belatedly, the PLO began to understand what was happening, and Yassir Arafat began to influence the action.

In fact, the UNC would finally lose influence. The combination of repeated sweeps by the Israeli security forces and Arafat's determination to retain power by neutralizing the UNC leadership finally relegated UNC to a minor role. Yet even the combined efforts of Arafat and the Israelis could not neutralize the leadership before it created a virtually self-sustaining resistance.

Like previous new tactical approaches, this variation of 4GW developed out of the efforts of practical leaders to solve practical tactical problems in a real situation.

One of the interesting aspects of the Intifada is the way it forced Yassir Arafat to modify his long-held positions in order to appear to be leading the movement. First, he accepted U.N. Security Council resolutions 242* and 338.**

Then, on November 15, 1988, the PLO released the Palestinian Declaration of Independence. Finally, on December 14, 1988, Arafat declared

* The key elements of U.N. resolution 242 (passed in 1967) state that the U.N. "affirms that the fulfillment of Charter principles requires the establishment of a just and lasting peace in the Middle East which should include the application of both the following principles:

"a. Withdrawal of Israeli armed forces from territories occupied in the recent conflict.

"b. Termination of all claims or states of belligerency and respect for and acknowledgement of the sovereignty, territorial integrity and political independence of every State in the area and their right to live in peace within secure and recognized boundaries free from threats or acts of force."

** The key element in U.N. resolution 338 (passed in 1973)

"1. Calls upon all parties to the present fighting to cease all firing and termi-

that Israel had a right to exist—a fundamental shift from his previous position. Arafat, a consummate tactician and survivor, was reacting to the changing tactical situation wrought by the Intifada. Although there is no apparent acknowledgment of employing 4GW warfare, the actions of both parties on the ground reflect the changes inherent in this new generation of warfare.

Another interesting aspect of the Intifada is the way the local leadership turned Arafat's own "theory of entanglement" against him. His theory of entanglement subscribed to the idea that "the weak and the few could manipulate their betters in strength and numbers."[6] Arafat had used this in 1967 to entangle the major Arab powers in his struggle with Israel. Now the leaders of the Intifada were using it to entangle Arafat and his Fatah organization in their internal struggle with the Israelis.

In addition to these operational-level techniques for involving Fatah, the leadership in the territories quickly adopted tactical techniques to neutralize the armed might of Israel. Reinforcing their use of stones wielded by teenagers, the Palestinians often interposed women and children between the Israeli security forces and the men they wished to arrest. This technique was effective only if it was covered by international media—preferably TV, but print journalism was also effective, if not so immediate.

The presence of cameras often triggered Palestinian action—because they understood the impact these images had on international and even internal support for the Israeli security forces. Day after day, the world saw pictures of Palestinian teenagers in T-shirts openly defying Israeli soldiers

---

nate all military activity immediately, no later than twelve hours after the moment of the adoption of this decision, in the positions they now occupy.

"2. Calls upon all the parties concerned to start immediately after the ceasefire the implementation of Security Council resolution 242 (1967) in all of its parts.

"3. Decides that, immediately and concurrently with the ceasefire, negotiations start between the parties concerned under appropriate auspices aimed at establishing a just and durable peace in the Middle East."

in flak jackets. Day after day, they saw images of these young, unarmed people being fired upon by Israelis. The sheer repetition of these images, along with the almost daily burials of Palestinian "heroes" complete with weeping mothers, slowly but surely changed Israel's image in the eyes of the world.

The Palestinians had a sophisticated plan to ensure that the media could be in position to cover the disturbances. They provided drivers, translators, vehicles, access, passports, contacts, and transportation in and out of the occupied territories. The combination of the competitive drive of the press and good planning by the Palestinians ensured that despite major Israeli efforts, the media were present within the territories.

The Israelis understood the impact the media was having on both world and Israeli public opinion. Yet, as an occupying colonial power, they were inevitably in the role of Goliath—and the Western media are always more sympathetic to David. The Palestinians were quick to capitalize on that fact.

The Palestinians hammered home two messages. The first was for international consumption. It was simply the portrayal of Palestinians as an oppressed, impoverished, but brave and resolute people fighting for human dignity. They asked only to have the occupying power go home and allow the Palestinians to be citizens of their own country.

The second theme was for Israeli consumption. It, too, was simple. The Palestinians made it clear that as long as the Israelis occupied the territories, there would be no peace. Because all Israelis serve in the armed forces, all Israeli parents knew their sons and daughters would face continual unrest. Although these parents were prepared for their sons and daughters to fight to preserve Israel, they were not as certain they wanted them to face continual bombardment with rocks, bottles, and hate in a questionable attempt to hold onto the occupied territories.

These simple and powerful themes were carried via multiple channels. The most obvious were the international media. But the Palestinians were astute enough to reinforce that message through a number of other channels.

One of the most powerful was the international academic and professional communities. Highly respected Palestinians in each community presented their message via international forums, meetings, emails, conferences, and television interviews. They made articulate, sympathetic, rational spokespersons. Used to seeing radicals with checkered headdresses railing against Israel, Westerners were now seeing highly educated people in Western dress providing coherent, calm, rational arguments for the Palestinian position.

Another channel was the soldiers of the Israeli army. Steeped in the traditions of a moral army that fights only to protect its nation, these young soldiers had trouble reconciling that image with constantly firing rubber bullets at teenagers and systematically harassing women and children trying to go about their daily business. They saw this image fed back to them by the international and even left-wing Israeli media. Adding to their frustration was the most recent and only failure of the Israeli Defense Force (IDF): Operation Peace for Galilee, the ill-fated invasion of Lebanon. Given the small size of the country, these soldiers communicated easily with family and friends and could reinforce the feelings of frustration.

The initial effect of the sudden Intifada uprising was to paralyze the Israeli response. In contrast, the Palestinians felt a surge of confidence and pride at their open defiance of the Israeli forces. They moved quickly to exploit the weaknesses inherent in an occupying force of a democratic nation attempting to suppress a civil population.

The initial Israeli response was confused and disjointed. They were baffled with the problems of dealing with mass demonstrations led by waves of women and children. They simply had no training or contingency plans for such an event. The previous "easy" twenty years of occupation duty did not prepare them for what they now confronted.

Complicating the problem for the soldier or policeman on the street was the complete failure of the political and military leadership to understand what was going on. By the end of December, it was clear that the Israeli policy for the occupied territories was bankrupt—but they had nothing to put in its place.

Although the Israelis could not develop a coherent strategic approach, they did respond tactically—although somewhat slowly. Their attempts to conduct door-to-door searches and enforce curfews were two examples. Yet they both showed the impotence of the Israeli forces. Often the searchers were turned back by mass demonstrations. Even when they succeeded, the searches were hasty and destructive—driving the occupants of the searched houses more firmly into the arms of the Intifada. Because they could not force their way into some neighborhoods, the curfew was simply impossible to enforce—and therefore a source of derision for the Arabs.

Suddenly, the Israeli security forces were not invincible. They were no longer universally feared. As with all occupying armies, the psychological aspects of the occupation were as important as the physical aspects. The Israelis had lost their psychological edge.

The Israelis were so slow to respond that it was the summer of 1988—fully six months into the Intifada—before the Israelis put out their first intelligence analysis of the roots of the revolt. Unfortunately, even then it did not have a major impact on the way the Israeli government conducted business in the occupied territories.

Although slow to understand and react, the Israelis did develop some highly effective tools against this new kind of warfare. One of the most important was the creation of the IDF Field Intelligence Corps. They came to the realization that unless each level of command has its own intelligence element, all intelligence simply flows up the chain, with little flowing down.

They also realized that unlike intelligence for a conventional fight in the desert, almost all intelligence in the Intifada must come from human intelligence (HUMINT) and signals intelligence (SIGINT). To assist their tactical forces, the Israelis invested heavily in increased HUMINT and SIGINT for all levels of command. They also added unmanned aerial vehicles (UAVs), balloons, thermal sights, language capability, and even began experimenting with visual intelligence, such as face recognition technology. They understood that this was a contest of human skills at the tactical level—technology could help, but it was not the solution.

Although both sides adapted tactically, the Palestinians did a better job of adjusting on the strategic and operational levels. Their ability to keep the Palestinian youth in the streets, combined with their ability to keep the story alive in the Western media, slowly but surely ground down external support for Israel. Even the seemingly unbeatable Israeli lobby in the United States was unable to maintain unequivocal support for Israel. The AFL-

CIO, in no uncertain terms, protested the treatment of Palestinians by the Israeli security forces.

Another early, and unexpected, blow came from Jordan when King Hussein renounced all claims to sovereignty over the West Bank on July 31, 1988. This completely eliminated the "Jordanian option"—which many moderate Israelis saw as the preferred solution. They planned to give the West Bank and its fractious Palestinian population back to Jordan. In his renunciation, King Hussein foreclosed that option—and showed an understanding of the changing nature of the Palestinian demands. He understood that the Palestinians were no more willing to be absorbed by his nation than they were to be absorbed by Israel. The adversity of the previous twenty years had created a genuine Palestinian nation where none had existed before.

It was this sense of nationhood that sustained the Intifada through the next four years and the run-up to the Israeli elections. The Palestinians knew they could not negotiate with a Likud government, simply because the Likud Party was fundamentally opposed to any form of Palestinian self-rule. In contrast, the Labor Party under the right leadership might be able to negotiate with the PLO.

The stage was set for the next four years. The Palestinians worked hard to maintain a consistent level of resistance—and keep it largely nonviolent. The instinctive early reaction of the internal Palestinian leadership had proved correct for the first part of the revolt—and was maintained. According to Israeli figures, the Palestinians inflicted only sixteen civilian and eleven military fatalities on the Israelis during the Intifada.[7]

During this period, the Palestinians developed a strategic approach that addressed three different audiences. They then used 4GW techniques to communicate a message tailored to each of those audiences. For their Palestinian supporters, the message was that they could sustain the resistance to the occupation. This took the form of economic support for those in the street, resistance to Israeli-enforced "business hours," continuing civil disturbances, and roadblocks. Thus they kept alive the support of the frustrated populace by proving that this time they would not fold under Israeli pressure.

The message for the external audience was different. The Palestinians set out to do nothing less than change world opinion on Israel. Israel had been consistently viewed as a distinct underdog in its conflict with the Arabs. After World War II, the Western nations watched in admiration as the Israeli pioneers, with almost no resources, fought and defeated the combined armies of the Arab nations—not once, but four times. Also, Israel, for all its flaws, is the only democracy in a nest of brutal dictators.

The Palestinians had to overcome all those perceptions if they were to gain the sympathy of the West and, more important, have the West apply political pressure to Israel to negotiate seriously with the Palestinians. They achieved this goal by using 4GW techniques. They controlled the images that would be sent by controlling the level of violence. The early decision not to use weapons was critical. As a result of this decision, the vast majority of all photos taken of the Intifada show Palestinian teenagers armed only with rocks facing down heavily armed Israeli troops and tanks.

Even more problematic for the Israelis is that the use of rubber bullets and the use of real bullets looks much the same on TV. Often when Israeli forces used nonlethal tools to disperse crowds, the resulting images looked exactly like lethal force. In fact, the Palestinians made extensive efforts to ensure full picture and video coverage of any casualties. The repeated images of bloody Palestinian teenagers and the Palestinian mothers weeping over their sons' bodies were a strong contrast to the relative lack of Israeli casualties.

The result was to change Israel's image in the eyes of the world. It changed the political aspect of the conflict completely. In a matter of months, Israel was transformed from the tiny, brave nation surrounded by hostile Arab nations to the oppressive state that condoned killing children in the street.

For the Israeli audience, the Palestinians turned Moshe Dayan's strategy of "facts on the ground" against them. They showed that there would never be complete peace in the occupied territories. At the same time, they limited the violence, particularly the killing, and ensured that most of it took place in the occupied territories. The more liberal and secular elements of Israeli society were deeply disturbed by this combination. Israel was an oppressor of an occupied area. They began to question the value of the occupation.

In the end, the Palestinian message to Israeli voters got through. They believed there could never be peace until the Palestinians had their own country. The problems were in the occupied territories, not in Israel proper. Their long-term resistance caused a rift in the Likud over what tactics to employ against the Palestinians. The result was the election of a Labor government, which then agreed to and conducted the Oslo negotiations.

Thus the Intifada brought together the key elements of 4GW to allow a people without a state, an army, or a government to take on and defeat the most powerful army in the Middle East.

In the words of Schiff and Ya'ari, two of the most astute observers of the Israeli-Arab struggle:

> The Intifada was an assertion of defiance that bubbled up from below, a statement by the legions of Palestinian youth who felt bereft of a future; the high school and university students doomed to choose between indignity and exile; the tens of thousands of laborers who made their living in Israel but were expected to remain invisible; the veterans of Israeli prisons who were more convinced than ever of the justice of their cause but saw their people sinking deeper and deeper into hopelessness. In short, it was the work of the Palestinian masses, and that is why it surprised everyone; the complacent Israeli authorities, the over-confident Jordanians, the self-satisfied PLO leadership, and even local Palestinians regarded as influential figures in the territories. A popular revolt with all the hallmarks of a genuine revolution, it erupted suddenly and created a new strategy for the Palestinian struggle that confounded both the PLO establishment, scrambling wildly to keep up with events from afar, and the native leadership whose constituents were suddenly spinning out of control. Above all, however, it delivered a sharp reminder to the Israelis that they simply could not go on blithely ignoring the twenty-

year-old Palestinian problem festering right in the middle of their collective lap.[8]

With the signing of the Oslo accords in 1993, the Palestinians, using 4GW, achieved what the combined armies of the Arab nations had failed to accomplish: they had forced the Israelis to yield territory. Although the Palestinians' subsequent inability to enact the formal agreement has greatly limited the intended results, the fact remains that the Intifada forced the Israelis to the negotiating table and won concessions. How the Israelis reversed this 4GW Palestinian victory is the subject of the next chapter.

# CHAPTER 9

# The al-Aqsa Intifada

With the Oslo accords of September 13, 1993, the Palestinians had apparently started down the path to statehood. After decades of conflict, it appeared that the Palestinians would finally have a land to call their own. The six-year Intifada set the internal and external conditions necessary for both sides to accept the unthinkable: recognition of the blood enemy. Yet at the time of this writing, that dream has faded to dust.

Since September 2000, the Palestinians and Israelis have been locked in the bloodiest conflict of their history—the al-Aqsa Intifada. Although exact numbers are difficult to come by, and unbiased numbers even more difficult, as early as August 2003, the *Washington Post* estimated the dead at more than 2,500 Palestinians and about 900 Israelis.[1] These estimates align closely with the Amnesty International figures of 2,300 Palestinians (including 400 children) and 900 Israelis (including 100 children) killed through the end of 2003. It is difficult to comprehend what losses of those magnitudes can mean to small populations. However, we can use the *Washington Post* figures to provide a sense of the scale of the conflict and the suffering of each side.

To understand the impact these numbers have on the Israeli population, consider how America would react if we had watched more than 40,500 people killed on our streets by terrorists. That may sound like an absurdly high number but is proportionate to our population. Israel has a population of about six million. The U.S. population is 270 million[2] or forty-five times the size of Israel's. The Israelis sustaining 900 dead is the same as the United States having 40,500 killed.

Palestinian losses are even more devastating. Although their population is more than about 2.8 million,[3] less than half that of Israel, the Palestinians have sustained over three times as many casualties. Comparative figures for the United States would be more than 225,000 Americans killed—by an occupying force. It will be extraordinarily difficult to overcome the hate and distrust that so many deaths have generated.

The obvious question is, What happened? How did the Palestinians squander their 4GW victory over the Israelis? How did the Israelis arrive at a point where they have essentially no security in their own homes?

It required major efforts by peacemakers on both sides to achieve the level of confidence necessary to sign the accords. It also required major efforts by hardliners on both sides to reverse conditions to what confronts us today. In fact, it took almost seven years to go from Oslo to al-Aqsa. Over that time, hardline Palestinians took control of the Intifada and restated their goal of destroying Israel. For their part, hardline Israelis took, and continue to take, aggressive, bloody action against the Palestinians. Essentially, Israeli hardliners, in conjunction with hardline, centralized, entrenched, and out-of-touch Palestinian leadership, led their peoples to this place. They were actively assisted by radical fundamentalists on both sides.

On the Israeli side, hardliners led by Ariel Sharon and Binyamin Netanyahu consistently opposed the Oslo accords and worked aggressively to undermine them. Their position from the beginning was that the accords were the first step in the Palestinians' ultimate goal—the destruction of the state of Israel.

As early as 1991, even before the Oslo accords were signed, the Likud Party (led by Netanyahu and Sharon) worked to defeat any possible compromise with the Palestinians in the occupied territories. One of their key tools was encouraging the immigration of a million Soviet Jews. With the fall of the Berlin Wall, the Soviet Jews were eager to emigrate to the West. The Israeli government did its best to encourage these people to come to Israel. In doing so, they achieved two goals. First, they reversed the population trend that saw Palestinian and Sephardic (non-European) Jews growing rapidly in proportion to the Ashkenazim—Jews of European descent. Second, they provided the people needed to populate the West Bank settlements the Likud Party was rapidly building.

At this time, Ariel Sharon was housing minister and architect of the program to settle Israelis in the occupied territories. He had always been a vocal proponent of Greater Israel and saw the settlements as becoming "facts on the ground." By establishing numerous strong Israeli settlements on the West Bank, he planned to present any future Israeli government with a fait accompli. He believed no Israeli government could remove significant numbers of the newly established settlements without violent action—and no government will survive such action against its own people. (Keep in mind that the Israeli right does not consider Israeli Arabs full citizens, so it is perfectly all right to forcibly move them to make room for Jewish citizens.)

Thus under Sharon's leadership, the Likud government worked to rapidly build and fill those settlements—even though it meant heavily subsidizing the residents to convince them to move to the isolated locations. As housing minister, Sharon ensured that virtually all new subsidized housing was built in the West Bank. Although new immigrants may not have particularly favored the West Bank, it was often the only place they could afford to live. Once settled, the new immigrants were virtual economic prisoners. If they left the heavily subsidized West Bank settlements, they could not afford similar housing—and often could not afford housing at all. Thus Sharon succeeded in building and populating many of the new settlements before the Oslo accords were signed.

Despite the efforts of the Israeli right, voter unhappiness with Likud's inability to bring peace to the occupied territories led to the election of a Labor government. The Palestinian Intifada had convinced the Israeli people they must negotiate. These negotiations led to the signing of the Oslo accords in 1993. With that signing, the Israelis and Palestinians agreed to:

> an IDF withdrawal from Gaza and the West Bank town of Jericho, which would then fall under the civilian control of a Palestinian autonomy government headed by Yassir Arafat. All Israeli settlements would remain intact, and the new Palestinian police would work together with the IDF to guarantee internal security and fight Hamas. In nine months, the IDF would redeploy throughout the remainder of the West Bank to prepare for Palestinian elections and the extension of autonomy to the entire West Bank.[4]

This prospect of peaceful coexistence drove both Israeli and Palestinian hardliners to redouble their efforts to derail the implementation of the accords. Their efforts provide a study in how a minority on each side can use 4GW techniques to change both internal and international political conditions to defeat a peace initiative.

On the Israeli side, the Likud, as the opposition party, ensured that the Labor government could not meet the timelines promised in the accords. Nor could the Labor government address the numerous genuine Palestinian complaints about their economic plight and severe restrictions on personal freedoms. Likud could and did successfully block any efforts to improve the conditions of the Palestinians in the occupied territories. They maintained this stance throughout the Labor administration.

Despite its inability to make progress with the Oslo accords, Labor was still in the running to win another term in 1996. Then, on November 4, 1995, Prime Minister Rabin was assassinated by a Jewish right-wing activist.

The Palestinian fundamentalists also did their part. In February and March 1996, they executed a series of suicide bombings in Jerusalem and Tel Aviv. The combination shook Israeli support for the peace accords, and Binyamin Netanyahu led Likud's return to power in May 1996. The right was now in position to further slow the fulfillment of the peace accords and consolidate Israel's hold on the West Bank.

During the election campaign, Netanyahu claimed to support the accords. He did admit he wanted to slow the process but claimed he did not want to stop it. However in his first hundred days in office, "He reiterated his opposition to the notion of a Palestinian state and even the Labor-enshrined principle of trading land for peace. He has vowed to never give up Jewish control of the Golan Heights and Jerusalem, and has broken the freeze on new Jewish settlements."[5]

Ariel Sharon, now foreign minister but still the unofficial "king of the settlers," reinforced the government's position when "he publicly urged settlers to seize the hilltops. 'What you hold, you'll keep,' he declared."[6]

After reassuring the settlers that they would never have to leave the West Bank, Netanyahu deliberately sought further confrontation with the Palestinians:

> The spark that ignited . . . the explosion was Netanyahu's decision to open a new tourist exit from an ancient tunnel near Jerusalem's holiest Muslim shrine, the Al Aqsa Mosque compound on the Temple Mount. For Arafat, Netanyahu's move was an insensitive attempt to display Israel's sovereignty over the contested city—and a perfect pretext to unleash Palestinian anger and frustration over the stalling of the peace process. . . . An emotional Arafat urged his people to protest against a regime that he claimed was undermining Muslim control over sacred sites and violating an Israeli commitment not to alter the status of Jerusalem until its ultimate fate had been negotiated by the two sides.[7]

Netanyahu's attempt to open a new tourist gate provoked an emotional Palestinian response that led to fifty-six Palestinian and fourteen Israeli deaths in the first week of disturbance. Increasing the tension was the fact that Arafat had moved from Tunisia into the occupied territories and had imposed the PLO's authority over the men and women who had led the Intifada. The combination of Israeli arrests and Arafat's political maneuvering neutralized the leadership that had come of age inside the occupied territories and made the Intifada a success.

As a result, when the Israelis failed to meet the timelines for the withdrawal and opened the tourist gate, the Palestinians did not return to their

4GW tactics. The leadership who understood and guided those tactics had been eliminated. In their place were Arafat and his old PLO lieutenants. Therefore, the world did not again see teenagers with stones facing down the Israeli forces. They did not again see educated, reasonable Palestinian academics and spokesmen articulating legitimate grievances. Instead, they saw the familiar, bearded face of Arafat the terrorist sending an unclear message.

Unimaginative and apparently unable to learn from Intifada I, Arafat suppressed the new generation of leaders and implemented the failed Palestinian tactics of old. He orchestrated a muddled response that combined outward reconciliation with orders to his 30,000-man security forces to shoot back. As Morris points out:

> To many experts, the undisciplined performance of the Palestinian police was precisely where the Palestinian leader lost points. "Arafat was given a golden opportunity by Netanyahu to focus on the 100 days of failure by the Israeli government to engage him in the peace process," said Joseph Alpher, a former director of Tel Aviv University's Jaffee Center for Strategic Studies. "While he may have succeeded in focusing everyone's attention, the fact that his security services went out of control has now placed him on the defensive." Arafat, says Alpher, took a good hand and overplayed it in a way that poses a major challenge to the future of the Oslo process.[8]

Unlike Mr. Alpher and the leaders of the first Intifada, Arafat did not understand 4GW. In a single month, he managed to destroy the Palestinian's hard-won image as a peaceful people resisting a brutal occupying force. Besides the damage to the Palestinians' international image, he caused great damage to the Palestinian internal political situation. First, he gave the Israeli security forces an enemy they could deal with—organized, adult, male, armed, and partly uniformed. In short, he played to the strength of the Israeli security services. Second, he reinforced the Israelis' legitimate fears that the Palestinians would not be content until Israel was destroyed.

One of the basic fears Likud played to in the election was the presence of an armed Palestinian security force inside Greater Israel. They portrayed this 30,000-man force as representing a corps-sized Arab force inside Israel's boundaries. Thus the military action of the Palestinian security forces was perceived by Israelis as yet another Arab military force threatening their existence. That perception steeled the resolve of the Israeli people to take whatever action was necessary to preserve Israel.

In their efforts, Likud and Arafat actually supported each other. Arafat had been slipping badly in Palestinian eyes but was given a tremendous boost by his aggressive public posturing during the 1996 riots. While he was rapidly destroying all the Intifada had gained, he was perceived by the Palestinians as standing up to the Israelis—and his popularity surged. This was of overriding importance to Arafat and the factions that relied on the resources of the Palestinian Authority. The huge setback to the peace process was not nearly as important to them as the enhancement of Arafat's prestige and control.

The two sides developed an unintentional symbiotic relationship. Arafat needed, and still needs, an external enemy to retain his control. Without such an enemy, the outrageous corruption of his regime and his inability to improve the conditions of his people might well lead to his removal from power. That corruption has certainly been a major reason for his "promotion" to president and the "election" of a prime minister. However, his continued defiance of Israel and his long-term survival skills have prevented his complete removal, so far.

Similarly, if Likud were to achieve their goal of annexation of key parts of the occupied territories, they had to convince the Israeli people that the Palestinians could never be trusted. They had to convince them that despite Likud's failed policy of invading Lebanon and their failed policy in dealing with Hamas in South Lebanon, Likud still had the correct vision of the future. In short, the right wing had to portray the Palestinians as seeking the annihilation of Israel; that "land for peace" was a false and dangerous dream. They had to return Israeli opinion to that which existed before Intifada I.

The old-line, despotic PLO leadership assisted in this effort. Authoritarian leadership such as the PLO cannot undertake a sustained 4GW campaign,* so they turned back to their old position of seeking the elimination of Israel. It is obvious to even the most liberal Israelis that you cannot deal with someone whose goal is your annihilation.

This pattern of confrontation, frozen negotiations, timid moves toward negotiation, then new confrontation continued to play out, with a crisis every few months. In each cycle, the hardliners gained ground. On the Israeli side, they continued to build settlements, then linked the settlements with protected roadways. They began to move into the Arab sections of Jerusalem and to build Israeli sections on the fringes of the old borders of the city. Daily, they were creating "facts on the ground." The ultimate fact will be the encirclement of Jerusalem and portions of the West Bank with an Israeli security fence.

This pattern of low-level violence interspersed with attempts at negotiation continued throughout Netanyahu's Likud administration. The high point from a negotiation point of view was the October 23, 1998, land-for-peace deal that came about as a result of the Wye River Conference. In it, the Israelis agreed to withdraw from another thirteen percent of the West Bank, while the Palestinians agreed to reduce the number and type of weapons in their police force. This was required to assure the Israeli right-wing elements that the agreement would result in increased security.

In fact, neither side honored the agreement. Arafat either could not or would not reduce the armament of his police forces, and Israel refused to withdraw. The primary result was the withdrawal of extreme right-wing support from Netanyahu. The extreme right felt he was not aggressive enough in making the West Bank a permanent part of Israel. This resulted in Netanyahu's subsequent defeat by Ehud Barak in the May 1999 elections.

* Authoritarian leadership can use some of the tools and techniques of 4GW—as Saddam Hussein proved in the fall of 2002. However, such a regime cannot fully exploit 4GW, simply because it can't trust enough people to create an effective, self-sustaining network. Its existence is based on hierarchical power structure, corruption, and fear.

With the election of a Labor government and the impending end of his own term, President Clinton called Arafat and Barak to Camp David in an attempt to restart negotiations. Despite intensive efforts from July 11–25, 2000, the negotiations failed. The net result was to greatly weaken Barak's position in Israel while simultaneously damaging Arafat's control over the Palestinians.

Then Ariel Sharon reentered the picture. Still dedicated to the idea that Israel must include the entire West Bank, he took two major steps. First, he bought a home in the Arab part of Old Jerusalem. Although he has never actually lived there, he has hired security forces to protect his property and to make the point that Jews are free to move into Arab neighborhoods. He also knew that the Palestinian population would interpret it as an effort to take all of Jerusalem for the Jews—yet another perceived violation of the Oslo accords.

With the failure of the peace talks, a weakened Barak administration, and steadily increasing tension in Jerusalem, Sharon, now leader of Likud, took the extremely provocative step of visiting the al-Aqsa mosque. On September 28, 2000, escorted by a thousand riot police, Sharon made highly publicized visit to the third holiest site in Islam.

Although he stated that he was concerned only with the security of the site, Sharon knew exactly what the Palestinian reaction would be. He was a cabinet minister in 1996, when Netanyahu opened a new tourist gate near the mosque—and it resulted in massive riots that left seventy dead and a thousand injured. It is inconceivable he did not know that his visit to the al-Aqsa mosque with a thousand riot police would touch off massive rioting in the West Bank. Clearly he had adopted a 4GW strategy and was counting on Arab violence to provide international cover for his plans. The Palestinians responded as he expected, even to the point of naming the new Intifada the al-Aqsa Intifada, to make it perfectly clear it was in reaction to Sharon's visit to the mosque.

Sharon understood that by pushing the Palestinians to open defiance and violence, he could shift the world's perception of their struggle for independence. He knew that Arafat's weakness and Hamas' opposition to any recognition of Israel would result in armed attacks on Israeli citizens. Those armed attacks could well lead to a vote of no confidence for the Barak administration and Likud's return to power. He also knew that the homegrown Palestinian leadership that had controlled the violent plans of Arafat in 1986 had been neutralized.

Sharon stimulated exactly the response he knew would come. The Palestinians took to the streets. And, exactly as he had done in 1996, Arafat sent a series of confused signals: "He condemned the mob violence in his telephone talks with President Clinton, according to U.S. officials. But in public, he called on Palestinians to 'continue the march to Jerusalem, the capital of the Palestinian independent state.'"[9] Israelis could only interpret this as a call for the destruction of Israel. Arafat continued to play the role Sharon intended.

With both Sharon and Arafat encouraging the radical elements of their respective peoples, violence rapidly escalated. Soon Jews and Arabs were attacking and burning mosques and synagogues. The rock-throwing Palestinian youth disappeared, to be replaced by Palestinian security forces carrying rifles and rocket-propelled grenades. The escalating violence, combined with the Israeli perception that the Palestinians would settle for nothing but the destruction of Israel, killed any possibility of further negotiation.

Complicating matters, the Palestinians believed the recent defeat of the Israeli army in South Lebanon showed a path to a Palestinian victory. They felt that the Israeli occupation of South Lebanon, initiated by then minister of defense Ariel Sharon in his 1982 Operation Peace for Galilee, had failed. After eighteen years, the Hezbollah had driven the Israeli army out of South Lebanon.

The Palestinians saw the victory in Lebanon as a model for what they could achieve in the West Bank and took courage from it. In their excitement, they failed to see that the Israelis now perceived a Palestinian victory would result not just in Israeli withdrawal from the occupied territories but in the destruction of Israel.

The ensuing violence escalated as hardliners on both sides rode it to power. In a series of escalating responses to Palestinian suicide bombers, Israel employed troops, armor, armed helicopters, and even jet fighters in an attempt to achieve security. The complete failure to provide security resulted in Ariel Sharon's election as prime minister on February 6, 2001.

Since his election, Sharon has continued to pursue his plan for security for Israel. Because he is a firm believer in Israeli possession of the West Bank, a key aspect of his plan has been strengthening the settlements. As Jackson Diehl observes:

> Following the same tactics he has employed for a quarter-century, Sharon has been asserting in public that he accepts Bush's diplomacy—and meanwhile is quietly overseeing a plan of settlement construction designed to make any two-state solution impossible. Since Sharon took office less than 18 months ago, 44 new settlement sites, including more than 300 units have been established in the West Bank—including nine in the past three months. . . . Despite a budget crisis caused by the continuing bloodshed, Sharon's government is pouring new money into the program. The new budget calls for $64 million in subsidies this year to induce Israelis to move to settlements, plus $19 million in funding for settlement development. That doesn't count the nine roads Israel is building for use by settlements, at a cost of $50 million, or the border fences being constructed around greater Jerusalem—fences that are advertised as security measures but will have the practical effect of roping off new tracts of land for settlement expansions. On June 20 [2002]—four days before Bush's peace initiative speech—tenders were announced for the construction of 957 new units in the settlements.[10]

The technique Sharon has chosen to secure the West Bank is essentially the same railroad-and-blockhouse technique the British used successfully against the Boers in South Africa. He is making use of "secure roadways" to link the settlements he helped create over the last fifteen years. The result is a network of Israeli outposts cutting the Palestinian controlled area into a series of small enclaves. Further, the intensive security measures, particularly the new roads, make it difficult for average Palestinians to move between these enclaves. In the name of security, Sharon has reduced the Palestinian area to what are essentially refugee camps. These camps are not self-sufficient, are steadily losing employment, and are daily becoming more crowded.

To date, the al-Aqsa Intifada has reversed the international perception of Israeli and Palestinian roles of Intifada I. The Palestinians are now the side with major image problems in the West. Resorting to suicide bombings and declarations about the destruction of Israel squandered the international image they built up during the six painful years of the Intifada. Instead of effective messages sent to their internal, Israeli, and Western audiences, the Palestinian leadership has sent incredibly damaging messages to each group. The only large bloc openly sympathizing with the Palestinians are the Arab nations that still see the Israelis as brutal, unjust aggressors.

As damaging as the external message of suicide bombing has been, the internal message to Palestinian citizens has been worse. The leaders of the Intifada had their roots in service organizations that focused on making life better for Palestinians. In contrast, the Arafat leadership clique has projected an image of corruption and lack of concern for the plight of the common Palestinian. Arafat and the "Tunisians"* seem focused on protecting their income and privileges, regardless of the cost to the Palestinian people. Their infighting and resulting ineffectiveness at every turn have squandered their capital with their own people.

On the international front, the Palestinians have projected tired rhetoric laced with impossible demands. They have talked about peace while actively encouraging the bombers. Apparently out of touch with and befuddled by their own people, the Palestinian leadership squandered the support of Western nations. It was not until the George W. Bush administration's

* The "Tunisians" are PLO members who sat out the first Intifada in the safety of Tunis and returned to Palestine only after the Oslo accords were signed. They had completely missed the first Intifada and did not adapt those 4GW tactics to the new struggle.

efforts to secure peace in the Middle East that any Western nation put pressure on the Israelis during the al-Aqsa Intifada.

As serious as these failures are, the Palestinians' worst mistakes have been in their relations with Israelis. After Oslo, many Israelis were seeking accommodation and were willing to trade land for peace. However, repeated Palestinian claims to all of Israel and slogans crying out for the destruction of Israel leave the moderate Israelis nowhere to turn. Palestinian-controlled radio even refers to Tel Aviv as a settlement.

By default, the right wing took control of Israeli policy—and imposed its version of a Greater Israel on both the Palestinian and Israeli people. The Palestinian suicide bombing campaign succeeded in transforming the image of Israeli settlements from an impediment to peace to a key component of Israel's survival. Before the al-Aqsa Intifada, the mass of secular Israelis saw the settlers as fringe radicals, who expected the general Israeli population to risk life and limb to protect the settlers' narrow view of the future of Israel. The Israelis were getting tired of subsidizing the settlers at three times the rate of any other Israeli. Then the Palestinian leadership's blundering execution of the al-Aqsa Intifada transformed the settlers into the first line of defense for Israel's population.

Clearly, the Palestinian leadership does not understand the conflict they are engaged in. They have ceded the initiative to Sharon by returning to the old, brutal bombing campaigns. They seemed to have reverted to the idea that ultimate victory will be won by the "womb of the Palestinian woman." Based on the high Palestinian birth rate, they believe they will simply overwhelm Israel with numbers. Current demographic studies indicate that this may be inevitable, but it will take a generation and the loss of thousands more Palestinians and Israelis alike. It may turn out to be a Pyrrhic victory.

In contrast, the Israelis apparently learned from the battering their public image took during the Intifada. Since then, they have made major efforts to portray themselves as the victims in the struggle between Israel and Palestine. They have shown an understanding of how they "lost" the previous Intifada and are ensuring that they never let the Palestinians gain such a powerful position again. They are careful to portray each step they take as a peaceful, logical way to improve security for the Israeli public.

Further, they have been careful not to depose Arafat. Although stating they are afraid radicals will replace him, in fact Likud must also know that Arafat is perfect for their needs. He ensures that the Palestinians will maintain armed resistance and terror attacks against Israel (or at least is too weak to stop them). In doing so, Arafat justifies Israeli security measures in the eyes of the world. At the same time, he is not effective enough to unify the Palestinians and make real progress to solve their problems or provide a unified Palestinian front to the world.

It is almost impossible to overstate how perfectly Arafat and the radical elements in Palestinian resistance have supported the Israeli effort. Their suicide bombing campaign has given Israel complete freedom of action. As Diehl puts it, "The self-destructive achievements of the Palestinians' suicide bombers keep rolling in. They have succeeded in uniting Israelis and the Bush administration behind a once-unthinkable military reoccupation of the West Bank. They have created the first U.S.-sponsored Middle East peace initiative ever that envisions major reforms and concessions by one side—the Palestinians—before any serious action is taken by the other."[11]

Since the signing of the accords, where Israel agreed not to expand the settlements, they have doubled the number of Israelis living in the West Bank. Even more remarkable, they have succeeded in placing numerous new settlements on strategic ground throughout the West Bank while simultaneously massively expanding the Israeli population in East Jerusalem. With the settlements in place, they then responded to the security needs of those new settlements by expropriating Palestinian land to build security roads between the settlements. There has been little objection in the West to the fact that the settlements themselves create the "need" for security.

In effect, the Israelis have cut the Palestinian-controlled territory into three major and several minor areas. Nablus in the north, Ramallah in the central area, and Hebron in the south are each cut off from the others by the expanding network of Israeli security roads.

According to the Palestinians, seventy-nine percent of the Israeli settlements have a thousand or fewer residents. Yet the Israelis are expending huge resources in linking them with Israeli-only roads. The emerging "facts on the ground" show that Israeli settlement policy has subdivided Palestinian-controlled territory into sectors much easier to control.

Also, the Israelis are using water, the most basic of all necessities, as a weapon. In the West Bank, water is rationed, but the ration for Israeli settlers is three times the amount allowed per Palestinian.

Finally, 2003–04 has seen a significant rise in the number of Israeli settler attacks on Palestinian civilians. These normally take the form of a mob of Israeli settlers entering a Palestinian area and randomly executing people. In essence, they are conducting the same types of random terror attacks as the Palestinians, yet they do so mostly without comment from the West. Many, if not most, of these attacks originate from Israeli settlements that are themselves violations of the Oslo accords. Even as the Israelis accuse Arafat and his security services of being unable to prevent terrorist attacks, they fail to note their own inability to stop their settlers from attacking Palestinians.

There has been no Western outcry at either the Israeli failures to live up to the Oslo accords or the oppressive security measures they have imposed on the Palestinians. Why? The Palestinians have made themselves pariahs in the West by unequivocally supporting suicide bombing, terror, and the complete destruction of Israel. The Palestinian message during the al-Aqsa Intifada has proven disastrous for two major reasons.

First, internationally, the injustice against the Palestinians—economic, political, human rights, even death—pales beside the potential annihilation of the entire Israeli nation. By their actions and statements, the Palestinians have framed the argument in exactly those terms. After winning the international opinion arena so thoroughly during the first Intifada, they have essentially ceded the 4GW message to the Israelis during the al-Aqsa Intifada. Rather than focusing on their needs and aspirations, they have focused on the complete destruction of Israel—an unacceptable goal for the West.

Second, they have completely transformed the message they are projecting to the Israelis. Their message to the Israeli people has changed from one of land for peace to one of destruction of Israel. Sharon's administration is more than happy to reinforce that message to its own people, to solidify annexation of the West Bank. Under Arafat, the Palestinian leadership does not appear to understand that terror is an effective 4GW technique only to convince your opponent that holding onto your land is not worth the price he is paying. However, it does not work when it is used to tell your enemy you plan to destroy him completely.

The Palestinians are no longer sending the message that if you give up our land, we will leave you alone in yours. Instead, they are stating they will settle for nothing less than the destruction of Israel. No state can negotiate its own demise, particularly when it means the massacre of its citizens. As a result, the Palestinians are failing to project a winning message to either the international or the Israeli audience. Even many of the Palestinians do not feel this is a winning strategy.

With the Bush administration's focus on the Middle East peace process since the spring of 2003, there were some indicators progress could be made. The Palestinians elected Mahmoud Abbas as prime minister, and he was striving to move them to a more moderate position. The Israelis, responding to major pressure from the United States, had at least offered the appearance of compromise. The key Palestinian terrorist groups agreed to a cease-fire. Hopes for peace went up. Then Arafat blocked all Abbas' initiatives. Realizing he could wield no real power, Abbas resigned on September 6, 2003, after only four months in office.

The Israelis have shown a much clearer understanding of 4GW than they did during the first Intifada and have used effective 4GW messages. They publicly state that they will dismantle some of the settlements in the West Bank, and do so with great publicity. As early as January 15, 1997, Israel announced it would withdraw its forces from Hebron. In fact, they managed to consistently delay that withdrawal—always based on legitimate security concerns. At the same time, they continued to support and expand the Jewish settlements on the West Bank. Thus they had their cake and ate it too. They portrayed to the West their willingness to withdraw while simultaneously continuing to build in the West Bank. Despite the intervention of President Bush and repeated promises to dismantle West Bank settlements, the Israelis are building them faster than they dismantle them.

In March 2004, Sharon stood next to Bush and announced he was unilaterally withdrawing all settlements from the Gaza Strip as well as four from the West Bank. In return, President Bush supported continued Israeli occupation of West Bank settlements and denied the Palestinian right of return. For removing 7,500 settlers from Gaza (an area that was becoming more and more difficult to defend) and giving up only four small settlements on the West Bank, Sharon has received American support for two of his most important goals.

In addition, Sharon has unilaterally continued to build a physical barrier between the Israelis and the Palestinians. What is not clear is the exact area the wall will encompass. Early indications are that it will include major segments of the West Bank and all of east Jerusalem. This is more likely now that Israel has U.S. concurrence.

The combination of frustration with Palestinian intransigence and fear of continued attacks justifies Israeli efforts to separate itself from Palestinian society. The question is whether enclosing significant portions of the West Bank does not simply put the problem inside the wall rather than outside.

If the alignment protects certain Israeli settlements, it will enclose large numbers of Palestinians. The question then becomes, How does Israel secure itself against attacks from within? This may well be the crucial weakness in any Israeli plan to hold significant portions of the West Bank. Constructing a wall will put so many Palestinians inside Israeli territory that population demographics will result in a Palestinian majority—if not nationally, at least locally. This would force the Israelis to choose between creating an apartheid society forever or letting democracy run its course and giving up the unique Jewish aspect of the Israeli state. Neither is an acceptable choice.

The opposition in Israel has begun to argue exactly this point during discussions about future location of the security wall. The recent investigation into corruption on the part of Sharon adds even more uncertainty to the situation. Fighting the charges, even if he eventually prevails, will weaken him for the rest of his term.

Although the two sides remain separated by the huge cost in lives each has suffered, the cycle of violence rolls on. Palestinian bombings and Israeli attacks on Palestinian leaders continue in an apparently unending conflict. Adding to the confusion, Palestinians began fighting among themselves much more openly during the spring of 2004, and Israelis are arguing intensely about Sharon's apparent strategy. Although the final outcome is still much in doubt, the al-Aqsa Intifada has illustrated a number of tenets of 4GW:

- The image of an organization or nation can be shifted. Although the al-Aqsa Intifada may be a unique case, because the Palestinians are being particularly self-destructive, it is an important point to note. Because one side is dominating the public-relations fight does not mean it will always be that way. Like all aspects of war, it is a continual struggle of wills—and is subject to reversal, as are all advantages. The Palestinians were highly effective in getting their message out during Intifada I, while the Israelis stumbled badly. Yet the situation has completely reversed since the start of the al-Aqsa Intifada. The Israelis have maintained an effective, coherent 4GW strategy, while the Palestinians have regressed to the earlier, incoherent, ineffective approach of pure terror.
- Not all sides will see the same message, even if they see the same dynamics. For instance, while the West focuses on the suicide bombing campaign, most of the Arab world sees an Israeli repression of the Palestinians. Each image is filtered not only by the experiences and prejudices of the viewers but also by the method in which the information is transmitted. Clearly al-Jazeera has a very different editorial slant from ABC News.
- The political message and image remain central to 4GW. The Israelis mended theirs for the international and domestic audiences—with a great deal of assistance by bad Palestinian decisions. Projecting the image of a small, brave nation struggling for survival, they have been able to virtually re-create apartheid—and without any significant Western outcry. In contrast, the Palestinians have managed to project the worst possible image to their own people,

the Israelis, and the Western community. They have ensured that even their legitimate grievances are buried in the avalanche of outrage over the suicide bombing campaign and stated desire to destroy Israel. Compounding the damage, the actions are being taken by corrupt, incompetent leaders who clearly care more about themselves than about their people. The Palestinians have proven to be their own worst enemy.

• If one side declares a war of annihilation, defeating the minds of the enemy decision makers will not be enough to achieve victory. Facing annihilation, even the most defeatist politician must continue to fight. In a war of annihilation, the 4GW practitioner must be prepared to execute a final offensive by conventional forces to destroy the enemy nation. No technique can convince a people to negotiate away their own existence. Certainly a suicide bombing campaign that trumpets the destruction of the target nation cannot convince that nation to negotiate. Thus the Palestinians have chosen a tactical approach that has no chance of success.

One final point is essential. It is difficult for a despot to effectively use 4GW as a strategic approach. Although many of the tactics and techniques of 4GW can be effective even for a dictator, the fundamental strength of 4GW lies in the idea or message that is the heart of the concept. Each successful 4GW practitioner—Mao, Ho, the Sandinistas, and the first Intifada leadership—had an underlying, appealing, unifying idea. Although in each case that idea was abandoned upon victory, it does not change the requirement for an idea to drive 4GW warfare. Arafat has utterly failed to develop such a message. His approach to warfare cannot succeed.

In the next chapter, we will consider a 4GW organization that is almost entirely based on an idea: al-Qaeda.

# CHAPTER 10

# Al-Qaeda: A Transnational Enemy

As stated in the introduction to this book, the 9/11 attack on the World Trade Center should not have come as a major surprise. Rather, it should be seen as the logical progression of a style of warfare that has evolved over the last seventy years. The attacks were conducted by al-Qaeda (the Base), which could serve as a model for a 4GW networked, transnational enemy.

To examine both the capabilities and the limitations of al-Qaeda and future organizations based on this model, it is necessary to take a look at how al-Qaeda evolved. To understand that, we need to look to the leader who brought it to prominence on the world stage: Osama bin Laden.

Bin Laden is the seventeenth son of fifty-one children of a wealthy Saudi businessman. His father, Muhammed bin Laden, is a self-made man. Of Yemeni descent, Muhammed started out working on the docks, then started a business in which he became the preferred builder for the Saudi royal family. Due to his father's wealth, bin Laden had a comfortable early life, but he was steeped in his father's stern Wahhabism, reinforced by his attendance at Wahhabi schools up until college. He then attended King Abdul Aziz University in Jeddah, Saudi Arabia, graduating in 1981.[1]

Upon graduation he set out for Pakistan, to participate in the jihad against the Soviet invasion of Afghanistan. While there, he renewed his relationship with Sheikh Dr. Abdullah Azzam, one of his college professors. They began the close association that would lead to the birth of al-Qaeda.

Dr. Azzam was already a leading figure in the Islamist movement. He was a senior member of the Jordanian Muslim Brotherhood and had also journeyed to Pakistan to aid the Afghans in their fight against the Soviets. An Islamic scholar as well as an activist, with a doctorate in Islamic studies from al-Azhar University in Cairo, Azzam had a major influence on bin Laden.

Working together, they established the Afghan Service Bureau (MAK) in 1984, to serve as a training and logistics establishment in support of the Arab mujahideen who came to fight the Soviets. Azzam and bin Laden solicited donations from influential friends, family members, Islamic charities, and governments supporting the Afghans in their fight. Bin Laden also contributed from his personal fortune. The lessons they learned in establishing and funding a training camp for insurgents would serve bin Laden well when the Taliban took over Afghanistan and permitted him to establish a base there.

In addition to serving as a training organization, MAK also served as an information service for the families of the Arab jihadists. MAK registered the home addresses of the men who came to fight. This was the beginning of a worldwide network of Arab veterans of the Afghan jihad. When the Russians withdrew from Afghanistan, bin Laden maintained the list of contacts for future use.

When setting up MAK, bin Laden initially focused on tasks for which his training as an engineer and businessman best suited him. He moved heavy equipment into the country and focused on building the logistics infrastructure to sustain the fighting forces. As the logistics network evolved, so did bin Laden's contacts throughout the worldwide network of Islamic charities and businesses supporting the fight. These contacts, too, would come in handy later.

As the war reached its height in 1986, bin Laden moved from Pakistan to Paktia Province inside Afghanistan. He clearly was not one of the "Gucci muj" so distained by real fighters in the country. Bin Laden lived beside the men, sharing their rations, accommodations, and work. He established himself as a leader who shared their hardships—a rarity among Arab leaders. During this period, his religious convictions also deepened, and he became more convinced than ever that all Islamic nations had to be unified under a single, borderless Islamic government.

Not content with just leading the logistical aspects of the operation, bin Laden took part in several major battles against the Soviets. By displaying physical courage and leadership in these encounters, he increased his credibility with the Arabs and other nationalities fighting to eject the Soviets.

In 1989, Azzam and bin Laden founded al-Qaeda—Arabic for "the Base." Azzam "envisioned it as being an organization that would channel the energies of the *mujahideen* into fighting on behalf of oppressed Muslims worldwide, an Islamic 'rapid reaction force,' ready to spring to the defense of their fellow believers at short notice."[2]

Although they agreed on the strategic purpose of al-Qaeda, Azzam and bin Laden disagreed on the tactics. Azzam, as an Islamic scholar, did not support terrorist actions, because they targeted primarily women and children. He stated that if innocent casualties cannot be avoided in an attack on enemy forces, they were acceptable. However, children and non-fighting women could not be deliberately targeted. Azzam believed this to be the correct interpretation of the teachings of the Prophet Mohammed. Bin Laden clearly disagreed.

The matter came to a head when Egyptian jihadists wanted to use one of the camps in Afghanistan for training terrorists to conduct attacks in Egypt. Bin Laden supported their plan. Azzam refused, because he felt that the Egyptians would target women and children as part of their attacks. Shortly thereafter, on November 24, 1989, Azzam and his two sons were killed by a remote control bomb. The attack has been traced to members of the Egyptian faction of the jihadists but has never been conclusively tied to bin Laden.

However, from this point forward, bin Laden was free to shape al-Qaeda into the much more aggressive, worldwide terrorist organization it has become. About this time, no longer welcome in Pakistan, bin Laden returned to Saudi Arabia. The demise of Azzam ensured that even from a distance, he could fill key positions in al-Qaeda with his people.

From Saudi Arabia, bin Laden remained active in the affairs of al-Qaeda. Although the Soviets had withdrawn from Afghanistan, Najibullah, the last Afghan president the Soviets put in power, continued to fight the mujahideen. In turn, bin Laden continued to support the Islamic resistance. In 1990, besides continuing his involvement with al-Qaeda, bin Laden spoke out frequently in mosques, warning that Saddam Hussein would involve himself in the Gulf states. He even warned the Saudi royal family that Hussein was about to invade Kuwait.

When they did nothing and Saddam invaded, bin Laden proposed that the Saudi armed forces, supported by his al–Qaeda, were sufficient to protect Saudi Arabia. The Saudi government did not share his optimism and invited the United States to send troops to protect Saudi Arabia and evict the Iraqis from Kuwait. The royal family assured bin Laden that when the Iraqis were driven out of Kuwait, the Americans would go home. Bin Laden's anger and sense of betrayal by the Saudi royal family only increased when the Americans did not go home after the war but settled in for a long-term stay. Even today, Bin Laden clearly feels that the royal family is failing in its religious duties to protect the holy sites. He refuses to refer to Saudi Arabia by name, because it includes the family name of the royal family. He now refers to it only indirectly with terms, such as the Land of the Two Mosques.

The presence of infidels—both male and female—in the Land of the Two Holy Mosques (Mecca and Medina) infuriated bin Laden. Once the Iraqis were ejected from Kuwait in February 1991, he became a vocal opponent of the presence of American troops on "sacred soil." Bin Laden agitated against their presence and, by implication, the king's decision to permit U.S. bases in Saudi Arabia. In essence, he joined forces with the anti-royalist opposition. He became vocal enough that the Saudis essentially placed him under house arrest.

Chafing under the restrictions, bin Laden used his influence with the royal family to get permission to leave the country on a "business trip." He used it to flee to Sudan in 1991 and continue his work in support of his vision of an Islamic caliphate. Sudan was ideal for his purposes. In 1989, Dr.

Hasan al-Turabi led the National Islamic Front to power in Sudan, his stated goal to establish an Islamic republic ruled purely by Islamic law. He invited bin Laden to establish a base in Sudan and bring the 1,000 to 1,500 Arab Afghan veterans from Pakistan to Sudan. There he would be free to continue his mission to spread Islam to the world.

In Sudan, bin Laden pursued dual tracks. First, he worked at expanding his business interests worldwide. This not only generated income but also established a worldwide network of banks, resources, and contacts for future action.

Second, he continued to support acts of terror whenever possible, with a particular emphasis on American targets. With businesses in Europe, Asia, Africa, and the Middle East, he was in a position to provide funds, safe houses, communications, contacts, transportation, and expertise to his expanding network of associates. He was ready to put that network to use in conducting attacks against Americans wherever he found them.

With the entrance of U.S. forces into Somalia in December 1992, bin Laden stated that it was part of a continuing American effort to take control of the Middle East and destroy Islam. Ten years after the fact, he claimed that he focused his effort on this opportunity to attack and defeat U.S. forces in an Islamic country.

The first step was a December 1992 attack on a hotel in Yemen that was the billeting location of American forces in transit to Somalia. No Americans were killed in the bomb blast, but one Australian tourist was.

Bin Laden claims that his support to the Somali clans continued and that his troops were involved in the defeat of the Rangers in Mogadishu in October 1993. At the time, bin Laden, as a matter of policy, did not claim responsibility for the attack. However, after the Somalis drove U.S. and U.N. forces out of that country in 1994, he could not resist bragging. He told CNN that he was very proud of the role his Arabs had played in the daylong fight against the Rangers and Special Forces.

At the same time, al-Qaeda was providing support for the first attack on the World Trade Center. On February 26, 1993, a truck bomb was detonated in the underground parking garage, killing six Americans, injuring more than 1,000, and caused $500 million in damage. Bin Laden was elated with the success of this attack, but once again, al-Qaeda did not claim responsibility.

Clearly, al-Qaeda was an organization that could manage multiple operations simultaneously—even complex ones requiring long-term planning, surveillance, and preparation. Bin Laden had built a simple but resilient and highly effective organization. He was the unquestioned leader and carefully picked a staff of talented subordinates. He appointed as his deputy Dr. Ayman al-Zawahiri, an Egyptian with more than thirty years' experience as a terrorist. In addition to being bin Laden's deputy, al-Zawahiri became the primary influence on his religious beliefs and strategy.

Bin Laden also formed a consultation council of Islamic elders. These men functioned as his shura—providing advice, heading the subordinate committees, and approving major attacks. A highly capable administrator, bin Laden organized his worldwide network into the three functional areas of Islamic study, military, and finance. He formed a committee to supervise al-Qaeda's efforts in each area.

The Islamic study committee is responsible not just for providing religious guidance to the movement and its Muslim followers but also for the Islamic schools that all al-Qaeda members attend as part of their training. Both roles are critical. The Islamic study committee debates Islamic law and, on the basis of their interpretation, issues the *fatwas* that provide the religious and propaganda underpinnings for al-Qaeda's actions. Because al-Qaeda relies heavily on religious supporters worldwide, this is an essential part of their propaganda message to their own forces. In much of the world, Islam is primarily an oral tradition, because few can read the original Arabic. Therefore, the stamp of well-respected, famous Islamic scholars validates al-Qaeda's actions for a huge number of Muslims.

The Islamic study committee's second task is to supervise the extensive network of religious schools they run—and in particular, the religious training of the al-Qaeda recruits. In the same way Mao created a unifying philosophy and intensive, repetitive study of the same, the Islamic Action Committee provides a specifically tailored version of the teachings of Mohammed, to strengthen the resolve of their soldiers. They also provide the schools that steep al-Qaeda recruits in that philosophy.

The finance committee supervises the most complex aspect of al-Qaeda. They handle all financial assets, including legitimate businesses, front businesses, non-governmental organizations, charities, and criminal activities. The legitimate businesses are worldwide (as are the other enterprises) and include pharmaceutical companies, fruit companies, livestock firms, fishing boats, construction companies, and dozens of other enterprises throughout Africa, Asia, and Europe.

The finance committee is also responsible for the distribution of funds based on directions from the operators. Distribution includes setting up accounts, moving assets, and ensuring that personnel have access to those accounts. To assist in this work, the finance committee has a section responsible for documents—both legal and forged. This committee can establish an identity for a member, complete with passport, addresses, background, credit cards, bank cards, bank accounts, and so on.

The military committee is responsible for all individual and unit training. The one major unit they formed, the 055 Brigade, apparently took heavy casualties in Afghanistan and is no longer an effective force. However, during its existence, it served not only as a major combat element for the Taliban (the embodiment of the rapid-deployment force bin Laden and Azzam envisioned) but also as a training unit to prepare mujahideen to fight in other countries, such as Chechnya. Despite the major damage inflicted by the U.S. campaign in Afghanistan, the military committee apparently continues to run terrorist training camps that take their recruits through basic, advanced, and specialized training.

The military committee also seeks to be a source of training for terrorists around the world. To achieve that, they have produced an eleven-volume, 7,000-page training manual. Although most of the manual is copied from Western military sources, particularly U.S. Army field manuals, it includes many of the harsh, practical lessons the mujahideen learned fighting the Russians. To ensure ease of distribution and use, they have placed the first ten volumes—which cover all conventional and guerrilla military operations—on CD-ROMs. A final volume, chemical and biological warfare, they reserve for restricted distribution to key elements of the force. Clearly, they take seriously their role as trainers for the world's Islamic terrorists.

Once bin Laden put this organization in place, al-Qaeda functioned much like a venture capitalist. They surveyed the world for organizations with "ideas" to attack American or Western interests. Then, based on their evaluation of the validity of the plan, al-Qaeda determined the level of support they would provide. For minor attacks or those without much chance of success, al-Qaeda might provide only some funding and advice. For those with major possibilities, they provide significant funding, training, advice, and perhaps supervisory personnel.

Just like a venture capital firm, they know the majority of their enterprises will not succeed. However, they also believe enough will succeed for them to achieve their goals. Also, like a venture capitalist firm, al-Qaeda expects sweat equity from the terrorists it sponsors. The terrorists have to work while they prepare, even if it means a minimum-wage job. They live in low-rent apartments and in some cases even have to engage in petty crime to fund their preparations. Many work for years to support themselves as they plan, prepare, and execute a mission.

This venture capital approach gave al-Qaeda a number of major advantages in its fight with the United States. For those ventures with either high payoff or high probability of success, al-Qaeda, in return for providing major resources, can take fairly direct control. They gain the benefit of local knowledge and capabilities while maintaining control over the target, timing, and methods. The locals gain from access to the worldwide network of assets, people, and expertise.

For attacks with a low probability of success or low payoff, al-Qaeda maintains a distance but still gets credit for the attack within the radical Islamic world. Further, the presence of these additional terror cells forces Western intelligence and police activities to spread their resources. They have to investigate a much larger number of terrorist groups while protecting a much longer list of potential targets. Thus, the low-payoff operations al-Qaeda supports are exceptional economy-of-force operations.

Besides initiating global attacks on American interests, this approach allowed al-Qaeda to strengthen their ties with dozens of terrorist organizations worldwide. Like a true multinational corporation, al-Qaeda used these local organizations to perform key functions in their home nations. They also use this network of contacts to move personnel, equipment, and money around the world. It is obviously much easier for a Filipino to move around Cebu than for an Egyptian.

To appreciate how aggressively bin Laden has sought this worldwide reach and how widespread al-Qaeda has become, consider that, post-9/11, cells have been arrested in Italy, Germany, Spain, Britain, Canada, the United States, South Africa, Tanzania, Kenya, Yemen, Albania, Singapore, Malaysia, the Philippines, Jordan, Algeria, Libya, Pakistan, and France. These represent only cells authorities could identify and move against.

Throughout his time in Sudan, bin Laden continued his opposition to the Saudi regime. As a result, the Saudis monitored his activities and ordered him home in 1994. When he refused, they revoked his citizenship, froze his assets, and encouraged his family to make statements condemning his actions. Bin Laden responded by founding the Advice and Reformation Committee, whose purpose was to publish papers and issue press releases attacking the Saudi government as illegitimate. In addition, bin Laden's anger was reflected in his own speeches and teachings. His conflict with the Saudi royal family was escalating.

Evidence indicates that in response, the Saudis funded an assassination attempt against bin Laden in February 1994. It failed but killed and wounded a number of his followers. Bin Laden, convinced that the Saudis were behind the attempt, responded by providing arms, explosives, and advice to Saudi insurgents.

Al-Qaeda's successful attacks motivated the international community to pressure Sudan to evict bin Laden and his followers. Although the Sudanese resisted the pressure, bin Laden took it upon himself to relocate to Afghanistan in 1996.

In the five years he had been in Sudan, the Taliban had transformed much of Afghanistan. Essentially composed of young male Afghan refugees who were graduates of strict Islamic schools, the Taliban were determined to make Afghanistan a pure Islamic caliphate and pursued that goal with a vengeance. In the areas they seized, the Taliban installed a ruthless, fundamentalist regime that enforced repressive "moral" standards on the people. All women were forced back into the burqua; men were forced to grow beards. All music, movies, and forms of entertainment were banned. Standards and enforcement were based on the arbitrary decisions of a self-appointed, religious elite. In short, the Taliban had built the society bin Laden wished to impose on the entire Islamic world.

Upon arrival in Afghanistan, bin Laden allied himself with the Taliban and, along with the Pakistani Inter-Services Intelligence (ISI), supported them during their final drive to seize Kabul. The Pakistani ISI had supported the Taliban all along, in an effort to ensure that a friendly government was installed in Kabul. The Taliban captured Kabul in September 1996 and established their caliphate. Although they had not been able to conquer the north of the nation, the Taliban held Kabul and most of the country south of the Salang Tunnel. They claimed to be the legitimate government of Afghanistan—and were recognized by Pakistan as such.

The Taliban-controlled area was easily large enough for al-Qaeda to establish and run full-fledged training camps and religious schools. This allowed for the rapid expansion of both the schools of the Islamic study committee and the training camps of the military committee. In addition, al-Qaeda supported the Taliban's continuing campaign against the Northern Alliance (mostly Tajik and Uzbek tribesmen from northern Afghanistan, led by Ahmad Shah Masood). By doing so, both the schools and training camps gained favor with the Taliban and had access to a superb finishing school for their warriors.

Bin Laden quickly made Afghanistan the center of his worldwide network. Inside Afghanistan, protected by the Taliban, he increased the training of terrorists as well as planning and supporting attacks by his personnel and by affiliated terror groups. He also an the aggressive religious programs that were an essential part of training members of al-Qaeda. Despite the apparent security provided by his location in this remote, austere, and dangerous part of the world, bin Laden continued his policy of not claiming credit for attacks against American targets:

> In keeping with the guidelines laid down by its Emir-General Osama, Al Qaeda's code forbade its membership from publicly identifying its organization or claiming credit for its attacks: "By

> claiming credit, we were told that the groups will earn the wrath of the target state. Everyone knows that we were behind it and responsible for the attack. Why claim credit and become identified and hunted down?" As such, Al Qaeda did not claim credit for its bombing of the National Guard Building in Riyadh on November 13, 1995, that killed seven people, or of the Khobar Towers military facility in Dhahran that killed nineteen Americans and injured several hundred more. However, he added: "I have great respect for the people who did this action. What they did is a big honour that I missed participating in."[3]

To further confuse his enemies, bin Laden had his operatives give credit for the attacks to various front organizations, such as the World Islamic Front or the Jihad Against Jews and Crusaders. His tactic of not claiming credit ran contrary to the policy of virtually all previous terrorist groups, where even non-articipants were eager to claim credit for any terrorist action.

His policy worked. Despite developing a worldwide network, being behind numerous successful attacks and being implicated in unsuccessful attacks and assassination attempts, al-Qaeda was not heavily targeted by U.S. and Western intelligence agencies. Even after the first World Trade Center attack, both the FBI and the CIA concluded that the terrorists who conducted the attack were not part of any major organization but were an isolated cell operating on their own. Not until after the simultaneous bombing of two U.S. embassies in Africa in 1998 were U.S. intelligence and law enforcement agencies willing to believe al-Qaeda was a worldwide organization with the capability to coordinate complex attacks.

It is also important to note that al-Qaeda is truly a modern organization. It learns from mistakes, incorporates the lessons learned into its training and future operations, and literally re-attacks the problem. Consider the attacks we have successfully identified as supported by al-Qaeda:

> **1991:** Attack on a tourist hotel in Yemen. The target was American servicemen, but only one Australian tourist was killed.
>
> **1993:** February 26 truck bomb attack on World Trade Center,

New York. This was a highly successful attack that targeted one of the symbols of Western capitalism. There are even indications that al-Qaeda attempted to chemically contaminate the rubble but was unsuccessful. They also failed to collapse the structure. Captured documents indicate that they have continued to study the employment of chemicals for potential attacks. Obviously, they continued to study how to attack the World Trade Center.

**1993:** Al-Qaeda claims to have supported the October 3–4 Somali attack on U.S. forces in Mogadishu. If the claims are true, this was highly successful. No key al-Qaeda personnel were hurt in the attack nor in the American operations afterward, but the attack resulted in American troop withdrawal that led to the failure of the U.N. effort. Although this was a disaster for the average Somali, it did remove any chance of Western influence in this Islamic country.

**1994:** On December 11, al-Qaeda operatives bombed Philippine Airlines Flight 434, en route from Cebu to Japan. This bombing was not attributed to al-Qaeda until a fire in the Philippines led authorities to capture Abdul Hamid Murad and his laptop. The interrogation and the laptop files showed that the bombing was a dry run for a much bigger operation: Oplan Bojinka. Under this plan, five terrorists were to board a series of flights, check luggage through, then get off at an intermediate stop. They were to target eleven airlines on the same day. Each suitcase would contain a bomb set to explode over the Pacific as the airliners headed to America. If it had succeeded, approximately four thousand people could have died. Murad also claimed that al-Qaeda was planning suicide attacks using airliners as the weapons. Even with this information in its hands, the United States did not take aggressive action to eliminate al-Qaeda operations. Again, bin Laden's approach of not taking credit for attacks paid off. Although Oplan Bojinka was not executed, the planning and thought that went into simultaneously bombing eleven airliners was useful in the preparation for 9/11.

**1994:** Al-Qaeda failed in assassination attempts against President Clinton and President Ramos in the Philippines.

**1995:** Al-Qaeda failed in an assassination attempt against President Mubarak of Egypt. However, in a separate operation by an entirely different cell, they successfully bombed the National Guard Armory in Riyadh, Saudi Arabia.

**1996:** Al-Qaeda supported a successful attack on the Khobar Towers in Dhahran, killing nineteen U.S. servicemen. Again, they did not claim credit.

**1998:** On August 7, al-Qaeda suicide bombers nearly simultaneously detonated truck bombs at the U.S. embassies in Dar es Salaam, Tanzania, and Nairobi, Kenya, killing more than 200.

**2000:** On January 14, al-Qaeda failed to execute a small-boat suicide attack on the USS *Sullivan* in Yemen. Their boat was overloaded and sank before it could attack. They obviously learned from the experience, and on October 12, 2000, they succeeded in a small-boat suicide attack on the USS *Cole* in Yemen.

**2001:** On September 9, two al-Qaeda members assassinated Ahmad Shah Masood, leader of the Northern Alliance in Afghanistan. This was a complex operation that involved recruiting assassins in North Africa, moving them through Britain to establish credentials, then on to Pakistan, and finally convincing the Northern Alliance they were genuine journalists.

**2001:** On September 11, al-Qaeda conducted a successful reattack on the World Trade Center and the Pentagon. They failed to complete another suicide attack when the passengers of Flight 77 fought to retake the aircraft. In the struggle, it crashed in western Pennsylvania.

Since 2001, al-Qaeda cells have succeeded with bombings at a synagogue in Tunisia and the U.S. consulate in Karachi. Cells have been arrested in Singapore for plotting to blow up the U.S. embassy, in Morocco for planning a small-boat suicide attack on a U.S. ship, and in the air, when Richard Reid, the incompetent shoe bomber, failed to detonate his bomb. They succeeded in a massive bombing in a nightclub in Indonesia—killing hundreds, mostly Australian tourists—as well as a near-simultaneous attack on five trains in Madrid, killing more than 200.

They carried the fight into Saudi Arabia with three near-simultaneous truck bombings against housing complexes during May 2003 and multiple assassination attacks against government officials.

Through one of their associated organizations, they changed the outcome of the election in Spain, with the near-simultaneous detonation of ten bombs on trains.

At first glance, there does not seem to be a strategic vision behind these attacks. Rather, they seem to be the violent lashing out of disparate terrorist groups.

In fact, when one reviews the development of the goals and techniques of al-Qaeda, it becomes apparent that this is a genuine 4GW strategic approach.

Al-Qaeda's strategic goals are reflected in bin Laden's statements and writing. When he formed al-Qaeda in conjunction with Azzam, he was focused on driving the Soviets out of Afghanistan and building a "rapid reaction force" to go to the aid of Muslims anywhere in the world they were threatened by infidels. Although al-Qaeda was initially conceived as a guerrilla combat force, bin Laden began to believe he needed to add terror to his arsenal—even though it meant he had to murder Azzam, his mentor and partner, to move the organization in that direction. Up to this point, his focus had been primarily against the Soviets. With their defeat and his return to Saudi Arabia, his strategic goals began to expand significantly.

Bin Laden was angered by the Saud family's rejecting his offer of help, inviting the Americans in to defend Saudi Arabia, seizing his assets, defaming his character, and attempting to assassinate him. He decided they were unfit to be keepers of the Two Holy Mosques and must be removed from power.

Although this was a primary goal, it was not the only goal. In keeping with running a truly transnational terror organization, bin Laden also sought the overthrow of Arab regimes he did not feel were Islamic enough. In essence, all Arab regimes became targets.

Throughout the late 1990s, bin Laden campaigned with the other Islamic groups to expand the war to include America. He argued strongly that Americans were the only crusaders ever to have occupied the holy places, that they had massacred thousands of Iraqi Muslims and were bent on killing more, and finally, that although much of their interest in the Gulf was economic, they were still the tools of the Jews and were working with them to destroy Islam.

This campaign to expand the war to include America would serve two purposes for bin Laden. First, he would achieve his personal goal of shifting the attack to America as both the strongest supporter of the Saudi government and the defilers of the Holy Land. Second, he would shift the attacks out of the Middle East, where the totalitarian governments were cracking down on the families and supporters of terrorists.

Given the brutality and virtually unrestricted power of the police agencies in the Middle East, the Arab governments were crippling al-Qaeda operations inside their nations. Al-Qaeda was getting fewer and fewer results, at greater and greater cost both in casualties and money. As more al-Qaeda members were rounded up, al-Qaeda was obligated to support their families. Bin Laden knew that only when he shifted the attacks out of the Middle East would the Arab governments relax the security measures that were costing al-Qaeda so much treasure and talent.

In February 1998, bin Laden announced the formation of the World Islamic Front for Jihad against Jews and the Crusaders. At that time, he published the fatwa calling for war against Americans. He called on all Muslims to conduct a personal jihad against Americans and kill them wherever they might be.

> [Through] an Arabic newspaper [he] announced the formation of the "World Islamic Front for Jihad against Jews and the Crusaders," a new organization with Al Qaeda at its core. This statement remains the central call to arms and the best document for understanding its ideology. It describes the presence of U.S. troops in the Holy Land (Saudi Arabia), the suffering inflicted on Iraq by sanctions, and the occupation of Jerusalem, as a "clear dec-

> laration of war by the Americans against God, his prophet, and the Muslims." It invokes its own interpretation of Islamic law to conclude that "to kill Americans and their allies is an individual duty of every Muslim who is able, in any country where this is possible." Faced with the overwhelming military might of the United States, the only option they believed would work was terror.[4]

Any doubts about bin Laden's anger over the continued presence of American troops in Saudi Arabia were erased by the bombing of the two U.S. embassies in Africa on the eighth anniversary of the arrival of U.S. troops in Saudi Arabia: August 7, 1998. American intelligence finally agreed that bin Laden was a major threat and, unless eliminated, would continue to plan, sponsor, and execute attacks against American targets worldwide. On August 20, President Clinton ordered cruise missile strikes against bin Laden's base in Afghanistan and a pharmaceutical plant in the Sudan.

Unfortunately, the cruise missiles failed to kill bin Laden. Instead, the failed assassination attempt enhanced his prestige throughout Islamic lands. The consensus in the Arabic press and street was that he had stood up to the United States and succeeded. The strike on the pharmaceutical plant just made the United States look foolish. Also, the fact that both attacks were conducted immediately before Monica Lewinsky was due to testify to the special prosecutor made it look like an attempt to distract the U.S. public.

This fact, combined with a complete failure to follow up, indicated that the United States would not strike back hard even when directly attacked. Despite bin Laden's being declared the number 1 enemy of the United States, our public response was limited to a single night of cruise missile attacks. Although President Clinton did sign an executive order authorizing his assassination, our inability to track bin Laden made that a purely academic exercise.

In continuing his pattern of escalating against enemies that attack him, bin Laden initiated the planning and positioning of forces for the 9/11 attacks. In keeping with his past declarations of intent, he informed the world, through the media, of his plans to attack America.* On December 22, 1998, he summoned Rahimullah Yusufzai, a reporter for both Pakistan's *The News* and *Time,* to Afghanistan for an interview. In that interview, he restated his disdain for Saudi Arabia, issued a clear call for revolution against the Saud family, restated his reasons for hating America, his plans to attack us, and his plans to use weapons of mass destruction.

> ***Time:*** How do you react to the December attacks on Iraq by U.S. and British forces?
>
> **Osama bin Laden:** There is no doubt that the treacherous attack has confirmed that Britain and America are acting on behalf of Israel and the Jews, paving the way for the Jews to divide the Muslim world once again, enslave it and loot the rest of its wealth. A great part of the force that carried out the attack came from certain gulf countries that have lost their sovereignty. Now infidels walk everywhere on the land where Muhammad was born and where the Koran was revealed to him. The situation is serious. The rulers have become powerless. Muslims should carry out their obligations, since the rulers of the region have accepted the invasion of their countries. These countries belong to Islam and not the rulers.
>
> ***Time:*** What can the U.S. expect from you now?
>
> **Osama bin Laden:** Any thief or criminal or robber who enters another country in order to steal should expect to be exposed to murder at any time. For the American forces to expect anything from me personally reflects a very narrow perception. Thousands of millions of Muslims are angry. The Americans should expect re-

* This is a critical aspect of al-Qaeda's image among Muslims. He is careful to fulfill the requirement to declare his intent *before* attacking. After the attack, even though he does not openly claim responsibility, he makes it known that he supported the attack. However, the attack cannot be considered unjustified, because he had openly warned his enemies that they were going to be attacked.

actions from the Muslim world that are proportionate to the injustice they inflict.

*Time:* The U.S. says you are trying to acquire chemical and nuclear weapons.

**Osama bin Laden:** Acquiring weapons for the defense of Muslims is a religious duty. If I have indeed acquired these weapons, then I thank God for enabling me to do so. And if I seek to acquire these weapons, I am carrying out a duty. It would be a sin for Muslims not to try to possess the weapons that would prevent the infidels from inflicting harm on Muslims.[5]

Once again, bin Laden skillfully applied 4GW techniques to war. He used open media to broadcast his message not only to the U.S. government but also to all Western governments and their people. More important, his followers worldwide received the message. He emphasized that this was a mass movement against America's infringement on the holy places. He called on Gulf Arabs, particularly Saudis, to revolt against their rulers. He intimated that he had, and was willing to use, weapons of mass destruction. However, he kept it ambiguous, making any firm Western response much less likely but forcing us to consider the possibility in any action against al-Qaeda.

Finally, he still did not take responsibility for the attacks on U.S. embassies. Although U.S. agencies have proved it to the satisfaction of Western leaders, the ambiguity in his statement allows the Arab world to see him as "standing up to America." This allows Arabs to claim that the attacks were orchestrated by Jews to discredit Arabs.

To understand bin Laden's strategy, consider it from the viewpoint of a 4GW conflict. The key problem is to destroy support for the government you are trying to overthrow. In this case, he seeks to overthrow the government of Saudi Arabia. Apparently he hopes to become the caliph of the holy places and then, using that prestige and his existing organization, begin absorbing all Islamic areas into a worldwide Islamic caliphate.

Fortunately for us, Islamic fundamentalism is simply not a story that sells well with voters of the Western democracies. If the voters won't buy it, they will not force their governments to cut off aid to the target nation. Because he cannot sell Americans on the idea that an even more fundamentalist Saudi Arabia would be the most just option available, he must take action to convince us it is simply too expensive to continue to support them.

Given that bin Laden's target was the government of Saudi Arabia, he had the additional problem of the tremendous U.S. reliance on imported oil. Until the invasion of Iraq, successive U.S. governments proved more interested in governmental stability in the Middle East than in the evolution of democracies. Even worse for bin Laden is that Iran provides a daily reminder of the problems inherent in dealing with an Islamic republic.

Thus, any 4GW campaign to drive Americans out of Saudi Arabia would be a long one. It must wear down American resolve to the point where the American people decide to let the House of Saud stand or fall on its own. With his early targets—U.S. military personnel overseas, U.S. embassies, international flights, U.S. warships—he was constantly reminding America of the price we were paying to prop up a corrupt and despotic regime.

This strategy seemed to be working. After the embassy bombings in Africa, public opinion in the United States was beginning to shift. Our citizens were tired of what appeared to be an endless commitment in support of one despotic state against another. For the first time, public discourse began to consider the possibility of U.S. forces leaving Saudi Arabia.

At this point, bin Laden made a fundamental error. He seems to have concluded that if killing a few Americans at embassies overseas stimulated discussion of withdrawal, killing thousands in New York would certainly lead to that withdrawal.

In this analysis, he failed to understand the American psyche. In attempting to send a final, expensive message to force the United States to withdraw from the Middle East, he conducted a "sneak attack" in the United States. Perhaps his misunderstanding came from our relatively mild reaction to attacks on U.S. citizens and U.S. embassies overseas, or perhaps his hatred blinded him to our cultural strength in times of adversity.

Whatever the reason, he committed a fundamental strategic error in 4GW. Rather than sending the message he intended—that maintaining forces in Saudi Arabia means the United States will continue to suffer casuaities—he sent the message "I am attacking you in your homeland." This is a message Americans do not react well to. Perhaps he should have examined more closely our response to the last nation to conduct a sneak attack on our homeland: Japan. He might have noticed how it unified our people and drove them through four years of high-intensity warfare—and ended in the nuclear attack on two Japanese cities.

Al-Qaeda has suffered a major setback. The Allied offensive in Afghanistan has hurt them badly. Although they continue to operate out of the tribal areas of northwest Pakistan, they cannot be as effective as they were with a government sponsor. In addition, the focused Allied attack on their network, finances, and contacts worldwide has also damaged them a great deal. However, like true networks, they are well designed to absorb damage.

Al-Qaeda's prestige in the Islamic terror network increased with each attack, from the hotel in Aden right through the 9/11 attacks. With increasing prestige, bin Laden became the unifying voice for the fundamentalist Islamic movement. Much like the CEO of a modern multinational corporation, he was focused at the macro level. His most important function was to provide a clear, coherent, executable vision of where he saw the movement going.

In addition, he appealed greatly to the masses of Muslims who were puzzled and frustrated that the great Islamic civilization should have fallen so far behind the West. He provided some answers, several scapegoats, and a possible, if drastic, solution to the West's domination of the Middle East.

Clearly a man who understood the necessity of providing inspiration to his followers, bin Laden wrote and disseminated poetry at critical junctures in his campaigns. He was also careful to select auspicious times in his personal life to release poetry. At the wedding of his eldest son, in January 2001, bin Laden narrated the following poem, praising the suicide bombers who attacked the USS *Cole:*

> A destroyer, even the brave might fear,
> She inspires horror in the harbour and the open seas,

> She goes into the waves flanked by arrogance, haughtiness and fake might,
> To her doom she progresses slowly, clothed in a huge illusion,
> Awaiting her is a dinghy, bobbing in the waves.[6]

In this simple poem, he stressed how the courage of the suicide bombers can defeat the arrogance and fake might of the United States. It sent several messages: praise for the terrorists, contempt for the United States, and a warning that the might of the United States is really an illusion.

Despite a massive effort that has eliminated many cells worldwide, al-Qaeda's continued operations and the arrest of newly revealed cells indicate that we do not have a clear idea of the extent of the organization nor how resilient it really is.

Even two years after the United States finally commenced a serious, worldwide attack on al-Qaeda, we cannot predict the future of the conflict. Our invasion of Iraq has allowed al-Qaeda personnel to get in close to U.S. personnel, while they remain essentially invisible to us in a sea of Arabs. The result has been a significant rise in U.S. casualties with an unknown amount of damage to al-Qaeda.

For conventional powers, this is one of the frustrating and cautionary aspects of 4GW. The massive conventional victory over Saddam's forces actually exposed U.S. forces to much greater risk. In addition, the occupation offers a critically important battlefield to al-Qaeda. If the latter can prevent Iraqis from forming a unified government and drive coalition forces out, it will not only destabilize Iraq but will serve as a huge psychological victory over the United States. Aside from creating a pool of recruits, this would provide the ungoverned regions essential for establishing training facilities and bases.

Conversely, if a secure, democratic government can be established in Iraq, it could well serve as an example for other Arab nations. The emergence of true democracy, if prosperity followed, would vastly undercut the support al-Qaeda receives from the masses.

In short, Iraq has moved from being peripheral to the U.S.–al-Qaeda struggle to a central battlefield that will test the endurance of the two sides.

Al-Qaeda is making the most of this opportunity to attack U.S. forces. Developing and executing an attack in the West requires a high degree of skill and significant assets, not the least of which is operatives capable of moving about without attracting undue attention. The U.S. presence in Iraq means that the Arabs supporting al-Qaeda, even non-Iraqi Arabs, can move about the country much more easily than can the Western security forces hunting them. The invasion of Iraq places a strategically significant American effort in the Arab heartland, with all the risks that implies.

Although we cannot predict the outcome of this decades-long war with al-Qaeda, we are undoubtedly witnessing a major struggle between a nation and a transnational organization. Clearly, we are fighting a fourth-generation war. Knowing that, what lessons can we learn from the struggle up to this point?

The first and most important lesson is that, prior to 9/11, al-Qaeda succeeded by staying on message for both their internal Islamic and external U.S. audiences. The key was maintaining a low profile while slowly increasing the cost to the United States of supporting the Saudi government. In addition to the cost in blood and treasure, they were extracting a cost in the perception of America in the Islamic world.

Bin Laden was successfully painting the Saudis as a corrupt regime that the Americans supported purely for access to cheap oil. He stated that the United States supported the Saudis and other corrupt Arab regimes only to ensure stability in oil prices. He hammered at the theme that America did not support democracy and would never support the Arab people against their tyrannical masters. The Arab people could only turn to al-Qaeda to achieve their dreams of a just society.

The combination of messages was playing to a U.S. cultural weakness: patience. Americans were tired of bearing the fiscal and emotional cost of supporting stability in the Middle East—and being hated for it. Bin Laden's dogged persistence and low-level attacks in the area (most Americans considered the African embassies to be close enough to be considered in the area) mirrored the Palestinian approach during the Intifada. Like the Palestinians' Intifada I message to the Israeli public, bin Laden was making the point to the U.S. public and our decision makers that the problem was the presence of U.S. troops in an area where they were not wanted. Therefore, the only solution to being hated and attacked was to simply go home and let the Arabs resolve among themselves who would rule in the Middle East.

The second major lesson we can draw from al-Qaeda's campaign is the sheer duration of 4GW. Despite heavy casualties in Afghanistan, the losses of dozens of cells worldwide, the seizure of significant funds, and the freezing of other assets, al-Qaeda's networked nature allowed it to absorb the damage and remain a threat. The 2004 attacks in Spain and open support for insurgents in Iraq show that they remain a tough opponent. Like all 4GW wars, this one will be long, and we are only two years into our response.

The final lesson is that 4GW opponents are as likely to make major mistakes as we are. With the 9/11 attacks, al-Qaeda showed the danger in not understanding the culture of the nation you are fighting. Fourth-generation warfare is based on getting a clear message through to the target audience. Although the message may be sent by any number of channels, it will always be filtered through a person's or nation's cultural references. Bin Laden failed to understand America's cultural abhorrence and anger toward "sneak attacks" directed at American soil. He completely failed to understand the visceral reaction a direct attack would provoke from the people of the United States. His failure has shown that a direct attack on the minds of decision makers requires an understanding of the history, culture, and attitudes of the people involved.

# CHAPTER 11

# Afghanistan: A Tribal Network

On October 7, 2001, U.S. forces initiated a counterattack against the perpetrators of 9/11. After unsuccessfully negotiating with the Taliban to turn over al-Qaeda terrorists, the Bush administration acted. Boldly striking into Afghanistan, the sustained U.S. air campaign caught the al-Qaeda and Taliban leadership by surprise. They were even more surprised when the U.S. committed ground forces to control the aerial firepower and directly assist the Afghans who allied themselves with the coalition.

Despite the predictions of failure and the dire reminders of the fate of both the British and Soviets in Afghanistan, the initial campaign succeeded in rapidly removing the Taliban government and inflicted significant damage on al-Qaeda. The U.S. actions proved that a nation can still surprise 4GW insurgents.

The terrorists had assumed that the United States would fight in a predictable fashion, with conventional forces. Instead, the U.S. campaign focused on unconventional forces forging alliances with Afghan commanders. Those commanders, supported by overwhelming U.S. firepower, drove the Taliban from Kabul. In less than two months, the Northern Alliance went from controlling less than one-sixth of the country, in the extreme north, to controlling all but a fragment of the mountainous south and east.

Although the enemy seemed to have withdrawn, we could not find them nor confirm their destruction. They had recovered from their surprise and reverted to classical Afghan tribal tactics. The U.S. continued to hunt but, with lack of contact, assumed the enemy had been dispersed and was now ineffective.

With the threat of the Taliban apparently gone, the U.S. government shifted its focus elsewhere. We perceived that the bulk of the fighting was over. In keeping with the president's oft-stated policy that the United States doesn't "do" nation building, we essentially left the Afghans to rebuild their own country. The interest we did maintain in the country was focused on pursuing the remnants of the Taliban in the south. We used most of the 10,000 troops we kept in the country for that purpose alone. Now it was our turn for a surprise: suddenly our progress seemed to stop.

Inevitably, the confused tribal politics of Afghanistan reasserted themselves. The old ethnic conflicts moved to the foreground. Some Afghans took advantage of our pursuit of al-Qaeda to settle old scores. Their efforts, combined with the lack of U.S. focus and poor interagency coordination, resulted in very odd actions on the ground. Within six months, U.S. aircraft were conducting bombing missions supporting one Pashtun tribal element against another. Farther south, U.S. Special Forces, focused on hunting the remnants of al-Qaeda, were employing tribal elements that were officially enemies of the U.S.-supported government in Kabul. We lacked the regional knowledge to anticipate when one tribal group was using us against another. U.S. and Afghan government efforts were very poorly coordinated.

In an effort to improve that coordination at a local level, the small U.S. element working with the Afghan government began planning nation-building operations in other sections of the country. Despite the fact that President Bush had repeatedly stated that the United States didn't "do" nation building, people on the ground understood that if we failed to establish some kind of nation, Afghanistan would revert to the lawlessness that gave rise to the Taliban.

The obvious question is, How did we find ourselves in such strange circumstances? How did we get embroiled in a 4GW struggle without any apparent long-term national strategy or unified U.S. effort? Why are we simultaneously chasing an elusive insurgent enemy and engaging in nation building when we have stated we don't do either?

To understand how we got here, we have to understand the recent history of Afghanistan. The first thing to understand is that all Afghan politics are tribal. Also, because the borders are artificially imposed by the Russians and the British, the tribes are not contained within Afghanistan but straddle the borders with surrounding nations, most of which have a direct stake in Afghanistan. Thus, Afghan politics are simultaneously tribal and international. Further complicating the situation are internal migrations, so even inside Afghanistan, the tribes are mixed. A tribe may be a majority in one area and a minority in another. Finally, numerous international and transnational players, such as religious movements and drug dealers, have vested interests in Afghanistan.

We have to start with the tribal structure of the nation. The Pashtun are the largest tribe and live primarily in the south and southeast parts of Afghanistan. Unfortunately, the Afghan-Pakistani border divides their traditional tribal lands. In fact, more Pashtun live in Pakistan than in Afghanistan.

The Tajiks are the second largest tribe. They live primarily in the north and northeast of the country, with the leaders coming from the Panjishi valley. Thus, the Tajiks are often referred to as the Panjishiris. They obviously have ethnic ties to Tajikistan.

With only ten percent of the population, the Hezara are just barely the third largest group—and the most isolated. They are a Mongol people and, in contrast to most Afghans, are Shia rather than Sunni. They live in the center of the country, in the mountainous region northwest of Kabul. They maintain a strong relationship with Iran and control the trade routes between Iran and Kabul.

The Uzbeks are the fourth largest tribe but make up only eight percent of the population. However, they have strong ties to Uzbekistan, so they receive support from both Uzbeks and Russians.

The balance of the country is a mix of very small groups.

With this basic understanding of the tribal nature of the country and rough makeup and location of each tribe, we can conduct a quick review of recent Afghan history.

Modern Afghanistan was established by Ahmad Shah, a Pashtun tribal leader. In 1747, he completed the conquest of the lands between Persia and the Indus River. From then until 1978, the Durrani tribe (so named for Ahmad Shah's propensity for wearing pearls, or "durranis") provided the kings of Afghanistan. This kingship was based on the power of the Pashtun tribes, of which the Durrani were one branch.

Continual tribal and international wars resulted in frequent changes in power. New kings came to power based on temporary alliances with both internal and external allies. Further complicating the power-sharing arrangements was that outside powers felt free to interfere in Afghan politics in an effort to put "their" man on the throne. In particular, the British and the Russians thought of Afghanistan simply as a pawn in the Great Game. Despite all these complications, the Pashtuns maintained an unbroken hold on the crown. Although the king changed, the tribe he came from never did.

The first blatant attempt by a modern foreign power to rule directly occurred in 1839. To cut off a perceived Russian move south, the British invaded Afghanistan and established themselves as the ruling power. However, a combination of Afghan aggressiveness and British ineptitude led to the near-total destruction of that British invasion force in 1842.

Defeated in Afghan proper but determined to protect the jewel of their empire, the British incorporated the Baluchistan region of Afghanistan into British India in 1859. By seizing this area, now southwest Pakistan, the British cut Afghanistan off from the sea. The Afghans did not have the power to resist the British move. Baluchistan is a long way from Kabul and is populated by the Baluch, who did not owe any loyalty to the Pashtuns. Therefore, the Pashtuns could not resort to their normal tribal tactics to defeat the British. Baluchistan remained under British control until it was incorporated into modern-day Pakistan upon the latter's independence.

Even after the annexation of Baluchistan, the Afghan boundaries, both north and south, remained vague. It wasn't until 1875 that the Russians unilaterally fixed the northern boundary.

In the south, the British once again invaded in 1878, to start the Second Anglo-Afghan War. They quickly seized the cities and remained in Afghanistan until 1880, when a new ruler took the Afghan throne. Satisfied with this ruler, the British withdrew from most of Afghanistan. They did keep some key terrain on the Afghan-India border, and they retained the right to control Afghan foreign policy. Just because they saw the new king as cooperative didn't mean they wouldn't take out insurance against yet another change in regime.

Although the Russians did not attempt to change the regime, in 1885 they suddenly seized Afghan territory north of the Oxus River. This was despite the fact that they had unilaterally drawn the previous border. The Russians then declared this to be the new border.

A decade later, the British, in yet another unilateral action, established the Durand line as the boundary between British India and Afghanistan. Unfortunately, the Durand line was devised solely by the British for the security and protection of British India. It resulted in a southern border that divided the traditional territory of the Pashtun tribes between Afghanistan and British India (later Pakistan). To this day, the actual border in the south remains a source of contention between Pakistan and Afghanistan—and is largely ignored by the Pashtun in daily business.

Finally, in 1895, the Russians again unilaterally reestablished the border—but this time, they stuck to it. That line is now the border with the Republics of Turkmenistan, Uzbekistan, and Tajikistan. Here, too, the international boundary divided traditional tribal areas.

In short, Afghanistan, both north and south, was artificially carved from traditional tribal areas. The artificial boundaries imposed in 1895 insured that Afghanistan could be only a loose confederation of tribal chieftains pledging various levels of loyalty to the Durrani king in Kabul.

In fact, the king remained in power only through a delicate balancing of the needs of the various tribes—and never trying to rule with too heavy a hand. The system, although not modern, worked. The last king, Zahir

Shan, ruled from 1933–73. In 1973, Prince Daud Khan, his cousin, seized power while the king was on vacation in Italy.

Daud was backed by the People's Democratic Party of Afghanistan (PDPA), a Communist organization. As Daud consolidated his power, he decided he did not need the support of the Communists and began removing them from key government posts. In 1978, the PDPA struck back and, in a Soviet-backed coup, overthrew Daud. Nur Mohammed Taraki, a self-proclaimed Marxist, seized power.

In keeping with his adopted party's philosophy, Taraki attempted to introduce reforms across the country. In particular, he attempted to change tribal traditions concerning marriage, weddings, women's rights, women's education, land ownership, and the power structure in rural Afghanistan. In the conservative Afghan culture, these reforms were seen as striking at the very core of Afghan society. Compounding the problem, the PDPA personnel were incompetent. The combination led to a countrywide rebellion against the PDPA government later the same year. The Communists responded with increasingly violent efforts to coerce the population.

Thus, even before the arrival of the Soviets, the pattern was established for strong tribal resistance to efforts by the central government to expand its control, and reforms, into the countryside. Simultaneously, the Communists' internal power struggles continued, leading to another coup in September 1979. Hafizullah Amin, the prime minister, named himself president. Unfortunately, he proved as incapable of stabilizing Afghanistan as his predecessor.

Fearing that Afghan instability would spread to the adjacent, heavily Islamic areas of the Soviet Union, the Soviets invaded Afghanistan. On December 27, 1979, the Soviet Fortieth Army invaded and rapidly seized every major population center, executed Amin, and installed a puppet regime. They were confident they could restore stability to the country and thus prevent any spread of instability to their Islamic regions.

At first, it seemed as if the Soviets had achieved an easy victory. Their conventional forces quickly took control of all major population centers. Initial resistance was sporadic and not particularly intense. However, just like French, British, Portuguese, Belgians, and Americans in other parts of the world, the Soviets completely failed to see that they had embarked on a fourth-generation war. These wars have different timelines. The absence of initial resistance usually means the 4GW enemy is in his political-organization phase.

The Soviets had selected an even more challenging enemy than those that defeated Western powers. The Afghans have a long tradition of interrupting their constant intramural struggles only long enough to combine against an international invader. In keeping with that tradition, the Afghan resistance, organized around tribally based militias called mujahideen, began attacking Soviet forces shortly after the invasion.

For the next ten years, the Soviets tried to pacify Afghanistan. They, like their Western counterparts, used primarily conventional forces and tactics against a completely unconventional enemy. They controlled the cities but never controlled major sections of the countryside. They attempted to destroy an idea with firepower.

The Afghans fell back on their traditional tribal tactics against invaders, using ambushes, assassination, and sabotage to inflict casualties on the Soviets. But, for Afghans used to resolving their own fights, they added a new twist. They took their message to the world and sought assistance both from Islamic nations and the West. In keeping with the networked nature of 4GW, they found allies with similar interests and made what were clearly temporary alliances. Even fundamentalist Islamic parties were happy to take U.S. funds and weapons to eject the Soviets from Afghanistan. The basic nature of the tribal coalitions and history of shifting alliances meant that the Afghans were naturals at 4GW. Further, the mujahideen were determined to throw out the foreign invaders, no matter what the cost.

The Soviets responded with one of the most vicious, scorched-earth, counterguerrilla campaigns in history. They carpet-bombed villages, destroyed irrigation systems, and systematically sowed millions of mines across huge swathes of productive farmland. The Soviet attacks were so intense that they drove almost forty percent of the Afghan population into refugee status. Yet even this vicious campaign did not defeat the Afghans.

Frustrated at their inability to pacify the countryside, the Soviets tried installing a series of different puppet leaders in Kabul. They simply could not find one who could unify and pacify Afghanistan—even with the support of a 120,000-man Soviet army and billions of dollars in aid. After suffering 25,000 dead, the Soviets conceded defeat and withdrew in February 1989. Once again, a superpower had been defeated in a fourth-generation war.

Shortly after the Soviets withdrew, the United States lost interest in the region. Our primary reason for supporting the mujahideen had been accomplished. We frankly did not think it possible to establish an effective government in Kabul. When Saddam Hussein invaded Kuwait in August 1990, America completely lost interest and focused its attention on the Middle East.

As the Soviets withdrew, they passed control of Afghanistan to the last president they had appointed—Najibullah. Ruthless, highly capable, and politically astute, Najibullah combined effective military leadership with an exceptional ability to exploit divisions among the mujahideen. He remained in power until March 1992. Finally, he admitted defeat and agreed to resign to give way to a U.N.-sponsored interim government.

This interim government was supposed to be comprised of all the rebel groups. However, upon Najibullah's resignation, the Northern Alliance seized Kabul without waiting for the United Nations. Led by Ahmad Shah Masood's Tajiks and Abdul Rashid Dostum's Uzbeks, the Northern Alliance simply moved into the city before the Pashtuns were ready to move. The Northern Alliance knew their occupation of Kabul would be unacceptable to the Pashtuns, but they were determined not to be subjected to Pashtun rule again.

Pashtun pride could not allow a Tajik-Uzbek alliance to rule Kabul. Even Gulbuddin Hekmatyar, a fundamentalist Pashtun who had been appointed prime minister in the interim government, announced that the Pashtun must drive the Northern Alliance out of Kabul. His militia attacked Kabul with rockets. He thus became the first prime minister in history to rocket his own capital while serving as part of its government.

Unable to seize Kabul but continuing to fight, the Pashtuns had to watch as, in June 1992, the leader of the largest northern party, Rabbini, was appointed head of the provisional government, with Ahmad Shah Masood as his minister of defense. Operating on a U.N. timeline and with its approval, the Northern Alliance had in essence seized control of the government of Afghanistan. In October, the interim government gave way to government elected by the national assembly. Unfortunately for the Pashtuns, the assembly was also dominated by northern tribal members. The result was a heavily Tajik and Uzbek government in Kabul, with little Pashtun representation. It was supposed to be an interim government and give up power after eighteen months. It did not.

As a result, the Pashtuns refused to cooperate with the central government. Without Pashtun cooperation, the government could not establish order in the south. In the absence of a central government, individual warlords took control. Often these were the most violent and brutal of the Soviet-era mujahideen commanders. As a result, civil society broke down, and the Pashtun people were subject to hardships as severe as under Soviet rule.

Into this power vacuum in the south came the Taliban. As early as 1992, they began moving out of the madrassahs (religious schools) in Pakistan to assist their Pashtun cousins against the warlords. These madrassahs were largely funded by the Saudis. They taught, and still teach, the virulent and violent Wahhabi version of Islam. Supporting the students with funds, training, and leadership was al-Qaeda. During the Soviet-Afghan War and subsequent intertribal fights, the madrassahs continued to indoctrinate young men. In essence, they built a power base of absolutely dedicated footsoldiers ready to follow their religious leaders anywhere.

As aggressive and fundamental as the Taliban–al-Qaeda team was, they offered the only viable alternative to the warlords. Through a combination of fighting and preaching, they ended the random violence that made life impossible in southern Afghanistan. Although they governed under an incredibly harsh version of Islamic law, they brought stability to the areas they controlled.

Beyond stability, they also offered the Pashtuns' only chance to return to power in Kabul. This had enormous appeal. A fiercely proud tribe, they were seriously humiliated by the minority northern tribes' control of the capital. Even worse, those tribes represented themselves to the world as the government of Afghanistan. Pashtuns had ruled Afghanistan literally since its founding. To not rule now was simply unacceptable to a people who felt it was their tribe's natural right.

For al-Qaeda, Afghanistan represented a unique opportunity to seize a secure base. When bin Laden left Sudan, he needed a new place to train and prepare his campaign to reestablish a worldwide caliphate. He knew an Afghanistan ruled by the Taliban would provide sovereign territory to protect al-Qaeda from external attack. Both the Taliban and al-Qaeda benefited from the alliance.

With growing support from the Pashtun in the south, the Taliban progressed steadily—until, by 1994, they controlled almost a third of the country. Besides their heavily indoctrinated followers and al-Qaeda, the Taliban had the support of the Pakistanis, who saw them as the only force capable of creating a stable country on Pakistan's northern border. The Pakistanis' continued clashes with the Indians over Kashmir made a secure northern border doubly important to them.

The border clashes were only the latest manifestation of the long-term Pakistani-Indian conflict. By far the smaller and less powerful nation, the Pakistanis were concerned that India could use Afghanistan as a second front. In a worst-case scenario, they could even stir up the Pashtun tribes on both sides of the border, to create a civil war within Pakistan. The Pakistanis felt they had to ensure that Afghanistan was ruled by a sympathetic government. As an added bonus, the Taliban could provide training and support to Muslim insurgents in Kashmir as surrogates for the Pakistanis.

Steadily growing stronger, in 1995 the Taliban defeated Hekmatyar's Hezb-i-Islami (HIB) party and drove them into exile in Iran. The Taliban was now the only significant Pashtun force left in the country. As always in Afghanistan, when one faction began to emerge as a winner, each tribal, clan, or village leader felt free to negotiate a change of sides. Soon, all the southern tribes were united behind the Taliban. With the south unified, they moved quickly, and by 1996 took Kabul. They executed Najibullah in public and immediately imposed a harsh, uncompromising, fundamentalist rule. Al-Qaeda effectively had a front government and provided support to maintain the relationship.

As the Taliban tried to complete their conquest of Afghanistan, they ran into two major problems. First, they were trying to conquer Tajik and Uzbek areas with Pashtun troops. Second, they were fighting against Masood, the most effective of the mujahideen commanders from the north and a legendary leader from the Soviet-Afghan War. Still, the Taliban made progress, advancing slowly, negotiating as much as fighting, until they controlled all but a sixth of the country.

Al-Qaeda's long and complex effort to assassinate Masood reflected their determination to control all of Afghanistan. Apparently they believed that with his death, no other leader could hold the Northern Alliance together. In fact, the murder of Masood by two al-Qaeda assassins seemed to open great opportunities for the Taliban . . . except for the timing. Masood was killed on September 9, 2001. Two days later, al-Qaeda conducted its attack on the United States.

Less than one month later, the United States initiated its campaign to destroy the Taliban and al-Qaeda. Having failed to convince the Taliban to give up Osama bin Laden, President Bush ordered U.S. forces to enter Afghanistan and destroy both the Taliban and al-Qaeda.

Using a combination of high technology and ground reconnaissance, U.S. forces began striking Taliban forces. Once Northern Alliance forces could see that the United States was serious, they allied with our forces. In keeping with Afghan traditions, commanders on both sides maintained communications with each other throughout this new phase of the conflict. Modern radios simply allowed the forces aligned with the Taliban to shift sides more quickly when it became clear the United States was staying and the Northern Alliance was winning. Taliban resistance collapsed. Despite demands from the United States that they not enter Kabul, the Northern Alliance swept south and seized the city on November 17, 2001.

Faced with the fait accompli of a Northern Alliance occupation of Kabul, the United Nations called a conference in Bonn during December 2001. In an attempt to establish a stable government in Afghanistan, leaders from the Afghan opposition groups agreed on a plan for the formulation of a new government structure. As part of that plan, Hamid Karzai was installed as chairman of the Afghan Interim Authority (AIA) on December 22, 2001.

Under the agreement, the AIA was required to hold a *Loya Jirga* (Grand Assembly) within six months to elect a transitional government. The transitional government, would, in turn, be required to hold elections within eighteen months. The timeline is almost precisely the same as that agreed to by all parties prior to Najibullah stepping down in 1992.

Keeping to the schedule, the AIA held a nationwide Loya Jirga in June 2002. By secret ballot, Karzai was elected president of the Transitional Islamic State of Afghanistan (TISA). The Transitional Authority was given an eighteen-month mandate to hold a nationwide Loya Jirga to adopt a constitution and a twenty-four-month mandate to hold nationwide elections.

With this agreement accomplished, the Bush administration turned its attention to Iraq. Refusing to "do" nation building, the United States focused its scant interest in Afghanistan solely on killing the al-Qaeda elements hiding in Afghanistan and the adjacent Pakistan semiautonomous tribal areas.

Despite international promises of $5 billion in aid for the first year of the TISA administration, less than $1 billion was actually delivered. The United States did not make serious efforts to either deliver its promised aid or encourage others to deliver on their portions. In fact, the U.S. administration simply ceased paying attention to the needs of Afghanistan. It focused on Iraq instead.

As a result, the security situation in Afghanistan began to slip. One obvious indication was that by the summer of 2002, President Karzai's personal security detail had to be taken over by Americans. He could not count on security provided by Afghans.

By the spring of 2003, there was a resurgence in activity by antigovernment forces. The situation was strikingly similar to 1992, when the Northern Alliance occupied Kabul the first time. The Pashtuns had been driven from the capital. The Tajiks and the Uzbeks not only held power in the capital but seemed determined to minimize the influence of the Pashtuns. The Pashtuns did not have a strong, effective leader to represent their interests, either in Kabul or with the international community. Although Karzai is a Pashtun and the son of a tribal leader, the Pashtun consider him an outsider. They saw him as powerless and a figurehead for the Northern Alliance. In fact, they saw the Kabul government dominated primarily by the Panjishiri—those Tajiks from the Panjishir valley. The Panjishiri were molded into a team by Masood and are essentially the same people who fought the Pashtuns over Kabul between 1992 and 1996.

To make matters worse, U.S. forces concentrated their efforts on military attacks in the Pashtun tribal areas, because that was where the al-Qaeda and Taliban remnants fled for refuge. Thus, the Pashtuns saw themselves replaying their exile after the fall of Najibullah. They saw themselves alienated from both the government in Kabul and the United States. Further, the United States was interested only in killing al-Qaeda and Taliban (which to them meant Pashtun).

In fact, prior to the summer of 2003, the lack of attention to nation building was so obvious that Michael Ignatieff, writing in the *New York Times Magazine,* called it "nation building lite."[1] He saw U.S. Special Forces, backed by air power, as being imperial police. If a U.S. journalist perceived it this way, imagine how the Pashtuns, who were the targets of the "policing," perceived it.

The combination of American operations, tribal unrest, and lack of an effective Pashtun leader meant that the small amounts of international aid did not make it to the Pashtun areas. Finally, in keeping with their history, the Pashtun tribes fell to fighting among themselves as the international community ignored them. This further complicated any efforts to deliver aid or establish central government services in the Pashtun areas. It was a perfect opportunity for al-Qaeda and the Taliban to stage a comeback.

As early as July 2002, they began to take advantage of the opportunity. Fairly well established in safe portions of Pakistan's semiautonomous tribal regions, they began to move back into Afghanistan. They pushed a simple message: "We told you so." They noted that, just as they predicted, the Northern Alliance was back in Kabul. All foreign aid was flowing to the Tajiks and Uzbeks. Pashtuns were not even welcome in the capital city they had always ruled. There are no viable Pashtun leaders. The only choice for the Pashtuns was the same one they made in 1992—let the Taliban lead. The message clearly had appeal.

Falling back on the 4GW tactics that had beaten the Soviets, the anti-government forces (AGF) began to rebuild their political position first. They conducted small raids, focused as much on discrediting the government and keeping the aid organizations out as on killing. I use the term "AGF" simply because it is more accurate than either al-Qaeda or Taliban. It reflects more clearly the reality of Afghanistan, where alliances are always shifting based on the needs of the tribal, clan, or village leaders. If we see the enemy as only al-Qaeda or Taliban, it oversimplifies the problem. We have to understand that a wide spectrum of people do not want to see an effective central government in Afghanistan—al-Qaeda, Taliban, smugglers, drug dealers, foreign powers, and most Pashtuns—as long as the government is perceived as Northern Alliance. The AGF is a true networked, 4GW enemy and will display all the resilience characteristic of such enemies.

In March 2003, the AGF conducted a series of operations. They killed two U.S. soldiers in the south and wounded three Afghans. They also stepped up their rocket attacks in the capital region. Although they caused no serious casualties, each rocket announced to all who could hear it that the Taliban was still fighting.

Even more damaging, they killed a Red Cross worker in the south. This followed close on the heels of a temporary suspension of aid in the north, when Dostum's militia became too violent. The aid agencies had just resumed operations in the north, and then they had to halt them in the south, while they evaluated the new situation. Concern ran high among the aid workers.

The cumulative effect of these numerous small actions—despite continued U.S. military sweeps—finally made the Bush administration notice. Along with the $87 billion for Iraq, the Administration carved out $1 billion to double its support for the Karzai government during the summer of 2003. It also took action to reinforce the prestige of the central government by backing Karzai's orders to remove the governor of Kandahar. In addition, the United States moved aggressively to build a true national army and police.

The anti-government forces responded. Isolated attacks continued, but they were not directed at U.S. forces—they continued to focus on aid organizations and representatives of the central government. In particular, police stations and security forces were targeted. Even aid organizations with long-term service in Afghanistan were being hit. Although the AGF did not have the strength to attack U.S. forces directly, they conducted a campaign to undercut critical supporting elements essential to the government's efforts in 4GW.

They also consciously took the fight outside Afghanistan. In September 2003, a Taliban press agent called the Agence France-Presse news service and claimed they had control of four southern districts in three different provinces. This was a 4GW technique. The claims were impossible to confirm or deny—yet added to the general feeling of uncertainty among the international community.

On the positive side, over the summer of 2003, key U.S. and international leaders recognized both the complexity of the problems and the requirement for both U.S. interagency efforts and international coordination.

Both sides seemed to understand that Afghanistan has settled into a complex 4GW struggle. Like all such struggles, it has both a general outline and unique characteristics.

Like previous 4GW conflicts, the insurgent is a networked, flexible force that avoids contact except on its own terms. It focuses on low-intensity activities—those one expects to find in phase I of a classic Maoist insurgency. It is clearly long term. The Afghans have always been patient in their tribal wars. Al-Qaeda leadership has stated that it took ten years to drive the Soviets out, so they expect it will take at least that long to drive the United States out.

It also has some challenging, unique aspects that complicate the counterinsurgency effort. First, the "nation" of Afghanistan has no history of a strong, benevolent central government. Even the brief history provided previously shows that it has always been stressed by rivalries—family, clan, tribal, ethnic, and religious. The ethnic groups and tribes have been careful to keep the central government at arm's length and deal with it purely on the basis of what each group can get from its relationship with the government.

To this volatile mix one must add the interests of the surrounding nations. The traditional national rivalries among Iran, Pakistan, and India are all better served by a divided Afghanistan. Thus, these nations also have reasons to support their own factions inside Afghanistan.

Pakistan clearly sees a Pashtun-dominated Afghanistan as essential to protecting its rear in the struggle with India. India has had a long-term relationship with the Panjishiris and sees Afghanistan as a way to keep pressure on Pakistan in payback for the support Pakistan has provided the insurgents in Kashmir. The Uzbeks are interested in supporting Dostum and his ethnic Uzbek fighters. Iran likes having Ismail Khan and his Hezara, who are Shias, firmly established in western Afghanistan. They see him as a buffer between a U.S.-supported central government and Iran. And of course, Russia has a serious interest in Afghanistan, because it impacts her Islamic regions.

In addition to these traditional nation-state actors, numerous stateless actors have an interest in Afghanistan. Internally, many of the local tribal leaders and Islamic fundamentalists have goals they think can be achieved. The Islamists' goals vary from local religious control to support for al-Qaeda's vision of a worldwide caliphate. Local tribal leaders simply want to protect their interests and those of their family and clan.

For the drug lords, both internal and external, profit is the primary motive and leads them to any alliance of convenience. Further complicating the matter is that many of the drug lords are also local tribal leaders and have extensive international connections necessary in the business. The huge sums of cash involved also corrupt the governments in the region.

Thus, the struggle in Afghanistan is not a simple two-sided fight between the Taliban and the United States. There are numerous players. The vast majority are opposed to an effective central government, which would impinge on their interests. Even for a 4GW conflict, Afghanistan is unusually complex.

Adding to this complexity is the current approach the anti-government forces are using. While they conduct an occasional attack on allied or U.S. forces, these consist primarily of long-range rocket attacks and remote-control bombings. This allows the AGF to claim they are taking action against outsiders without much risk to themselves. They cause few casualties but contribute significantly to a general feeling of unease among the international contingent. They also remind any Afghans who might wish to cooperate with the coalition that the coalition might well leave, but the AGF won't.

Much more dangerous, and more effective at the operational level, are the direct attacks on the U.N., non-governmental, and isolated police outposts. These attacks represent a further refinement of 4GW techniques—and a huge complication for the counterinsurgents. With very few carefully targeted killings, the AGF have halted international aid operations in many areas of the country. This closes off one of the few ways the government can be seen to improve life in the rural areas. Worse, the withdrawal of aid agencies and government representatives confirms the propaganda that only the AGF can help the Pashtuns regain their prosperity and power and that only the AGF will always be there. The government currently lacks the resources to provide effective security for the non-governmental organizations (NGOs). Therefore, assassinating aid workers has become an economy-of-force operation for insurgents.

The AGF understand that 4GW requires effort across the political, military, economic, and religious domains to succeed. Although there are no indications that a single plan is motivating the actions, Afghans are combining their traditional resistance methods with modern communications systems to disseminate their actions.

The in-country coalition leadership has also recognized the transition to a 4GW struggle. They are working hard to establish a coordinated interagency effort to bring security and improved living conditions to the countryside. In particular, they have redoubled their efforts to build an effective, multi-ethnic army and police force. These security elements are being integrated with the coalition's Provincial Reconstruction Teams (PRTs) to establish security in selected towns around Afghanistan.

PRTs consist of elements of coalition and Afghan security elements, civilian agencies of the Afghan government, and NGOs, who deploy as a team to an area to assist in its reconstruction. These teams provide a complete package of government services to the Regional Development Zones they move into. In a *Daily Standard* article, Christian Lowe quotes Lt. Gen.

David Barno, U.S. commander in Afghanistan: "A PRT is really a catalyst. It forms a focal point in a particular area, with the goal of building not only relationships but also serving as an accelerator in the rebuilding of the nation and extending the reach of the Afghan central government."[2]

Based on the classic British concept of the spreading ink stain, early results of the PRTs are encouraging. By producing concrete improvements in people's lives, the PRTs foster trust between the population and the government. As the trust grows, the people provide the intelligence and local knowledge essential to any successful counterinsurgency effort. Over the fall and winter of 2003–04, the Afghan government and coalition have increased the total teams to twelve and have targeted some of the most unstable areas of the country.

One of the most positive aspects of the PRTs is that they allow the Afghan government to make its presence felt in the rural areas. In areas where the PRTs have been established, the Afghan government has began to replace corrupt local officials with new officials loyal to the central government—and focused on helping the people.

At the time of this writing, the outcome in Afghanistan remains unclear. There is still a good deal of instability in the south and the north. In the south, an unexpected outbreak of violence in Herat included the murder of Zahir Nayebzada, minister of aviation and son of Ismail Khan, governor of Herat. In the north, traditional warlord rivalries broke out in several areas. As a result, government forces were stretched even more as the Karzai government dispatched Afghan National Army troops to both the west and the north. This reduced the forces available in the Pashtun south just as winter ended and the traditional campaign season started.

In addition, the Pakistanis were conducting major operations in the tribal areas in support of U.S. operations in Afghanistan and were suffering scattered attacks throughout the area. These may be the first signs of the feared widening of the struggle to the tribal areas of Pakistan. The exceptional complexity of the Afghan situation is reflected in the wide-ranging and varied conflict and the numerous players.

In a positive development, coalition forces have recognized the nature of the war they are in and are developing much more effective responses.

The combination of supporting the Karzai government, building central government institutions, providing Provisional Reconstruction Teams, and maintaining a united front are all having an impact.

Unfortunately, the AGF have understood the nature of the war since early 2002 and have reverted to their traditionally successful methods of resistance, reinforced with 4GW techniques for attacking the minds of the coalition decision makers. They know it will be a long war. In fact, they are counting on the fact that the United States does not have the staying power.

> According to the premier historian on Afghanistan, the late Louis Dupree, four factors contributed to the British disasters in Afghanistan: having troops there in the first place; installing an unpopular emir on the Afghan throne; allowing "your" Afghans to mistreat other Afghans; and reducing the subsidies paid to the tribal chiefs. These fatal miscalculations, barely altered in form, were committed by the British in 1839 and again in 1878, and a century later by the Soviets. They are being committed today, and how we deal with them will determine the ultimate outcome of the American undertaking in Afghanistan.[3]

The United States made virtually the same mistakes—twice: first when the Soviets withdrew and again when we moved in to destroy the Taliban. Although we kept our troops out of the Soviet-Afghan War, we committed each of the other errors. And with the exception that Karzai was the best possible compromise leader to install, we made the mistakes again after U.S. forces routed the Taliban.

We have apparently learned from those mistakes and are developing an approach that demonstrates an understanding of all aspects of 4GW. However, the key question remains: Does the coalition, particularly the United States, have the political will to sustain a decades-long effort? Only time will tell.

# CHAPTER 12

# Iraq: High-Tech versus Fourth-Generation

> [T]he first, the supreme, the most far-reaching act of judgment that the statesman and commander have to make is to establish by that test the kind of war on which they are embarking; neither mistaking it for, nor trying to turn it into, something that is alien to its nature.[1]

Carl von Clausewitz wrote this almost two hundred years ago, but, as events in Iraq are proving, it is as valid as the day he wrote it. In March 2003, the Bush administration failed to understand the type of war they were embarking on. They tried to turn it into a short, high–technology, conventional war. Confident that things had turned out as they predicted, President Bush essentially declared victory on May 1, 2003, when "major hostilities ceased."

Unfortunately, the underlying nature of the Iraq War is not that of a high-tech war but rather that of a fourth-generation netwar. Hostilities did not end on May 1. They are continuing, with no apparent end in sight.

Complicating our problem is our slowness in recognizing that we had slipped into an insurgency. Despite the continued attacks on coalition forces, even after the official "defeat" of the Iraqi armed forces, U.S. leadership refused to accept that the war was continuing, much less that it had become an insurgency:

> "It's a very small group—one or two people—in isolated attacks against our soldiers." Maj. Gen. Buford Blount III, May 27, 2003

> "We do not see signs of central command and control direction. . . . These are groups that are organized, but they're small; they may be five or six men conducting isolated attacks against our soldiers." Administrator, Coalition Provisional Authority, Iraq (He is not an ambassador because he rules the country, the amabassdor title refers to his time as ambassador to Netherlands) L. Paul Bremer, June 12, 2003

> "This is not guerrilla warfare; it is not close to guerrilla warfare, because it's not coordinated, it's not organized, and it's not led." Maj. Gen. Ray Odierno, June 18, 2003

> "There's a guerrilla war there, but we can win it." Deputy Secretary of Defense Paul Wolfowitz, June 18, 2003

> "I guess the reason I don't use the phrase 'guerrilla war' is because there isn't one, and it would be a misunderstanding and a miscommunication to you and to the people of the country and the world." U.S. Secretary of Defense Donald Rumsfeld, June 30, 2003

> "[G]uerrilla and insurgency operations are supported by the people, and I've demonstrated to my own satisfaction that the people of Iraq do not support the violence that we're seeing right now." Gen. Tommy Franks, July 10, 2003

It wasn't until June 18, 2003, that Deputy Secretary Wolfowitz became the first to indicate that we might be involved in a guerrilla war. He was subsequently firmly corrected by both Secretary of Defense Donald Rumsfeld and Commander Central Command Gen. Tommy Franks. It was not until more than ten weeks after the president declared an end to major combat that Gen. John Abizaid, the new Commander Central Command, admitted that the United States faced an insurgency in Iraq. He was the first senior U.S. official to categorically state the obvious.

> "I believe there are mid-level Ba'athist, Iraqi intelligence service people, Special Security Organization people, Special Republican Guard people that have organized at the regional level in cellular structure and are conducting what I would describe as a classical guerrilla-type campaign against us." Gen. John Abizaid, July 16, 2003

Even after this statement by the man responsible for fighting the insurgents, the Pentagon would not refer to it as an insurgency and instead avoided defining the type of conflict on which we had entered:

> "The discussion about what type of conflict this is . . . is almost beside the point. . . . It's worth remembering that as we kind of have this almost kind of, you know, academic discussion, is it this or is it that." Pentagon spokesman Lawrence Di Rita, July 16, 2003

The Pentagon's efforts to avoid discussing the type of war we are fighting could not be more diametrically opposed to Clausewitz's caution that the single act of determining the type of war one is to engage in is the supreme act of the statesman and commander. Rather than identifying the war they were really in, the Bush administration continued to denigrate the resistance in Iraq as merely the aftermath of the short, decisive war they had planned.

Unfortunately, events during the fall and winter of 2003–04 confirmed General Abizaid's judgment. The insurgents in Iraq are clearly an intelligent, adept, and adaptable enemy.

During the months of August and September 2003, they attacked a police academy graduation; the U.N. headquarters (twice); the Jordanian embassy; the Turkish embassy; Ayatollah Mohammad Baqer, Baghdad chief of police (unsuccessfully); Red Cross facilities (twice); numerous police stations; an intelligence center in Irbil; the mayors of Fallujah, Haditha, and Khalidiya; the deputy mayor of Baghdad; Italian soldiers; Japanese aid workers; Korean contractors; hotels where relief workers and Western officials stay; and numerous U.S. military positions and convoys. Their choice of targets showed the clear strategic concept of destroying American will by attacking U.S. forces, any government or NGO supporting the United States, and any Iraqis working for or believed to be collaborating with the United States.

Buoyed by their success in driving the United Nations and many aid agencies out of the country, the insurgents stepped up operations against U.S. forces. Their attacks increased in both sophistication and deadliness. They successfully shot down U.S. helicopters, damaged a commercial aircraft flying out of Baghdad International Airport, and continued to kill Iraqis who cooperated with the United States. However as U.S. forces became more effective at countering insurgent tactics, the insurgents' casualties went up.

In response, the anti-coalition forces (ACF) shifted their campaign from international agencies to the Iraqi security services and individuals assisting the coalition. During December, their bombing and assassination campaign began to focus on police personnel and Iraqi civilians working with the Coalition Provisional Authority. By March, they were killing a minimum of one policeman per day. Throughout this period, they continued to use improvised explosive devices (IEDs) against coalition forces, but their focus had shifted to the Iraqi security forces.

Expanding on this campaign, they began an active effort to create distrust and suspicion among the various elements of Iraqi society. The near-simultaneous bombing of the political headquarters of the PUK and KPP during Id al-Adha, an Islamic holiday, was clearly intended to drive the Kurds away from Iraq. Similarly, the multiple bombings and mortar attacks on the Shia community during their holy day of Ashoura was intended to deepen the divisions between Shia and Sunni.

The ACF continued its relentless attacks with the assassination of Shia clerics. Increasing the tension, the ACF personnel began conducting attacks while wearing Iraqi Civil Defense Corps (ICDC) and Iraqi police uniforms, creating distrust both of and among the elements of Iraqi security forces. As a direct result of their actions, neither coalition nor Iraqis can assume that a uniform means a friend.

The subsequent difficulties in signing the Transitional Administrative Law (TAL), Iraq's interim constitution, indicate the increasing tensions and mistrust among the elements of Iraqi society. The Shia representatives delayed the ceremony and signed only after traveling to visit Grand Ayatollah Ali Sistani in his home. Although the signing of the TAL was a positive step, it was only the first step in what is an increasingly difficult path to preparing Iraq to govern itself.

In fact, the nationwide surge of attacks in April 2004 hammered home the fact that the coalition faces a competent, networked, and determined fourth-generation enemy. At the time, the U.S. leadership was emphasizing the transition to sovereignty. Although admittedly unable to explain what that meant or exactly whom they would turn the country over to, U.S. leaders were surprised by the extent and power of the resistance in April.

They should not have been. The nature of the early targets and results indicate that the ACF was conducting a well-thought-out operational campaign. Each tactical act was minor in itself. But orchestrated as a continuing campaign, they were moving toward the strategic goal of driving U.S. and international reconstruction elements out of Iraq while simultaneously setting the conditions for civil war.

By forcing out international aid organizations and intimidating Iraqis willing to work with us, the ACF intended to reduce the support of these organizations' key functional roles and drastically reduce U.S. capacity to establish stability. With the upsurge in violence, the seeming inability of the United States to provide security will aggravate the Iraqi people and continue to provide an arena for Islamists to directly attack Americans.

Decades of living under a dictator have taught the Iraqis the danger of backing the wrong side. Until the situation clarifies, the majority of Iraqis will remain neutral. And the fact that the United States has said it is leaving is always part of the equation. Why opt to support a force that has announced its intention to leave soon? Thus, U.S. policy reinforces the ACF campaign to separate the Iraqi people from the coalition and prevent the establishment of a stable, representative government in Iraq.

In conjunction with these attacks on supporting elements, the ACF maintained a steady campaign of improvised explosive devices to inflict casualties on U.S. forces. Although the focus of their campaigns has shifted with their successes on the ground, they have never let up in their continued effort to inflict U.S. casualties with these simple but deadly devices.

From their actions, the ACF clearly plan to drive the United States out of Iraq. Although their goal is clear, the nature of the ACF itself is not. At the time of this writing, the United States had not answered the key question of "Who are these anti-coalition forces?" To date, the administration has clung to the idea that they are only "bitter-enders" or, more formally, former regime loyalists (FRLs). Although some members of the administration mention al-Qaeda, the official line through April 2004 remained that it was FRLs behind the attacks. Given that the resistance has continued despite the capture of Saddam and the death of his sons, the concept that it is only regime loyalists who are fighting the United States is becoming a bit absurd. Eventually, the administration will have to admit that the anti-coalition forces represent a much wider opposition than simply FRL diehards.

The definitive answer will have to come from the U.S. intelligence services, but based on open-source reporting through the winter of 2003–04, the ACF seems to be a coalition of the willing—a diverse collection of those willing to attack the United States: Baathist loyalists, disgruntled military and security elements not necessarily Baathist, criminal elements of Iraqi society (including Saddam fedayeen), Sunni and Shia Arab religious extremists, factions such as Ansar al-Islam, and elements of al-Qaeda.

The ACF shows all the traits of a fourth-generation organization. They seek to win by wearing down the political will of the coalition. They know they must convince coalition members that any potential gains are not worth the cost, and they plan a long, drawn-out struggle to do so. The ACF are trying to convince America that we cannot prevail and are counting on defeating our political will as well as that of the coalition. They talk about U.S. aversion to casualties, as proven by Vietnam, Lebanon, and Somalia. They fully expect that when a sufficient number of body bags go home, the United States will withdraw.

The ACF are also working to convince the Iraqi people that supporting the coalition is not a safe or smart move. They portrayed U.S. announcements that we would turn over the government by July 1, 2004, and the administration's increasing focus on the upcoming U.S. elections as signs of weakness and unwillingness to stay the course.

Recognizing that the strategic centers of gravity for the coalition members are their people's willingness to accept casualties, the ACF exhibit a keen sense for projecting their message through the media. Further, they know that the real key to the coalition is the United States.

With the 2004 U.S. elections looming, the ACF believes it is a message that could alter the Bush administration's approach to the insurgency.

In late November 2003, they were rewarded with the U.S. announcement that we would turn control of Iraq over to the governing council not later than July 1, 2004. In December, Mr. Bremer even let it be known that the United States would not require a constitution or a free-market economy before the political handover.[2] This statement represented a major policy change from the administration's original position that it would take at least eighteen months more and require a functioning free-market economy and a written constitution before the United States would leave.

Then on March 11, bombers affiliated with al-Qaeda struck the Spanish rail system, killing 201 and wounding more than 1,400. Conducted just days before the national elections, the attacks resulted in the defeat of Prime Minister Jose Maria Aznar's government and the installation of a government dedicated to withdrawing Spanish troops from the coalition.

Finally, a marked increase in the number of attacks on coalition and Iraqi civilians during March and April indicates yet another step in the ACF effort to strip away all support for the coalition and the Governing Council. They are sending a clear message to the United States and its coalition partners: we are engaged in a long-term fight and will use 4GW techniques and tactics to destroy the will of your people and the people of Iraq who are assisting you.

The message the ACF are attempting to send to their fellow Iraqis is not nearly so unified. The diversity of the ACF makes it impossible to put out a unified political message. Instead, they have focused on the negative message that they will drive the United States out and that they are setting the pace of the fighting by selecting soft targets. They plan to defeat the United States by killing or driving out anyone who assists the coalition. The United States will leave, and the ACF will remain.

The ACF represents a genuine fourth-generation enemy—a loosely affiliated network joined in a temporary alliance to achieve a specific, short-term goal. Although we have seen indications of a command and control structure, the ACF do not seem to be centralized under a single leader. Rather, they remain a loose coalition of the willing. Each fights for its own goals. The goals of each group may be at odds with the others, but that does not keep the various elements from cooperating when it comes to fighting the United States. They know that their first and most difficult problem is to drive the United States out of Iraq.

Because the nature of the various elements of the ACF means they can have no unified goal other than the negative one of driving the United States out, the ACF cannot have a coherent plan for the political future of Iraq. All elements know that if the United States withdraws before establishing a stable government, they will still have to settle among themselves who will be in power. That struggle will escalate into a civil war, the consequences of which will have implications reaching far beyond Iraq or even the region's border.

The obvious question is, Why is there any resistance at all? Didn't we free the Iraqis from one of the most murderous regimes in history? Shouldn't they be eager to embrace democracy? In fact, this was the belief the administration brought into the war. The war would be a short, high-technology war followed by the Iraqis eagerly embracing democracy and serving as an example for the rest of the Middle East.

So what happened? History happened. As with every war, the roots of the struggle in Iraq lie in its history. One of the oldest settled regions in the world, Iraq inevitably has a long, complex history. The ancient history of the area gives the Iraqis a sense of who they are. However, it is the more recent history that is critical to the situation in which we now find ourselves.

In short, the key problem is that Iraq has no history of democracy. Nor have they developed the social and governmental institutions, the economic structure, or the bonds of trust necessary for a society to function as a democracy. This lack of institutions, trust, and protections means the various elements of Iraqi society believe that the only real protection for their interests is armed power under their control. In particular, the Arab Sunnis, a minority of twenty percent but the traditional holders of power in Iraq, are very concerned about their future. Over the centuries, they have ruled Iraq with a heavy hand and naturally fear reprisals from the majority Arab Shias.

Modern Iraq emerged from the ruins of the Ottoman Empire. Under the Empire, present-day Iraq was divided into three provinces: Mosul, Baghdad, and Basra. Mosul, though heavily Sunni Arab itself, was the capital of the Kurdish area; Baghdad was the capital of the central, primarily Sunni Arab area; and Basra was the capital of the primarily Shia Arab southern area of the country. The three provinces were not formally associated or administered together. The only unifying factor under the Ottoman Empire was the presence of Sixth Corps headquarters in Baghdad. It commanded the Ottoman army units in all three provinces.

Not until after World War I was Iraq unified as an administrative entity. In April 1920, the League of Nations granted Britain a mandate for Iraq. Britain, after lively internal British discussion, decided to unify the three provinces of Mosul, Baghdad, and Basra (after first separating Kuwait from the Basra province) under direct British rule until the Iraqis were prepared to rule themselves. The joining of the provinces into a single entity had much more to do with the British need for oil reserves than the political viability of the combined provinces.

This artificial creation of the British took Iraqi politics in a new direction. The Sunni and Shia landowning tribal sheiks emerged as the primary competitors for power against the previously dominant urban-based Sunni families and Ottoman-trained army officers and bureaucrats. The fact that Iraq's new "democratic" institutions were a British creation, combined with the fact that they were without precedent in Iraqi history, meant that the leader in Baghdad lacked legitimacy in the countryside. None could develop true constituencies.

Despite all the outward trappings of a democracy, Iraqi politics continued to be a shifting alliance of important personalities and cliques rather than a democracy in the Western sense. With no institutions to build the networks of trust necessary in a democracy, the Iraqis continued to rely on their traditional sources of security. Thus, Iraqi social structure never evolved to that of a democracy but clung to older forms of government based primarily on personal relationships rather than institutions.

Complicating the situation, British rule was not what the Iraqis had envisioned. They felt that the breakup of the Ottoman Empire should mean self-rule rather than rule supervised by the British. Therefore, in June 1920, armed revolt broke out in the Sunni center. The revolution was not a unified effort but reflected the decisions and aspirations of the diverse groups that made up the mandate area. The revolt spread both north to the Kurdish areas and south to the Shia areas.

The British, with long experience in putting down native revolts, quickly regrouped and restored British control. It was not cost free. The British lost roughly five hundred men and had to kill about six thousand Iraqis.[3] However, they did not destroy the aspirations of either the Shias or the Kurds to have a more significant say in their own government.

In the north, the Kurdish revolt had set the pattern for a long series of attempts to create a Kurdistan. Despite opposition not only from Iraq but also from Iran, Turkey, and Syria, the Kurds maintained the dream of a free Kurdistan. Although the level of resistance fluctuated from political activity to open revolt, the Kurds maintained their goal through the British mandate, the monarchy, the republic, and even throughout Saddam's rule. Yet despite their determination to rule themselves, the Kurds were largely unable to agree on which Kurdish party should be in power.

Unable to arrive at a peaceful accord, they have fought a long series of internal struggles, with each side sometimes seeking external help from either the Iraqi or Iranian government. The internal divisions allowed Baghdad to maintain control over the Kurdish region up until the imposition of the northern no-fly zone by the United States in 1991. The presence of U.S. and British aircraft prevented Iraqi security forces from continuing their pursuit of the Kurds, who had revolted against Saddam at the end of the 1991 Gulf War.

Immediately after the war, the first Bush administration encouraged the Iraqi people to overthrow Saddam. The Kurds rose up. Unfortunately, the United States then stood by as Saddam's security forces ruthlessly counterattacked against the Kurds. Only when a massive Kurdish refugee movement to the north faced catastrophic, inhumane living conditions did the Bush administration intervene to protect the Kurdish areas by establishing the no-fly zone.

The unintended result of creating a safe haven for Kurdish refugees has been the flourishing of a Kurdish-ruled region. Under the protection of allied air power, it developed self-government and in December 2003 was the most stable region of occupied Iraq. Backed by a large, well-equipped militia, the peshmerga, the Kurdish leaders have put aside their differences and are running an effective government in their section of Iraq.

The Kurdish experience under the British and then the various Arab-dominated Iraqi governments ensures that they will not surrender their current autonomy lightly. In fact, their insistence on dictating elements of the Transitional Administrative Law to protect their interests almost derailed the U.S. efforts to have the law signed.

In the south, the Shia Arabs have long simmered as an oppressed majority. Denied equal representation under the mandate, the monarchy, or the republic, they were brutally suppressed by Saddam. In 1991, they, too, answered the elder President Bush's call to revolt following the liberation of Iraq. They, too, were abandoned by the United States and paid a heavy price: perhaps as many as fifty thousand Shias were killed in Saddam's suppression of their revolt.

Beyond the immediate killing, Saddam drained the marshes that provided a way of life to the half-million Marsh Arabs. In his efforts to deprive Shia insurgents of a hiding place, Saddam nearly destroyed a marsh culture thousands of years old. When coalition forces defeated Saddam's forces, only a few thousand Marsh Arabs were left. Since then, efforts to restore the marshes have begun, and Marsh Arabs are returning to their old homes as rapidly as the marshes refill.

This is the situation in which the coalition found itself at the end of April 2004. Without any previous history of success, it had to form a government that would represent fairly the wishes of three distinct groups.

Compounding the problem was the active insurgency outlined at the beginning of this chapter. Given that one of the central characteristics of

4GW is its long duration, the immediate situation is not as important as the long-term strengths and weaknesses of the combatants. So the key question is, What are the relative strengths and weaknesses of each side?

### *ACF Strengths*

1. The greatest strength of any insurgent is the fact that he doesn't have to win. He simply has to stay in the fight until the coalition gives up and goes home. As long as the insurgents can stay in the fight, it is not over. Their forces are not going home. By simply not losing, they compel their opponent to choose—either continue to fight, perhaps indefinitely, or quit and go home. In Iraq, withdrawal of coalition forces will not result in political settlement. It will simply set the stage for the struggle among the various elements of the ACF, as each tries to attain its specific, and often mutually exclusive, goal.

2. The insurgents are a loose network. Networks are exceptionally resilient and difficult to destroy. As stated previously, the opposition appears to include elements of Saddam loyalists, disaffected soldiers, Iraqi criminal elements, Ansar al-Islam, al-Qaeda, Islamic volunteers from various countries, and possibly elements of the Syrian and Iranian intelligence agencies. The fact that they have different goals and different constituencies is both a strength and a weakness. It is a strength because the coalition cannot focus on a single cause or group in its counterinsurgency efforts. It is a weakness because, although indications are that they can coordinate their military actions, they cannot effectively coordinate their political agendas.

3. The high unemployment rate leaves a large number of Iraqi young men unemployed and angry. Angry young men with time on their hands and access to weapons are an ideal source of recruits.

4. Iraq serves as a magnet for Islamic fundamentalists who wish to strike back at America. Religious extremists, those who see the United States as the Great Satan, those who trained in the Afghan camps of Osama bin Laden, and volunteers who have served in the Algerian civil war, Bosnia, and Chechnya all see Iraq as a new battleground. Besides providing expertise acquired in decades of fighting around the world, they provide a significant pool of suicide bombers for the cause. Suicide bombing is not a tactic common to

Iraqis, but it is a signature of religious extremists. Its frequent occurrence in Iraq is a clear indicator of the presence of extremists.

5. Iraq is awash in weapons—in particular, rocket-propelled grenades, rockets, mortars, and SA-7 missiles, which are ideal for the suicide and hit-and-run attacks the ACF favor. Just as important, a huge quantity of explosives, timers, and detonators is available for either improvised explosive devices or car bombs.

6. Although there have been attacks on isolated roads, the ACF primarily operate in dense urban areas that, due to a lack of significant police or military presence, provide an ideal environment for their survival. The urban areas provide the necessities of life, intelligence, and concealment. By eliminating and threatening influential Iraqi leaders at the local level, the ACF ensure compliance from the local community. The urban terrain also restricts the use of U.S. firepower.

7. The Iraqis are a proud people and want to see the "occupiers" gone as quickly as possible. If the ACF can convince the people that the only way to get the United States out of Iraq is through armed resistance, this can be a powerful asset.

8. Every significant attack is immediately broadcast to the world. In addition to the primary goal of weakening U.S. will, it also impacts potential allies' political decision making concerning additional aid and forces for Iraq.

### *ACF Weaknesses*

1. The ACF lacks any unifying political creed. The only unifying element is a wish to kill Americans and anyone who assists them. Although this can motivate a network, it cannot unify them.

2. Each insurgent realizes that the fight will not be over if the coalition leaves. They know that a rushed departure of the coalition will likely lead to civil war. Therefore, each insurgent must consider whether the ensuing chaos is a goal he wishes to fight for. Some will be in favor of such chaos, particularly if it spreads to Saudi Arabia; others will fear it.

3. The "sea" the insurgents operate in is relatively small and, initially, was limited primarily to the largely Sunni-populated central part of the country. Further, because the ACF is not unified, they have no unifying political cause

to rally the rest of Iraq's people. Unfortunately, the attacks in both the south and the north over the winter of 2003–04 indicate that the ACF can at least operate in other sections of the country. This may also indicate that the situation is changing and that more of the Iraqi people are turning against the coalition.

4. Although the Iraqis are a proud people and want to see the "occupiers" gone as quickly as possible, if the coalition can convince the people that the fastest way to get the United States out is the defeat of the ACF, Iraqi national pride could be a powerful asset to the coalition. It will motivate common Iraqis to assist the coalition in defeating the ACF's terror and its criminal elements.

5. The majority of Iraqis do not want Saddam's party to return to power. This can provide a basis for cooperation, particularly among those who have suffered badly at Saddam's hands.

### *Coalition Strengths*

1. The coalition possesses the resources and technical capabilities to restore the Iraqi economy. More important, the Iraqis have an educated population that can absorb the resources, put them to work, and run a modern society. Given the long-term nature of counterinsurgency, it is essential for Iraqis to understand that the best prospects for improving their economy is a continued U.S. presence, until the new Iraqi government and military are capable of providing for their own stability and security.

2. The daily improvement in power, sanitation, water, and trade are having positive impacts, even in the Baathist triangle. They provide evidence that life can be better if Iraqis cooperate with the coalition. In contrast, repeated ACF attacks on the infrastructure show that the ACF is not interested in the economic well-being of Iraqis.

3. The long-term relationship with Kurds is a particular strength for the coalition, due to its protection of the Kurdish enclave during the last ten years. In the short term, this has greatly facilitated the coalition's ability to work with the Kurds in establishing and maintaining order in the north. However, the Kurds' strength and desire for self-rule may greatly complicate establishing a stable government in Iraq.

4. The Sunni and Shia have a long history of community ties, including extensive intermarriage. Many families have both Sunni and Shia branches. Improving relations between the two communities can greatly assist coalition efforts to build a free Iraq.

*Coalition Weaknesses*

1. Official U.S. statements focus more on the withdrawal of U.S. forces than on long-term support for a new democratic Iraq, leading some to suggest that the United States is more interested in pursuing its own domestic agenda than in stabilizing a volatile region in the war on terror. Any seemingly precipitous departure of U.S. forces would hand victory to the insurgents. In particular, discussion of early U.S. withdrawal strengthens the ACF's ability to intimidate Iraqis, to ensure that they don't cooperate.

2. The ratio of coalition forces to civilian population in Iraq is a fraction of that for forces initially employed in Bosnia and Kosovo. During the first year of operations in Bosnia and Kosovo, there were roughly nineteen troops per thousand inhabitants. In Iraq, the ratio is fewer than seven per one thousand inhabitants. Clearly, we have too few troops to provide security and nation-building assistance.

3. One response to the shortage of troops appears to be a rush to count hastily trained Iraqis as qualified security personnel. There is little evidence that a couple of weeks' training makes an Iraqi an effective counterinsurgent, yet that is essentially what the police and Iraqi Civil Defense Corps troops are getting. The potential for abuse by poorly trained and unsupervised police and ICDC is high. A pattern of such abuse will be a significant setback for the coalition.

4. Iraqi leaders are hesitant to be too closely aligned with the coalition. They fear not just reprisals but also loss of status and influence if they are perceived as American puppets. They also fear that the Americans will depart before a functioning government is firmly installed.

5. The coalition's apparent lack of understanding of the ACF's composition hampers efforts to effectively combat them. During Ramadan, bombings conducted by the ACF had key personnel at various command levels, from division to the Pentagon, giving varied and even contradictory

statements about who was behind the bombings. If we do not understand who the enemy is and what motivates him, other than killing Americans, it will be difficult to fight him.

6. Tactical responses to ACF attacks suggest a breakdown between tactics and operational-level aims. The U.S. response to the shootdown of the Blackhawk helicopter in the north closely resembled Israeli actions against the Palestinians. U.S. forces conducted a show of force, including aerial bombing, movement of armor, and the destruction of empty houses in the vicinity of the shootdown. The tactic of destroying homes has been used and has failed in Israel for almost two decades. Even worse, the perception that the United States has chosen to treat Iraqis as the Israelis treat Palestinians is a major setback for our "hearts and minds" campaign.

7. The lack of cultural awareness and language capabilities in coalition forces adversely impacts our ability to pacify Iraq. Repeated humiliation of Iraqis in their own homes and at checkpoints is turning many neutrals to the ACF. The lack of language skills means coalition personnel are isolated from the Iraqis even when they are surrounded by them.

8. The ineffective campaign to keep the people of the United States informed as to the critical nature of our goals and the strategy to achieve them threatens popular support for the war. If the U.S. government is not more adept at explaining our strategy and providing a long-term plan for success, the American people will increasingly object to the entire effort. This also applies to the Coalition Provisional Authority's relationship with the Iraqi people.

9. Coalitions and alliances possess inherent weaknesses, because they can be fractured. The ACF intend to isolate the United States by driving away all potential supporters, targeting international aid organizations and Iraqis who collaborate with the coalition. With the drawdown of U.N. and NGO personnel and the pending withdrawal of Spanish forces, the ACF campaign appears to have been at least partially successful.

10. Counterinsurgency is usually Darwinian. U.S. counterinsurgency operations kill the stupid or unlucky ACF fighters and, in doing so, improve the quality of those still fighting. Those who survive are smarter, more careful, and more effective. They have learned from the mistakes of others. As

the elements of the insurgent network observe the action-reaction-counteraction cycle, they are learning what works and what doesn't when it comes to fighting the U.S.-led coalition.

In contrast to the steady Darwinian process on the insurgent side, the United States regularly rotates personnel out of the theater. The current policy of unit rotation rather than individual rotation is a huge improvement over the truly devastating individual rotation policies of Vietnam. However, unit rotation does not solve the fact that our leaders usually rotate out of their units after each tour. Therefore, each unit returns with a different set of inexperienced leaders, who will always be behind the learning curve when compared to their adversaries.

At the time of this writing, it is impossible to predict with certainty the outcome in Iraq. However, the war has clearly become a 4GW struggle. Recent history shows that this type of struggle lasts a decade or more. Further, like the other complex struggles in Palestine and Afghanistan, there are not just two sides but numerous intensely involved communities: Shia, Sunni, Arab, Kurd, U.S., and other coalition members. This multi-sided contest requires patience, a long-term view, and slow, often painful, efforts to build trust among the communities. This type of effort does not lend itself well to timelines.

Unfortunately, as of late April 2004, the U.S. effort has focused on a single date—July 1—and the transition of control to an Iraqi government. The administration steadily pared back its prewar goals. Despite an initial position that the United States would not leave until the Iraqis had a working constitution and a free-market economy, the administration has quietly abandoned both those goals as unachievable by July 1. Worse, they have not yet articulated a plan for after the transition of authority. How will the United States, with the new Iraqi government as a partner, defeat the insurgents? How will they sustain the will and focus of the American people over the long timeline necessary to create a stable, free Iraq?

This chapter started with Clausewitz's caution about understanding the nature of the war one is fighting. Unfortunately, the U.S. focus on high technology and the power of precision weapons convinced our decision makers that we could prevail quickly and cheaply in Iraq. We could make it a rapid, high-tech, third-generation war of maneuver rather than the long-term, low-tech, fourth-generation war that is its underlying nature. Much to the surprise of the *Joint Vision 2020* proponents, the insurgents have proven largely immune to our technology.

However, the failure of information technology to give conventional forces an edge against 4GW opponents should not have been a surprise. It has been clear for a decade or more that, as always, the emerging technology favors the new generation of war rather than the old. We are getting a lesson in that fact now.

To understand the danger inherent in the Department of Defense's reliance on the technological aspects of war rather than its human aspects, we need to take a close look at how these new technologies favor the 4GW practitioner who uses them to reinforce the human skills of his organization rather than to replace the humans. That is exactly the subject of the next chapter.

# CHAPTER 13

# Technology: Not a Panacea

Today, America finds itself embroiled in 4GW in Iraq and Afghanistan as well as a worldwide struggle against al-Qaeda. These are long-term struggles that will be won or lost primarily with human skills and knowledge. Unfortunately for America, in its rush to embrace technology as the solution to all our problems, much of its defense establishment has ignored the importance of cultural and historical understanding. As discussed in Chapter 1, they are convinced that high technology will provide virtually all the answers for future warfare, regardless of the setting.

The current emphasis on transformation within the Department of Defense continues to expand on this theme, detailing how the information revolution can be harnessed to vastly improve military and political decision making, allowing technologically advanced nations to dominate all arenas of conflict. Airpower proponents and defense industry spokesmen in particular praise the capabilities of our sensors, computerized information processing systems, worldwide secure communications systems, and precision weapons. They inform us that these systems will allow us to "sense" the battlefield with near-perfect clarity, understand it, and strike with virtual impunity. Proponents of the high-tech systems assure our political leadership that our lead in this area is commanding and translates directly into an inherent advantage against any potential enemy.

In fact, these proponents are so confident that they state, "Network-centric warfare, where battle time plays a critical role, is analogous to the new economic model, with potentially increasing returns on investment. Very high and accelerating rates of change have a profound impact on the outcome, 'locking out' alternative enemy strategies and 'locking in' success."[1]

True believers in technology see warfare as being reduced to a one-sided contest where the technologically superior side dictates all action. They never discuss what happens if the enemy selects a strategy where time is not essential. How can battle time be critical in a war that lasts decades? Or what do we do if the enemy works hard not to produce any collectible signals?* In other words, the true believers ignore what is happening to U.S. forces around the world today.

Rather than deal with the complex political, economic, and social aspects of the conflicts we are currently fighting, they focus on technological solutions to problems at the tactical level of war. If there is one thing we should have learned from watching the Germans execute 3GW, it is that strategic victory is *not* the sum of incredible, tactical victories. Both Germany and Japan failed to understand the strategic context of the war—and despite exceptional tactical- and operational-level victories, failed abysmally strategically. They could win battles but not wars. In many ways, the United States mirrors this misunderstanding today. We continue to focus on technological solutions at the tactical and operational levels without a serious discussion of the strategic imperatives or the nature of the war we are fighting.

As indicated in Chapter 1, I strongly disagree with the idea that technology provides an inherent advantage to the United States. In this chapter, I will point out how the explosive growth of information technology

* Al-Qaeda has used this approach since the destruction of the Taliban government in Afghanistan. The ACF in Iraq have used it since U.S. forces occupied Baghdad. In fact, it was HUMINT, not technology, that led to the capture of Saddam and the killing of his sons, Uday and Qusay.

has actually eroded our lead. The information revolution allows our potential 4GW enemies to not only match our capabilities in many areas but actually exceed them in some. It provides those enemies with distinct advantages, from the tactical level to the strategic, in a conflict with the United States or other Western powers. This should not come as a surprise. As long as we insist on using 3GW tactics, we should not believe that 4GW technology gives us an advantage. New technology favors a new generation of war—not simply updating the old generation with new equipment.

You may be thinking that my view overstates the case—that I fail to understand the incredible collection, dissemination, collation, and analysis capabilities the Department of Defense and other national agencies possess. You may feel that our potential 4GW enemies could not have access to better information than our combatant commanders. After all, they are small, geographically separated entities that have no major bases or facilities to provide the kind of support our combatant commanders routinely receive.

I acknowledge that our systems are the most powerful, most capable, most technically advanced in the world. They clearly can collect more information across the spectrum of emissions than any single adversary and probably any collection of adversaries. However, this technological prowess does not translate into an inherent tactical, operational, or strategic advantage.

Why? Two reasons: our current organization and the changing threat we face.

### *Organization*

Our advanced information systems are still tied to an outdated, hierarchical organization that slows the dissemination of information. Although specific high-priority commands receive near real-time intelligence, most commanders must submit their intelligence requirements up the chain of command. Each level validates, consolidates, and prioritizes the requests, which are then fed through the centralized staff system to task the assets that will actually collect against the requests. The information is collected, passed to another section for analysis, then put in the form of a usable product, and finally disseminated through the same cumbersome system. Thus, the premier benefit of the Information Age—immediate access to current intelligence—is nullified by the way we route it through our vertical bureaucracy.

Not only does our bureaucracy delay the distribution of the intelligence products we develop, it actively discourages subordinate units from tapping into the information themselves, via the Internet. The result is a limiting of the variety and timeliness of the information available to our decision makers, from the strategic to the tactical levels. This is further exacerbated by the mismatch between a hierarchical system design and potential 4GW targets. Although shaving seconds off the sensor-to-shooter loop is not critical in a decades-long conflict, it is essential that intelligence be collected and distributed in a network rather than a hierarchy. Only then can each level understand enough of the situation to make the sound, informed decision essential to this type of war.

The U.S. intelligence community is currently working hard to establish web-based systems to provide rapid, simultaneous dissemination to all levels of command. They have had some remarkable successes in sharing intelligence by placing it on servers and allowing customers to pull just the intelligence they need. However, their efforts will continue to be hampered as long as we insist on a top-down bureaucratic process controlling the overall system.

A second major flaw in our systems further ensures that opponents can outstrip us in exploiting information technology. Our systems were initially designed to collect against nations and their assets—specifically, the Soviet Union. They were designed to find, identify, and track large, conventional forces, so they could not surprise us.

Unfortunately, most of our potential enemies are not nations. Our current and most likely future enemies are subnational (Iraqi resistance, Taliban, Bosnian, Serb, Croat, Muslim, Somali clan), transnational (Islamic Brotherhood, al-Qaeda, other terrorist groups), and international (drug cartels, organized crime).

In a nutshell, we face a fight between asymmetrical forces. While our opposition is still collecting against essentially conventional forces (our bases, units, ports, airfields), we are forced to collect against small cells, individuals, and even ideas. The cumulative effect leaves our collection assets severely handicapped. The target is fundamentally different from what our systems and organizations were designed to collect against.

Even worse, those systems, which used to be highly classified, are now commercially available to anyone with a computer, a modem, and a credit card. Because of the changed nature of war, these legacy systems are of decreasing value against our current enemies. However, the commercial systems they fathered can be a huge help to that enemy in tracking our movements.

The legacy systems, despite major faults, still provide significant intelligence. Unfortunately, they have yet another serious downside. At the political level, by providing a false sense of understanding, they encourage policy makers to overestimate our ability to control a situation. Throughout history, wars or campaigns have been started with goals in mind. Obviously, the person making the decision to initiate war believed his goals were achievable. Just as obviously, history has shown that they are rarely achieved. Wars almost never turn out as envisioned by those who start them.

With the assurance of "battlespace dominance" promised by the proponents of cyberwar, political leaders will be more inclined to commit U.S. forces to an unclear situation. After all, they "know" that our superior systems give us special insight and dominance across the spectrum of war. The plethora of "information" they produce may cause our leaders to believe they understand the situation.

A belief in these systems convinces some people that we can control even unclear situations because of superior "targeting" ability, thus increasing the willingness to commit U.S. forces to uncertain situations. Our confidence that we could track and capture Aideed in the chaotic environment of Mogadishu, that we could easily locate and destroy Serbian armor, and that we could easily capture Saddam are cases in point. This false belief in the power of our intelligence systems increases the potential for us to commit forces to situations we don't really understand.

At the tactical level, the quantity of information our systems provide has grown exponentially. Unfortunately, although vastly improved in raw amounts of data, our ability to turn that information into coherent intelligence products for our commanders has not kept pace. These systems provide so much information that they virtually force the commander to focus his intelligence staff on simply sorting the flow rather than on analysis or developing his own local sources and solutions.

Despite the huge increase in information available, Afghanistan proved that many of the "precision strikes" so beloved of *JV 2020* and network-centric warfare advocates required the presence of a Mark I, Mod 0 human eyeball on the ground. Similarly, even during the conventional phase of operations in Iraq, lead maneuver forces had to rely on their own assets to determine what was directly in front of them. In the unconventional operations that have followed, most of the high-technology systems have proven irrelevant.

### *Threat*

Potential enemies are not hampered by an entrenched bureaucracy. They are free to exploit the full range of commercially available information technology. They can use the rapidly expanding worldwide information system to collect information, store it on web sites, collaborate on analysis, and direct attacks on our interests. They can even use technology to directly assault our interests via cyber attack.

Collection and storage are the simplest tasks. Remember that much of the commercial technology available today is an outgrowth of the military systems designed specifically to collect and defend against conventional forces. Even small cells can exploit the information revolution to collect against our forces. A group trying to track U.S. forces can watch CNN or a dozen other news agencies for live footage of the movement of our forces from home bases—and often even in theater. They can tap into a wide variety of commercial satellite imaging services—many with resolution of less than one meter. These photos can be used to track our ships, identifying changes in our ports, as well as arrival and assembly areas. The resolution of these images is sufficient to assist tactical planning for specific operations.

In addition, they can get worldwide weather reports. They can conduct online research in port usage, shipping insurance rates (to indicate perception of threat by business), gauge market reaction to current events, and even watch our leaders express their positions to members of the media. Anyone with a computer, a modem, and a credit card is limited only by his own imagination and intelligence in developing information from the political level to the tactical. The last seventy years have made it clear that insurgents are imaginative, intelligent, and creative.

As part of their fight against the United Nations, the Serb leadership used CNN as a near real-time collection asset to observe Western reaction to the taking of U.N. personnel as hostages. After seizing the hostages and chaining them to various potential U.N. targets, they invited the media to film the scene. Thus, within hours, the Serb leadership not only ensured that their strong message would reach the United Nations, but they could watch the reactions of the ministers of defense and foreign affairs for the key players in the Untied Nations as they staked out their national positions in the media. Of course, all this happened long before the U.N. commanders on the ground had received any official guidance on the situation. Using modern technology and a flat organization, the Serbs were able to get way inside the Untied Nation's observe-orient-decide-act (OODA) loop.

Even more important for using 4GW techniques, today's terrorists are organized as networks rather than as hierarchies. This means that each entity can use the network simultaneously, searching for and receiving the information he is interested in without having to work through a bureaucracy. Ask yourself which you would rather have as a tactical commander: a one-meter-resolution image from a commercial source hours after you request it or a high-resolution image from one of our national systems days after you request it. Even more important, the insurgent knows what he can and cannot get. The U.S. commander has to submit his request and wait to see if it can be filled—further delaying his decision cycle.

The terrorist collection assets are limited only by their ingenuity. Once collected, the information can be stored free on a multitude of web sites, through worldwide providers such as Excite or Yahoo. After being placed on a web site, it can be viewed, processed, and manipulated by anyone to whom the terrorist chooses to grant access. Again, this reflects a 4GW approach to the collection, storage, manipulation, and dissemination of information. Although our intelligence and operations agencies are moving this direction, they have to adapt legacy organizations, software, and hardware from hierarchy to network. Even more difficult, they have to adapt risk-averse, hierarchical organizations to exploit the opportunities our systems do provide.

In contrast, an adept terrorist simply uses the existing networks created by the information-based economy. These networks provide a cheap, robust, redundant system and allows the information to blend into the trillions of legitimate transactions that take place every day. Using commercial networks, an intelligent opponent can even avoid moving incriminating documents with him as he moves from country to country by emailing them ahead or posting them on a web page. The combination of encryption and the minuscule size of his signal compared to the mass of commercial transactions ensures a low probability of interception.

In addition to using the collection technology available, potential enemies can exploit information technology to communicate easily, cheaply, and securely. From the beginning of the technology revolution, insurgents have made extensive use of the capabilities it provides. The Somalis used cellular phones to build an inexpensive communications system. Easy, cheap to establish and use, relatively secure using commercially available encryption technology and immediately available, these simple phones minimized the physical contact among cells while complicating our efforts to track the insurgents' communication. Somali use of readily available commercial technology vastly improved their tactical collection, dissemination, and command and control.

Besides providing excellent local communications, cell phones provided worldwide communications. Thus the warlords in Somalia could maintain contact with suppliers, financiers, and intelligence sources outside Somalia. In effect, they leveraged a full-blown worldwide communications system by purchasing a few phones, laptops, and modems. They gained those benefits without the overhead that makes conventional communications systems vulnerable to physical attack. Further, although these systems were vulnerable to exploitation, use of one-time pads, slang, and simple codes greatly increased their security.

Because warfare remains a conflict between opposing wills, we in the West learned to exploit those cell-phone signals. Although we could not intercept and interpret all of them, we could identify specific high-value targets, focus on them, and collect successfully . . . until our capability to do so was leaked to the press. At that point, use of cell phones by those targets ceased. Yet another example of how rapidly each side adapts to the changing circumstances of war.

From this early exploitation of technology, insurgents and terrorists have been quick to adopt any new development. By definition, commercial technology is available to anyone who can afford it—and the cost has been decreasing rapidly, while availability has increased geometrically. Using these commercial items and the agility inherent in a distributive decision-making system, potential enemies can develop a remarkable capability. By tapping into the Internet and using widely available encryption technology, anyone with a couple of thousand dollars has access to a secure, worldwide communications system. They don't even need to carry it with them but can access it through the widely available Internet cafes and public library systems.

With the advent of steganography, insurgents can hide their messages in a single dot in one of dozens of photos sent through the system—or perhaps even in the dot at the end of this sentence. They can further encrypt by using a commercially available 256-bit encryption system to encode the data before they reduce it to a dot, so that even if you find the right dot, you have to work at decrypting it.

In fact, we know that al-Qaeda is using the web this way.

> U.S. intelligence discovered Al Qaeda uses the Web as a communications network. Analysts believe Al Qaeda uses prearranged phrases and symbols to direct its agents. An icon of an AK-47 can appear next to a photo of Osama bin Laden facing one direction one day, and another direction the next. Colors of icons can change as well. Messages can be hidden on pages inside sites with no links to them, or placed openly in chat rooms. . . . For more direct communications, Al Qaeda uses commercially available encryption

> software or hides messages inside graphics files by a process known as steganography. "They are giving strategic direction to their supporters by using the Web [and] using [cryptographic software] to transmit email messages," says a British intelligence source.[2]

Yet, because war, regardless of generation, remains a contest between two wills, Western intelligence agencies are gleaning some information from the web:

> Some of the most valuable intelligence gleaned from the sites has been the connection between Islamic charities and Qaeda fundraising operations. Analysts found the same bank-account numbers listed in Islamic humanitarian appeals on sites raising funds for jihad against the enemies of Islam. Several U.S. based Islamic "charities" have been shut down thanks to the analysts' discovery of this fund-raising scam.[3]

We also know that once this intelligence method was revealed in the media, the terrorists ceased the practice of using the same account numbers. War will continue to be the action-reaction-counteraction cycle inherent in all human struggles. However, modern technology favors the organization built as a network rather than as a hierarchy.

The Internet also provides a superb system to acquire and move funds. We now know al-Qaeda has used Islamic charities and easily moved money around the world via formal, informal *(halawa),* or even tribal networks. Given the billions of dollars that move through these channels every year and the Byzantine nature of the system, it provides a virtually invisible path for the funds. Further, these funds do not travel just via Islamic routes. All immigrant groups have informal routes to send money back home. Given the worldwide, transnational, multi-ethnic nature of the al-Qaeda network, we must assume they are using multiple paths. Osama bin Laden was not the first to use charities to collect funds. The Irish Republican Army used essentially the same system for years to collect funds in the United States. The Internet simply makes it easier and faster.

Finally, the worldwide information system enables savvy groups to use the information revolution to directly attack the U.S. center of gravity: our political will. Once again, the Somalis showed us how. They recognized the power of a message sent via mass media. Based on this knowledge, they were ready to exploit any success they might have against U.S. forces in Mogadishu. Although the Somalis could not predict the exact date or time they would succeed against American forces, they had planned to immediately exploit the media when it did happen. The speed with which they escorted journalists to the scene of the October 3, 1993, battle indicates this. In addition, the escort was heavily armed and had enough authority to protect those white, Western journalists from mobs of angry Somalis. Further, they seemed to know the deadlines for the images to be uplinked to make the evening news cycle in the United States.

All this could not have been a coincidence. Their actions reveal a carefully developed plan to project a specific image to U.S. decision makers. As a result of this careful preparation, the Somalis delivered an explosive message (a dead American being dragged through the streets) to a targeted audience (U.S. decision makers) within minutes of the event—long before the official Department of Defense version of events could wend its way to the top and be released to the public.

Both al-Qaeda and the anti-coalition forces in Iraq understand the power of the media and often include coverage in their tactical plans. The individual events are part of the overall operational approach of directly influencing decision makers who view or read the reports. And by posting film directly to the Internet, they eliminate even the buffering effects of the mainstream media editors.

Recent events from Somalia to Beirut to the West Bank to New York City and Washington make it clear that commercially available systems allow a low-tech opponent to get inside our decision-making cycle. Although the commercial product may not be as refined as our professionally produced intelligence products, it moves much more rapidly, allowing our opponents to set the tempo of operations.

### *But Does That Make Them a Real Threat?*

At the strategic level, the combination of our perceived technological superiority and our bureaucratic organization sets us up for a major failure against a more agile, intellectually prepared enemy. It manifested itself clearly on September 11, when we found that our bureaucratic approach to intelligence gathering had never followed up on reports about men seeking lessons on how to fly a jetliner but not to take off or land in it.

In contrast, the al-Qaeda terrorists were able to use the information networks to move information successfully all over the world and coordinate, research, and fund their actions using 4GW techniques and commercial networks. This problem is both more subtle and more dangerous than those previously discussed.

Our dilemma is the same one that always faces leading powers as society undergoes major shifts in how it creates wealth—and therefore in how it functions day to day. The leading power's military strength is based on the previous generation of technology. Even as the way it generates wealth shifts rapidly to new sources, the society retains a huge investment in the basis of that military power.

In the case of the United States, we have huge sunk costs in conventional forces. Not only do we have the resources funding them, we have the culture, promotion system, schools, staffs, procurement systems, and so on. In short, we have an entire culture and industry built around second- and third-generation warfare. As a result, we have convinced ourselves that applying our technology to these older generations of war gives us a unique and virtually unassailable lead, through our ability to conduct precision attacks that surgically remove an enemy's ability to fight. Our official documents state that we have the sensors, processing systems, secure communications, and precision weapons that will allow us to dominate the battlespace via precision strike.

In fact, small, moderately well funded organizations have the same ability to perform all the steps necessary to conduct precision strikes. Their sensors are human intelligence contacts, open-source reporting, Internet mining, and commercially available imagery. They process information through the most subtle, sophisticated, and capable system in existence: the human mind. They have secure, worldwide communications through the use of the Internet and basic tradecraft. Finally, they have precision weapons, in the form of humans willing to ride the ordnance to the target.

They have repeatedly demonstrated all these capabilities in diverse locations, yet somehow our Department of Defense still touts the "superiority" of our high-technology systems. Unfortunately, DOD publications never address how our precision weapons can attack a target that blends into civilian society. In both Afghanistan and Iraq, the end of the conventional warfare phase essentially terminated our ability to conduct precision strikes. Although we occasionally launch a missile or a precision bomb against a target, these attacks have minor effects.

In contrast, the insurgent use of precision weapons in the form of car bombs drove the United Nations out of Iraq. The use of hand-placed backpacks on Spanish trains resulted in a change to the Spanish government and the impending withdrawal of Spanish troops from Iraq. Continued precision attacks on civilians involved in the reconstruction of Iraq has slowed the reconstruction and dramatically raised its cost.

What gives our 4GW opponents an even greater advantage is that we continue to apply most of our technology resources to third- and even second-generation warfare. History is replete with examples of technologically superior forces that employed new technology based on an outmoded understanding of war. The British had weapons equal to or better than the Boers, but they insisted on using 1GW tactics against an enemy who was developing and employing 2GW tactics. The result was disaster on the battlefield.

In the same way, the French took their superior numbers of higher-quality tanks and scattered them among the infantry forces of their army. The numerical and technical superiority of their equipment could not overcome their adherence to 2GW tactics. Instead they were decisively defeated by the 3GW warfare of the Germans.

Today, the terrorists themselves state that they understand and use 4GW. The February 2002 edition of the online magazine *Al-Ansar*, which purports to be an official al-Qaeda outlet, published an article on 4GW. In it, Ubeid al-Qurashi, one of bin Laden's close aids, wrote as follows:

> In 1989, some American military experts* predicted a fundamental change in the future form of warfare. . . . They predicted that the wars of the 21st century would be dominated by a kind of warfare they called "the fourth generation of wars." Others called it asymmetric warfare. . . .
>
> This new type of war presents significant difficulties for the Western war machine and it can be expected that [Western] armies will change fundamentally. This forecast did not arise in a vacuum—if only the cowards [among the Muslim clerics] knew that fourth-generation wars have already occurred and that the superiority of the theoretically weaker party has already been proven; in many instances, nation-states have been defeated by stateless nations. . . .
>
> In Afghanistan, the Mujahideen triumphed over the world's second most qualitative power at that time. . . . Similarly, a single Somali tribe humiliated America and compelled it to remove its forces from Somalia. A short time later, the Chechen Mujahideen humiliated and defeated the Russian bear. After that, the Lebanese resistance [Hezbollah] expelled the Zionists army from southern Lebanon. . . .
>
> Technology did not help these great armies, even though [this technology] is sufficient to destroy the planet hundreds of times over using the arsenal of nuclear, chemical, and biological weapons. The Mujahideen proved their superiority in fourth-generation

*The Western military experts quoted included were William Lind, Keith Nightengale, John Schmidt, Joseph Sutton and Gary Wilson who collaborated on "The Changing Face of War: Into the Fourth Generation" (*Marine Corps Gazette*, October 1989) and this author from his article "The Evolution of War: The Fourth Generation" (*Marine Corps Gazette*, September 1994).

> warfare using only light weaponry. They are part of the people and hide among the multitudes. . . .
>
> Thus, it appears that there are precedents for world powers and large countries being defeated by [small] units of Mujahideen over the past two decades, despite the great differences between the two sides. . . .[4]

Al-Qaeda understands 4GW and is using it. Their actions in Iraq, Afghanistan, and Spain demonstrate a keen understanding of how a militarily weaker power can attack a vastly more powerful enemy.

In sum, Information-Age technology has actually eroded our position relative to potential 4GW enemies over the last couple of decades. Our position is much weaker than the rosy picture painted by the advocates of advanced technology. Although we have technology superior to that of many of our potential adversaries, we continue to use it to support a third-generation style of warfare. In contrast, the most forward-thinking of our opponents have seized on fourth-generation warfare. They know that the new technology has evolved with and is perfectly suited to 4GW. Rather than applying new technology to an old style of war, they are using that technology to push the new form of war forward.

War since 1945 has shown what happens to large bureaucratic forces, even those of superpowers, that attempt to force a fourth-generation war into the third-generation mold: they get beaten. The Chinese, Vietnamese, Sandinistas, Hezbollah, Palestinians, and Chechnyans all triumphed over forces with superior military power. They did so by crippling that power through more effective uses of 4GW, from the strategic level through the tactical. The superior technology of the losers did not prove to be a magic solution.

The key point is that the winners focused the new technology on the emerging generation of war rather than trying to overcome the loser's lead in the previous generation. To comprehend fully the potential impact that could result from our bureaucracy focusing this perceived technological advantage on the previous generation of war, take a look at IBM versus the home computer industry at the dawn of the computer age. In the 1970s,

IBM had enormous labs and incredible resources. It dominated the computer business worldwide. The name IBM was virtually synonymous with computers. In contrast, personal computers were an idea in the minds of a few people operating out of their garages.

Thirty years later, the survivors of those early garages dominate the personal computer market and are launching the new software and hardware that will further increase their market share. They continue to network these increasingly powerful machines and are actually taking a share of the mainframe market. In stark contrast, IBM has been driven out of the PC hardware and software business and is even losing ground in its mainframe stronghold to these upstarts.

Quite simply, while IBM had dominant resources and information, its large, hierarchical, overconfident bureaucracy virtually ensured that it could not put those advantages to use. Decision makers far up in the hierarchy could not overcome their old prejudices in favor of mainframe computers. They applied the new technology to previous-generation concepts based around mainframe computers while paying only sporadic attention to the concept of personal computers. Even more damaging, they assumed that the rest of the world would also continue to believe in mainframes and buy accordingly.

Unfortunately for IBM, the rest of the world was not interested in IBM's reputation or its beliefs—only in results. The structure of IBM, which seemed to confer great advantages, turned out to be a major disadvantage.

Like IBM in the 1970s, our Department of Defense and regional combatant commanders have access to huge reservoirs of information, large staffs processing that information, and extensive distribution systems. Unfortunately, we also have the large bureaucracy that characterized IBM. Like IBM, we are busy making things more like we think they should be, 3GW updated through *Joint Vision 2020* and "transformation," rather than observing, understanding, and reacting to the major changes in society.

A perfect example is DOD's drive for ever-increasing centralization. They are forcing centralization simply because that is their vision of the future. In every area, from single-item managers for logistics items to the consolidated commissary system to experimentation about the future of war,

DOD is centralizing. Unfortunately, the political, social, and economic systems of the world are moving in a diametrically opposite direction. Successful organizations are employing information systems to improve strategic decision making while forcing all other decisions downward.

Despite this worldwide trend, accelerated by the spectacular failure of the Soviet Union's centralized planning, DOD, like IBM in the 1970s, continues to centralize and is losing any limited agility it had to ever-growing bureaucracy. It reflects the same intellectual arrogance and inertia that plagued IBM. If the smug tones of our professional journals and "idea" papers, such as *JV 2020,* "Network-Centric Warfare," and "Transformation Planning Guidance" are an accurate indication, we believe our systems exceed the capabilities of any opponent and will provide us with a near-perfect understanding of the battlefield. This is despite the contrary evidence presented by our difficulties in hunting down al-Qaeda, the Taliban, and other insurgents in Afghanistan and Iraq. Unfortunately, like all true believers, technologists never let facts get in the way of their beliefs.

# CHAPTER 14

# Characteristics of Fourth-Generation War

The evolution from second-generation firepower to third-generation maneuver matured over seventy years ago with the German offensives into France and Russia. Since then, every aspect of our civilization has undergone major changes. Therefore, despite the Pentagon's fascination with high-technology maneuver warfare, warfare, as an integral part of civilization, has also changed.

It is clear even from our brief study of previous generations of modern war that each generation evolved over time. Further, each evolved as practical people developed real-world solutions to specific tactical problems. Each solution required changes in the political, economic, social, and technical arenas before the solutions became practical. We can see that warfare is evolutionary rather than revolutionary. We can see that it evolves in response to major changes in society.

Beginning with Mao's concept that political will could defeat superior military power and progressing to Intifada I's total reliance on the mass media and international networks to neutralize Israel's military power and political process, warfare underwent a fundamental change. It shifted from an Industrial-Age focus on the destruction of the enemy's armed forces to an

Information-Age focus on changing the minds of the enemy's political decision makers. With the al-Aqsa Intifada and al-Qaeda, we have seen that 4GW can develop a variety of strategies, depending on the goals of the practitioner. With Iraq and Afghanistan, we have seen that 4GW can hold its own even against the most technologically advanced and militarily powerful nation in the world.

The fourth generation has arrived. It uses all available networks—political, economic, social, and military—to convince the enemy's political decision makers that their strategic goals are either unachievable or too costly for the perceived benefit. It is an evolved form of insurgency. Still rooted in the fundamental precept that superior political will, when properly employed, can defeat greater economic and military power, 4GW makes use of society's networks to carry on its fight. Unlike previous generations, it does not attempt to win by defeating the enemy's military forces. Instead, via the networks, it directly attacks the minds of enemy decision makers to destroy the enemy's political will. Fourth-generation wars are lengthy—measured in decades rather than months or years.

The following discussion looks at strategic, operational, and tactical characteristics of 4GW.

### *Strategic Level*

Strategically, 4GW attempts to directly change the minds of enemy policy makers. This change is not to be achieved through the traditional method of superiority on the battlefield. The first- through third-generation objective of destroying the enemy's armed forces and his capacity to regenerate them is not how 4GW enemies will attack us. Both the epic, decisive Napoleonic battle and the wide-ranging, high-speed maneuver campaign are irrelevant to them. Their victories are accomplished through the superior use of all available networks to directly defeat the will of the enemy leadership, to convince them their war aims are either unachievable or too costly. These networks will be employed to carry specific messages to our policy makers and to those who can influence the policy makers.

Intifada I showed how a sophisticated opponent can tailor specific messages to several audiences simultaneously, based on strategic requirements.

Although tailored for various audiences, each message is designed to achieve the basic purpose of war: change an opponent's political position on a matter of national interest. The fights in Iraq and Afghanistan are showing similar characteristics. In each, the insurgent is sending one message to his supporters, another to the mass of the undecided population, and a third to the coalition decision makers.

Subsequent developments in the al-Aqsa Intifada show how a central authority such as Arafat can destroy a successful 4GW campaign by not understanding the message he is sending or even the impact of that message. These developments also show how a country (Israel) can reshape its defensive efforts into a 4GW campaign by understanding 4GW techniques: developing appropriate messages and matching the strategic approach to the realities imposed by 4GW.

In contrast, the al-Qaeda campaign showed how a 4GW campaign can be derailed when planners do not understand the cultural biases of the nation being attacked. Al-Qaeda shifted from making steady progress toward their strategic goals to arousing the focused anger of the United States. Yet their ability to continue to operate, despite two years of focused American attacks, proves the incredible resilience of a 4GW enemy.

We have also seen that the use of 4GW networks does not imply a bloodless war. In fact, we know that most casualties of 4GW will be civilians and that many of these casualties will be caused not by military weapons but by materials available in a modern society. This is an aspect of 4GW that we must understand. The 4GW opponent does not have to build the warfighting infrastructure essential to earlier generations of war. As displayed in the Beirut bombings, the Khobar Tower bombing, the African embassy bombings, the Oklahoma City bombing, 9/11, and the ongoing bombing campaign in Iraq, 4GW practitioners are making more and more use of materials available in the society they are attacking. This allows the 4GW practitioner to take a different strategic approach. It relieves him of the strategic necessity of defending core production assets, leaving him free to focus on offense rather than defense. It also relieves him of the logistics burden of moving supplies long distances. Instead, he has to move only money and ideas—both of which can be digitized and moved instantly.

Alliances, interests, and positions among and between 4GW actors will change according to various political, economic, social, and military aspects of the conflict. Although this has been a factor in all wars (Italy changed sides in the middle of the biggest conventional war of all time), it will be prevalent in 4GW war. It is much easier for stateless entities (tribes, clans, businesses, criminal groups, racial groups, subnational groups, transnational groups) to change sides than for nation-states or national groups. A government usually ties itself to a specific cause. It has to convince the decision makers or its people to support it, so it can be awkward for that government to change sides in mid-conflict without losing the confidence of its people. Often, the act of changing sides will lead to the fall of the government. In contrast, non-state entities get involved only for their needs, and if the needs shift, they can easily shift loyalties. In Somalia, Afghanistan, Kosovo, Iraq, and innumerable skirmishes in Africa, alliances shift like a kaleidoscope.

If a democracy gets involved where its vital interests are not at stake, its overall situation will be both difficult and dangerous. Players with vital interests will have large incentives to attack the democracy's forces. They have an even larger incentive to ensure that the videos of those attacks make the news cycle. They know that in the past, such tactical attacks have been more likely to result in withdrawal than in retaliation, as in Somalia, Lebanon, and Spain. The fact that vital interests are not at stake makes it difficult for a nation to bear the pain inflicted in a 4GW conflict. The long timelines of 4GW require a nation to have a significant stake in the outcome of the conflict to sustain the effort. It also requires patience as a national trait.

The importance of the media in determining policy of the participants will continue to increase. We saw a demonstration of this when U.S. interest in Somalia, previously negligible, was stimulated by the repeated images of thousands of starving Somali children. Conversely, the images of U.S. soldiers being dragged through the streets ended that commitment. The media will continue to be a major factor in the future. This will be true from the strategic level to the tactical.

Strategically, the world is more and more closely tied together. Events in any region are increasingly likely to affect other, even distant, regions. If more of the world begins to meet the basic needs of its people, there will be fewer and fewer places for "movements" to get started. Simply put, people who are happy with their lot in life and have hope for the future generally do not follow revolutionary leaders. Although the leaders themselves usually come from the upper and middle classes, the mass following of a movement usually comes from those who feel disenfranchised. Conversely, areas of the world where society is collapsing and there is no hope provide ideal recruiting grounds for 4GW warriors. Unfortunately, such "ungovernable" areas are plentiful today.

The increasing integration of human activity across the spectrum, from politics to leisure activities, means wars will not be fought in isolation. The days of the Foreign Office conducting "splendid little wars" have long been over. On the positive side, the interconnection of all aspects of society and increasing globalization will place some limits on the type and severity of conflicts in the future.

One final point needs to be understood about using 4GW at the strategic level. If the strategic goal is the absolute destruction of the target nation or organization, there will have to be a final military campaign to achieve that goal. Remember, Mao and Ho used 4GW techniques to change the correlation of forces so that their significantly weaker conventional forces could defeat an enemy that was much stronger initially. They knew they would have to physically destroy the opposing government before they could take over the country. Only a conventional campaign could provide that destruction.

Thus, while the Palestinians (Intifada I) used 4GW techniques to collapse the will of their opponents, they had limited political objectives. They convinced their opponents that the political concession they sought would cost less to grant than continuing to fight. Conversely, the al-Aqsa Intifada is proving that when the goals are unlimited, even a 4GW effort will be resolved only by conventional combat. No nation or group will give up its right to exist as a result of 4GW techniques. The techniques can only weaken the enemy's will and reduce his resources to the point that a conventional military campaign can defeat him entirely.

In the political arena, 4GW will make use of international, transnational, national, and subnational networks. Internationally, a wide variety of networks is available: the United Nations, NATO, the World Bank, OPEC, and dozens of others. Each has a different function in international affairs, and each carries a different type of message to New York or to its own capital city. These organizations will be used in virtually all 4GW conflicts. Although they may not be capable of directly changing the minds of enemy decision makers, they can be used to slow or paralyze an enemy's response.

The obvious use is to create political paralysis in both the international organizations (not a difficult task) and in the target nation (difficulty varies with the nation being targeted). However in addition to normal political attacks, 4GW planners can influence other aspects of the target society. Thcy know that the security situation in a country has a direct effect on the ability of that nation to get loans. The international marketplace is a swift and impersonal judge of creditworthiness. This gives the attacker a different avenue to affect a target nation's position: the mere threat of action may be enough to impact the nation's financial status and encourage it to negotiate. Thus, if his objective is simply to paralyze the political processes of a target nation, he can use a number of avenues to create that effect. As the world becomes ever more interconnected, the potential for varied approaches increases.

A coherent 4GW plan will always include transnational elements. These organizations span borders but are not subject to national control. These would include belief-based organizations such as the Islamic jihad and mainline churches; nationalistic organizations such as the Palestinians and Kurds; humanitarian organizations such as Médecins Sans Frontières and Amnesty International; economic structures such as the stock and bond markets; and even criminal organizations such as narco-traffickers and arms merchants. The key traits of transnational organizations are that none is contained completely within a recognized nation's borders, none has official members that must report back to a government, and none owes loyalty to any nation—and sometimes very little loyalty to its own organization.

The use of such transnational elements will vary with the strategic situation. But they provide a variety of possibilities. They can be a source of recruits. They can be used as cover to move people and assets. They can be an effective source of funds: charitable organizations have supported terrorist organizations as diverse as IRA and al-Qaeda. Finally, entire organizations can be used openly to support the position of the 4GW operator. Usually this is done when the organization genuinely agrees with the position of one of the antagonists, but false-flag operations are also viable. Such support can lend great legitimacy to a movement and, as we saw in the case of Intifada I, can even reverse long-held international views of a specific situation.

National organizations also provide highly effective networks for 4GW messages. The Congress of the United States was both a target of and a network for the North Vietnamese and the Sandinistas. In our brief case studies, we saw how the Vietnamese and Sandinistas targeted their efforts to neutralize U.S. military power through Congressional action to remove funding for their opponents. A prudent planner will assume that parliaments and congresses of democratic nations will be natural targets in a 4GW struggle.

Just as clearly, non-governmental national groups—churches, business groups, and even lobbying firms—can be major players in shaping national policies. President dos Santos of Angola actually hired a U.S. lobbying firm to prevent Jonas Savimbi of Unita from meeting the president of the United States. This was despite the fact that, at the time, the United States was covertly supporting Savimbi in his efforts to overthrow the government of President dos Santos. This use of lobbyists is not an isolated case. Both the Jewish and Arab Anti-Defamation Leagues aggressively support their respective sides in the Arab-Israeli conflicts.

Subnational organizations can represent groups who are minorities in their traditional homelands, such as the Basques, and those who are self-selecting minorities, such as the Sons of Liberty and Aryan Nation. These groups are in unusual positions. They can be either enemies or allies of the established power. It depends on who best serves their interests. Even more challenging, because they are not in fact unified groups, is that often one element of a subnational group is supporting the government while another is supporting the insurgent.

To reach these networks, the 4GW operational planner must seek various pathways for various messages. Traditional diplomatic channels, both official and unofficial, are still important but are no longer the only pathway for communication and influence. Other networks rival the prominence of the official ones. The media are rapidly becoming a primary avenue. Fortunately, the media's increasing diversity and fragmentation makes it much more challenging for either side to control the message. Professional lobbying groups have proven effective too. A new avenue is the Internet and the power it can give to grassroots campaigns. The anti-landmine campaign was coordinated largely via the Internet by volunteers, yet it had a major impact on the nations of the world.

A key factor to remember in targeting a 4GW campaign is that the audience is not a simple, unified target. It is increasingly fragmented into interest groups that shift sides depending on how a campaign affects their issues. During Intifada I, the Palestinians tailored different messages for different constituencies. The Israelis were doing the same during that al-Aqsa Intifada, and the anti-coalition forces in Iraq seem to be doing so also.

We can assume that future opponents will do the same. They will have one message for their own supporters, their power base. They will have a second message for the general public of the target nation. Another message will focus on the decision makers of the target nation. If the target nation has allies, they will send yet another message to that nation. Finally, there will always be a message for neutral nations—in an attempt to either keep them neutral or obtain their tacit support.

Even 2GW enemies will use 4GW techniques. As discussed earlier, Saddam Hussein conducted a 4GW campaign to deflect future U.S. action against his regime. It failed, but the United States spent significant resources defeating it. Since the fall of his regime, a number of 4GW messages to the Iraqi people have emerged. Throughout the Shia regions of Iraq, there is deep concern that Saddam, or at least his party members, will return to control Iraq. The name of the "Party of Return" is clearly gauged to maintain the terror that was the base of his power for decades. Even the capture of Saddam has not completely put these fears to rest.

Similarly, during the spring of 2004, the Ṣadr organization portrayed itself as the one entity in Iraq that consistently resisted the coalition occupation. They portrayed themselves as the true protectors of the Shia majority.

Keep in mind that what looks like a major failure to us may be a victory in the minds of an opponent's power base. The clearest example of this is the difference in perception between Israelis and Egyptians over who won the Yom Kippur War in 1973. The Israelis remember that their armies crushed the Egyptians, crossed the Suez, and had completely surrounded an entire Egyptian army when the cease-fire took effect. To them, the Yom Kippur War was yet another decisive victory for Israeli arms. The Egyptians remember the same war quite differently. The fact that the Egyptian army crossed the Suez Canal and fought the Israelis successfully for a period of time in the Sinai is perceived as a victory for Egyptian arms.

Similarly, U.S. military spokesmen kept insisting that the early attacks on U.S. troops after the end of major combat operations in Iraq were "militarily insignificant." This was at a time when each attack was on the front page of the *New York Times, Washington Post,* and *Los Angeles Times.* This revealed a fundamental misunderstanding of how military action is used effectively in 4GW.

Further complicating the conduct of 4GW is that military action will range from precise to bloody. It may be a single bullet to the brain of a specific enemy, or it may be mass casualties inflicted by dedicated people willing to die to get to the target—even willing to ride the munitions to the target.

### *Operational Level*

Operationally,* the practitioners of 4GW will pursue various avenues to ensure that tactics lead to the strategic goals. Given that the target of all 4GW actions is the mind of enemy decision makers, campaigns must structure tactical events toward that end. Tactical events should be selected to target an audience with the message the insurgent is trying to send.

* U.S. military discussion divides war into strategic, operational, and tactical levels. The strategic level sets the goals, allocation of resources, and overall timeline for the conflict. The operational level develops the campaigns that tie a series of battles together to achieve the strategic goals. The tactical level covers the battles themselves: the techniques, procedures, and tactics for fighting.

To succeed, the 4GW operational planner must determine the message he wants to send, the networks available to him, the types of messages those networks are best suited to carry, the action that will cause the network to send the message, and the feedback system that will tell him if the message is being received.

Finally, this campaign must be devised with an understanding of the timelines involved in 4GW. Although we must still understand and use the decision cycle, it must be with the view that 4GW timelines are much longer. The focus is no longer on the speed of the decision but on a correct understanding of the situation. Observation and orientation become the critical elements of the observation-orientation-decision-action (OODA) loop.

Effective operational application of 4GW is difficult. It requires knowledge, experience, and the ability to sense patterns in the fog of war. Just as clearly, it is doable. During Intifada I, the Palestinian use of limited violence in the occupied territories allowed them to send messages to multiple target audiences. By doing so, they neutralized U.S. support for continued Israeli action, froze the Israeli defense forces, and affected the Israeli national election.

Similarly, the series of bombings conducted by the Iraqi insurgents throughout the fall and winter of 2003–04 carefully targeted the organizations most helpful to the Coalition Provisional Authority: police, the United Nations, neutral embassies, and Shia clerics. Each event was tactically separated by time and space, but each tied together operationally to attack America's strategic position in the country. The campaign continues, with each attack designed to prevent a stable, democratic government from emerging.

At the operational level, a 4GW opponent will examine our entire society to find vulnerabilities. He will then attempt to attack those vulnerabilities to defeat our will. Many said that coordinating such a complicated campaign was beyond the capabilities of any organization except a modern, sophisticated nation. In the wake of 9/11, everyone now realizes that even an organization as loosely tied together as al-Qaeda can put together a sophisticated, coordinated attack.

In fact, managing the 9/11 attacks was simple compared to managing a worldwide production, distribution, marketing, sales, security, and investment organization. Yet non-state, non-territorial narco-traffickers manage that enterprise on a daily basis. There is no doubt that 4GW enemies are capable of highly sophisticated and complex campaigns that potentially exceed even what we have seen to date.

To complicate matters, 4GW will include aspects of earlier generations of war in conjunction with those of the fourth generation. Even as Israelis struggled with the Intifada, they had to be constantly aware that major conventional forces were on their border. Similarly, in Vietnam, the United States and later South Vietnam had to deal with aggressive, effective fourth-generation guerrillas while always being prepared to deal with major North Vietnamese Army conventional forces. Fourth-generation warfare seeks to place an enemy on the horns of this dilemma. This is an intentional approach and goes all the way back to Mao.

Fourth-generation warfare will take place across the spectrum of political, economic, social, and military fields. It is essential that we understand this to analyze how an enemy will conduct a campaign against us. For instance, he may choose a tactical action directly targeted at a major economic target, such as the stock market or international trade. Although the individual action may look purely tactical, it can be part of a campaign to disrupt our economy and reduce the resources we have available to fight.

Only by looking at warfare as a 4GW event can we see the vulnerabilities to weapons of mass destruction. Even a limited biological attack with a contagious agent, such as plague, will result in a shutdown of major segments of air travel, shipping, and trade. Smallpox will require a total quarantine of the affected areas until the incubation period has passed. The potential for billions of dollars in losses to disrupted trade is obvious—as well as years of continuing loss due to subsequent litigation.

Thus, weapons of mass destruction may focus not on physical destruction but on area denial or disruption. The ability of a single person to shut down Senate office buildings and a post office with two anthrax letters is an example of an area-denial weapon.

Disruption can easily be made even more widespread. The use of containerized freight to deliver either a weapon of mass destruction or a high-yield explosive will have even more far-reaching and costly effects on the international trade network than the shutdown of international air routes.

Compared to the problem of inspecting seaborne shipping containers, security for airliners and air freight is easy. Containers are the basic component for the vast majority of international trade today, yet we have no current system to secure or inspect them.

By taking advantage of this vulnerability, terrorists can impose huge economic costs on our society for very little effort on their part. Worse, they don't have to limit their actions to the containers but can also use the ships themselves. Ships flying flags of convenience do so to minimize the ability of governments to regulate or tax them. It is logical to assume that the same characteristics will appeal to terrorists.

Action in one or all of the fields previously mentioned will not be limited to the geographic location (if any) of the antagonists but will take place worldwide. Al-Qaeda has forcefully illustrated this to us. No element of U.S. society, no matter where it is located in the world, is off limits to attack. The Bush administration actions in Afghanistan and against the al-Qaeda network show that effective counters to 4GW must also be worldwide.

Key players will have to give much greater consideration to regional and worldwide audiences in addition to their own national constituencies. On all levels—strategic, operational, and tactical—loosely coordinated groups will organize to oppose even reasonable action. The tremendous size and aggressiveness of the anti-globalization efforts against World Trade Organization meetings in Seattle show how groups with wide-ranging agendas and membership can be coordinated to oppose specific policies. Groups as diverse as unions and environmentalists came together to oppose globalization. As these groups become even more sophisticated in their use of the Internet to coordinate worldwide activity, they will become players in regional and even national crisis.

At the operational level, all an opponent has to move is ideas. He can do so through a wide variety of methods, from email to snail mail to personal courier to messages embedded in classified advertisements. He will try to submerge his communications in the noise of the everyday activity that is an essential part of a modern society. It will be extraordinarily difficult to detect the operational level activities of a 4GW opponent.

### *Tactical Level*

Tactically, fourth-generation war will take place in the complex environment of low-intensity conflict. Every potential opponent has observed the Gulf War, Operation Iraqi Freedom, and Afghanistan. They understand that if you provide America with clear targets, no matter how well fortified, those targets will be destroyed. Just as certainly, they have seen the success of the Somalis and the Sandinistas. They have also seen and are absorbing the continuing lessons of Chechnya, Bosnia, Afghanistan, and Iraq.

In attempting to change the minds of key decision makers, antagonists will use a variety of tactical paths to get their message through to presidents, prime ministers, members of cabinets, legislators, and even voters. Immediate, high-impact messages will probably come via visual media—and the more dramatic and bloody the image, the stronger the message. Longer-term, less immediate but more thought-provoking messages will be passed via business, church, economic, academic, artistic, and even social networks. Although the messages will be based on a strategic theme, the delivery will be by tactical action.

Tactically, 4GW will still involve a mixture of international, transnational, national, and subnational actors. Because the operational planner of a 4GW campaign must use all the tools available to him, we can assume we will have to deal with actors from all these arenas at the tactical level as well. Even more challenging, some will be violent actors and others will be nonviolent.

The term "noncombatant" applies more to conventional conflicts between states than to fourth-generation war involving state and non-state actors. Nonviolent actors, while being legally noncombatants, will be a critical part of the tactical play in 4GW. By using protestors, media interviews, web sites, and other "nonviolent" resources, the 4GW warrior can create tactical dilemmas for his opponents. These will require tactical resources in police, intelligence, military, propaganda, and political spheres to deal with the distractions they create.

Look at the effort the United States expended to overcome the simple al-Qaeda lie "We were beaten while being held prisoner." Despite the fact that we had copies of al-Qaeda training manuals that explicitly direct their operatives to make this statement when captured, it was still presumed to be true by many in the media. As a result, it required an official response. Further, the simple act of the United States creating an information organization to respond to this type of tactical action added fuel to already widespread discussions in the United States about whether anything the government says could be trusted.

Although the United States was eventually able to put this charge behind us, it was a classic example of an economy-of-force effort by al-Qaeda. By planning this response before the conflict started, they were able to ensure that even though their personnel were captured, they still contributed to the fight. Using 4GW techniques, they turned captives into combatants—and tied up major U.S. assets in responding to these charges. Of course, the actual abuse of Iraqi prisoners at Baghdad's notorious Abu Ghraib prison by U.S. forces will make it much more difficult to counter false charges of this sort in the future.

Military action (terrorist, guerrilla or, rarely, conventional) will be tied to the message and targeted at various groups.

Finally, at the tactical level, the 4GW opponent will often use materiel and tools available in everyday society. He will not have to manufacture, transport, store, or maintain his weapons and equipment. He will purchase them in the target country, hijack them en route, or simply use them in place. Although 9/11 made it painfully obvious, numerous truck bombings had already shown that 4GW opponents use commercial sources for destructive weapons.

As we look at protecting ourselves from chemical, biological, radiological, nuclear, and high-yield explosive (CBRNE) weapons, it is important not to overlook the readily available commercial sources of these weapons. The 1984 Bhopal chemical plant disaster killed more people than 9/11 and left many more with serious long-term injuries. Although Bhopal was an industrial accident, it presents a precedent for a devastating chemical attack.

The necessary existence of chemical plants and the movement of toxic industrial chemicals to support our lifestyle ensure that the raw material for a chemical attack is always present. In addition to the widely recognized potential for chemical attack, it is fairly certain that terrorists are today exploring how to use liquid natural gas tankers, fuel trucks, radioactive waste, and other available material for future attacks. These are just a few of the resources available to an intelligent, creative opponent.

### *Timelines, Organizations, Objectives*

The final critical characteristic of 4GW is that its timelines, organizations, and objectives are different from those of earlier generations. Of particular importance is understanding that the timelines are much longer. If you fail to understand this, you fail to understand the magnitude of the challenge presented by a 4GW enemy.

The United States wants to fight short, well-defined wars. We went into Vietnam, Bosnia, Kosovo, Afghanistan, and Iraq convinced we could "clean it up" quickly. In each conflict, our leaders told the people we would be out in a year or so. They felt this was important to convince the American people to go to war. For the United States, a long war is five years. That, in fact, is how long we had a major involvement in Vietnam—from 1966 to 1971. We came in when the war was already being fought and left before it was over. Even then, the U.S. public thought we had been at war too long. In other words, Americans want short wars.

Unfortunately, 4GW wars are long. The Chinese Communists fought for twenty-eight years (1921–49). The Vietnamese Communists fought for thirty years (1945–75). The Sandinistas fought for eighteen years (1961–79). The Palestinians have been resisting Israeli occupation for twenty-nine years so far (1975–2004). The Chechens have been fighting for more than ten years—this time. Al-Qaeda has been fighting for their vision of the world for twenty years, since the founding of MAK in 1984. Numerous other insurgencies in the world have lasted decades. Accordingly, when getting involved in a 4GW fight, we should be planning for a decades-long commitment. From an American point of view, this may well be the single most important characteristic of 4GW.

Next, we need to understand that 4GW organizations are different. Since Mao, 4GW organizations have focused on the movement's long-term political viability rather than its short-term tactical effectiveness. They do not see themselves as military organizations but as webs that generate the political power central to 4GW. Thus, these organizations are unified by ideas. The leadership and the organizations are networked to provide for survivability and continuity when attacked. And the leadership recognizes that their most important function is to sustain the idea and the organizations—not simply to win on the battlefield.

Finally, because of the long timelines, even the objectives are different. Fourth-generation-warfare opponents do not seek to service more targets faster to disrupt an enemy's OODA loop. They do not seek to destroy an opponent's industrial base using the U.S. Air Force's concept of targeting key segments of the opponent's society. Nor do they seek to dislocate the enemy's armed forces so that their decision cycle fails and the enemy collapses. In fact, it is essential to 4GW strategists that the opponent complete his strategic OODA loop—with the resulting decision that the war is too costly to continue.

Fourth-generation-warfare opponents focus on the political aspects of the conflict. Because the ultimate objective is changing the minds of the enemy's political leadership, the intermediate objectives are all milestones in shifting the opinion of the various target audiences. They know that time is on their side. Westerners in general, and Americans in particular, are not known for their patience. We are not a people who think in terms of struggles lasting decades. Fourth-generation-warfare enemies will not seek immediate objectives but a long-term shift in the political will of their enemies. They will accept numerous tactical and operational setbacks in pursuit of that goal.

Col. Harry Summers noted in his book *On Strategy: A Critical Analysis of the Vietnam War* that after the war he told a North Vietnamese colonel that the United States had never been beaten on the battlefield. The North Vietnamese replied, "That is true. It is also irrelevant." It is essential to understand that 4GW opponents do not focus on swift battlefield victories. They focus on a long-term strategic approach. They focus on winning wars, not battles.

In summary, fourth-generation war, like its predecessors, will continue to evolve with society as a whole. As we continue to move from a hierarchical, industrially based society to a networked, information-based society, our political, economic, social, and technical bases will evolve too.

With this evolution comes opportunity and hazard. The key to providing for our security lies in recognizing these changes for what they are. In understanding the changing nature of war, we must not attempt to shape it into something it is not. We cannot force our opponents into a cyberwar that plays to our strengths. They will instead seek to fight the netwar that challenges our weaknesses. Clausewitz's admonition to national leaders remains as valid as ever. We must ensure that our leaders heed it.

CHAPTER 15

# Where to from Here?

From the brief historical survey in Chapter 1, it is clear that 4GW is here to stay. Of even more immediate concern, the United States is currently involved in three 4GW struggles—Iraq, Afghanistan, and our global war on terror. The obvious question is, Where to from here? What must the United States do to deal with fourth-generation warfare? How do we provide security for our people and interests worldwide—particularly now that worldwide includes our homes? How do we win against a 4GW enemy?

The strategic concepts, operational execution, and tactical techniques of fourth-generation war require major changes in the way we think about defense. No longer is defense only about stopping foreign enemies overseas. Fourth-generation-warfare enemies do not see international boundaries as an impediment, nor do they see war as primarily a military function.

To respond, we must integrate all elements of our national power so we can deal effectively with 4GW enemies wherever they appear. In essence, we have to develop our defenses into a functional network rather than a pure hierarchy. Although we can be highly effective against a 4GW enemy, it will require a shift in mindset throughout the government. All changes in a large bureaucracy are hard. Major cultural change is even harder. Cultural change across multiple bureaucratic departments is the hardest of all.

As discussed in the Chapter 1, two visions of the future have evolved. The first—high-technology cyberwar, outlined in "Transformation Planning Guidance" and *Joint Vision 2020* is the current guiding philosophy for the Department of Defense. Given its focus on fighting an overseas, nation-state enemy, it anticipates no real change to DOD's organization to fight a 4GW opponent. Although the concepts talk about networks, they really mean the technology, not the organizations. They still view warfare as taking place overseas and homeland security as a domestic matter.

*JV 2020* means big defense projects with correspondingly large budgets. Its focus on technology and information superiority requires massive investment in information technology and high-tech weapons systems. Such largesse has hundreds of proponents in Congress, thousands of businesses, and millions of average Americans concerned for their jobs and way of life. Further, it means business and profits as usual for the vast bureaucracy and industry that supports our current approach to defense. The Department of Defense and the defense industry have huge sunk costs in equipment, training, and facilities designed to fight 2GW and 3GW opponents.

Under the rubric of "transformation," DOD is assuring America that it is in fact changing itself to deal with the enemies of the future. Yet when you go to the official DOD Transformation web sites (www.defenselink.mil/transformation or www.oft.osd.mil), it is obvious that DOD transformation envisions only one segment of the spectrum of conflict—high-technology conventional war.

The Department of Defense was conceived and designed to fight a massive conventional war by mobilizing large segments of the male population and managing the massive U.S. industrial base. *JV 2020* and its successor, transformation, are simply high-technology versions of this concept. Expanding beyond this limited but expensive role will require a major cultural shift within DOD.

Even more alarming, these "new" DOD concepts are about winning battles, not winning wars. They are based on the idea that if we service enough targets, we will win the battles. If we win the battles, the enemy will quit. As soon as he does, the war is over. In fact, as we painfully discovered in Vietnam and are rediscovering in Iraq and Afghanistan, you can win the battles and neither win nor even end the war.

In contrast to simply maintaining and marshaling massive assets to destroy enemy targets, 4GW, or netwar, requires the government to focus the intellectual capital of our people. We have to coordinate with the entire spectrum of agencies that have a role in these complex wars. Rather than just winning the battles, we must have a plan for winning the war.

This is much trickier. As we have discovered in Iraq and Afghanistan, to rebuild the enemy country as a democracy, we have to be prepared to assist in establishing a fully functioning government. This requires experts in every field.

Fortunately, the U.S. government has such experts. Unfortunately, we have no coherent organization to find and deploy them. Even if we can push our bureaucracy to find and deploy the right people, they still work in their individual departmental stovepipes.

Beyond getting the people to the field, we have to develop genuine networks to tie the various agencies together in the field and in Washington. We have to become organizationally networked to overcome the inertia and restriction of information flow characteristic of our 19th-century bureaucracies.

Developing those networks requires major changes in the way we train, promote, and employ our people across the government. It requires focusing on human aspects of society: languages, history, cultures, internal and international relationships. It also requires streamlining acquisition and aid, building fewer high-tech weapons systems, understanding the basics of a society, and reducing the walls between bureaucracies, to make them more agile and capable of genuine interagency operations.

Such changes will be extraordinarily difficult. It means uncertainty for every element of the national security structure: military services, civilian agencies, and the defense industry. Dozens of constituencies are threatened by the shifts in budget required by 4GW. In contrast, there is no identifiable constituency for the major shifts in personnel and budget required to deal with this type of war.

Yet from the brief historical survey earlier in this book, it is clear that our enemies have learned that only 4GW has a chance of succeeding against the massive conventional superiority of the United States. Anyone who has watched modern conflict on CNN can see that the United States easily dominates high-technology war. Although Americans may applaud the standoff range and videotapes of weapons shown in the news coverage of these conflicts, our enemies around the world see the futility of presenting any kind of target to American forces. They know it will be destroyed. In contrast, the daily video of our soldiers struggling to bring order to Iraq, the difficulty they have with unconventional forces and attacks, and the problems in understanding and establishing a government provide a living example of how to fight the United States.

Therefore, although major constituencies in the United States have an interest in perfecting high-technology war, none of our most dangerous enemies sees it as a viable way to compete against the United States. We simply have too great a lead, and the weapons cost too much. We have to give up our cyberwar fantasy and understand that our most dangerous enemies are those who are preparing to fight a 4GW conflict.

To respond to 4GW enemies overseas requires a genuine, effective interagency process. Currently, the United States has no formal process. Although we created effective interagency responses on occassion during Vietnam, the early phases of Somalia, and a very few other times, these successes have always been based on the personalities of the key people in charge of the agencies involved. It has never been a systematic approach but rather one of sheer chance that all the agencies involved were led by people who understood 4GW and the coordination required to fight it.

The normal U.S. response to 4GW has been uncoordinated and disjointed. With no unifying strategy, each agency performs its functions within its stovepipe, as it sees fit, often at cross purposes with the others. Fourth-generation attacks are coordinated across the spectrum of human activity: political, military, economic, and security. Our responses must be coordinated across these spheres too—but we currently have no mechanism to make this happen.

One of the most glaring examples of this is the short-term view all agencies take to these conflicts. The armed forces appear to be the worst, by insisting on limiting tours of duty to periods as brief as three months and never longer than one year, even during a conflict. In Iraq, civilian agencies have adopted the same policies. Worse, all agencies seem to see these wars as a distraction from their main bureaucratic functions. The unstated position seems to be that these wars cannot be allowed to interfere with normal bureaucratic practices, particularly not personnel policy or budgeting. Thus, we are fighting decades-long wars with personnel who spend at most a year in the fight and a budgeting process that looks less than a year ahead.

Clearly, we need a major cultural change in the U.S. government. Defending against 4GW enemies cannot be divided neatly into domestic and foreign, military and civil operations. Rather, we have to create effective interagency structures to deal with this new threat.

Those reluctant to change will note that North Korea still has huge sunk costs in the hardware, training, and organizations suitable for 2GW and must maintain those forces to keep the regime in power. They will claim we must maintain the forces capable of dealing with this large, Industrial-Age army. In fact, the mixture of second-, third-, and fourth-generation enemies obviously creates significant challenges for our national defense. Not all future conflicts will be fought primarily using 4GW.

However, if we can transition to 4GW, we can deal with the mixed threat. History has repeatedly demonstrated that nations organized and prepared to deal with an emerging generation of war can defeat those of earlier generations. To date, 4GW organizations have fared well against previous generations, but the converse is not true. If we do not transition to 4GW, we will not do well against those threats either.

Although the transition will be challenging, it can be done. It will require a major shift in culture within the government—and will likely take a generation to accomplish. Given the constituencies that support cyberwar throughout the government and society, it is too big a problem to attack directly. We must first change the culture within the national security community to raise a generation prepared to fight 4GW. These people will then drive the shifts necessary within their departments.

Further, a cultural and organizational shift to an interagency approach is vital. Only such a shift can provide the driving force behind the two aspects necessary for defense against a 4GW opponent: defending the homeland and learning to win wars instead of battles.

These are somewhat different problems. The first, securing the homeland, is a constant. It is a permanent strategic problem that will evolve continually. The second, winning a war overseas, is more immediate but somewhat episodic, and each challenge will have unique aspects.

### *Securing the Homeland*

The challenge in securing the homeland is to establish an interagency process that can function indefinitely against nonspecific and widely varied threats. The formation of the Department of Homeland Security (DHS) was a fundamental step. It brings together twenty-two of the key agencies needed for this mission. Supporting this has been the formation of the Terrorist Threat Integration Center (TTIC), to integrate the intelligence efforts of the various branches of government.

In the same way DOD and the services slowly learned to work together, the civilian agencies involved in homeland security must do so too. However, their coordination problems are even greater, because of the various departments involved. When the Department of Defense was formed, it had to absorb only two departments—the army and the navy. In addition, the two had essentially the same mission: defending the United States from overseas attack. Despite the apparently simple task, it still took more than forty-five years and multiple changes of the law to successfully integrate DOD. The task of integrating the twenty-two agencies with different missions into the Department of Homeland Security will be much more challenging.

Complicating the coordination problem further, many of the departments critical to effective homeland security are outside DHS. The Justice Department, Central Intelligence Agency, and Defense Department are all vital but independent entities.

With all these complications, we need an effective, tested process for interagency coordination. Fortunately, we have such a process. Presidential Decision Directive 56 (PDD 56), *Managing Complex Contingency Operations,* was written to provide a process and organization for coordinating the efforts of all U.S. agencies in complex operations short of war.

PDD 56 was developed in response to difficulties the United States encountered in Somalia, Bosnia, and northern Iraq. Signed in 1997, it was designed to deal with "complex contingency operations" overseas. In fact, the PDD states it does not apply to "domestic disaster relief . . . nor to . . . counter-terrorism and hostage-rescue operations and international armed conflict."[1]

However, the disclaimer about not using it for crises in the United States was written before 9/11 and the new understanding of the threat to the homeland. Once we understand that 4GW is network-based and does not respect borders of any type, we will see the need to always apply an interagency approach. Given the long timelines of 4GW, we know our homeland security problem will be a constant factor of life for decades to come. Therefore, our interagency response must keep evolving and improving. It, too, must be constant.

PDD 56 provides a superb starting point for processes and procedures to coordinate the wide variety of federal, state, local, and private agencies that must be involved in the day-to-day defense of our homeland—and in the response to any successful attacks. The combination of building the relationships among and within the agencies and developing a formal interagency process are both the most essential and most challenging actions we have to take.

### *Winning the Wars*

Now it's time to turn to the second half of our security problem: winning wars. Fortunately, the primary steps for winning wars instead of just battles are the same as those for securing the homeland. We need to develop interagency planning and execution each time we choose to fight. Whether we are seeking regime change or a small-scale stabilization operation, we must learn to function as a practical network.

History has shown our fourth-generation opponents how to fight us. Fortunately, it has also shown us how a democracy can defeat such an enemy. The British experiences in Malaya, Kenya, Oman, and Borneo all show that an integrated, coordinated, interagency approach can win the war of ideas rather than just winning battles in the field.

To achieve success, we must be prepared to fight across the spectrum of political, economic, social, and military spheres. We not only have to win battles, we have to fill the vacuum behind them—starting with rapidly establishing security. This means just not police and security forces but also the court system and prison system to support them. We have to establish banking, currency, customs, public health organizations, public sanitation, air traffic control, business regulation, a system of taxation, and every other process needed for running a modern society. And all of these must be done in conjunction with the people of that nation. We know that solutions imposed from outside rarely remain in effect once the occupying power leaves.

Although some will claim such activities have nothing to do with waging war, history indicates that to win wars, a nation has to be prepared to do exactly that. After World War II, we executed those functions in both Germany and Japan. The British didn't leave Malaya until the Malaysians were confidently running all aspects of their societies. Those are clear examples of winning the wars after winning the battles.

These requirements greatly exceed the range of knowledge and skill available within the Department of Defense. Therefore, we need to adopt the interagency approach to planning and execution, even in combat, proposed in PDD 56.

We must understand the long timelines involved. Using PDD 56 as a starting point, we can develop a genuine interagency system for coordinating our actions across governmental and non-governmental organizations over many years. Then we have to train the people to make that interagency system function and simultaneously educate them as to why the systems are a good way to govern. Like all major changes in large bureaucracies, it will take almost a generation before our efforts to reform are fully effective. However, 4GW wars last decades, so our efforts to defeat them and establish a functioning society will last that long too.

The exception will be where U.S. policy makers decide our strategic position does not require a viable nation to replace the regime we destroy. In that case, we can win the battles, pack up, and come home. Of course, what happened to Afghanistan after they drove the Russians out illustrates that we may then have to be prepared to go back in and repeat the operation periodically, to prevent the ungoverned space being used as a terrorist haven.

The fact that both domestic vigilance and overseas fights require the same organization is actually an advantage to our government. We can learn from each other. Each department has its own culture and must adjust in its own way to the challenges of 4GW. However, the military services are uniquely positioned to lead that process. They are organized to educate and train; they have a large number of young, thoughtful officers and NCOs; and they have a clear charter to deal with 4GW threats. They should step out to help lead the transition within the government necessary to protect our citizens.

To initiate the transition, the military services must take three major steps. First, we have to focus on people rather than technology. Second, we have to honestly analyze the threat and organize our forces and processes accordingly. Finally, we have to realize that no one predicts the future with perfect accuracy, and we must therefore build flexibility into our forces.

### *Focus on Our People*

The first and by far most important shift we must make is to stop emphasizing technology and start focusing on people. Technology does not solve problems; people do. This sounds incredibly simple. It fact, it is an oft-repeated slogan in DOD. Unfortunately, it is mostly lip service. Note all the emphasis in *JV 2020,* "Network-Centric Warfare," and the "revolution in military affairs" discussions on replacing 1990s weapons systems, while there is no discussion on replacing our 1890s personnel system. Even the "transformation" discussion is primarily about technology. So far, there has been little discussion or study into what makes effective leaders in a chaotic, 4GW environment.

As we have seen from our brief study of the development of 4GW, technology is largely irrelevant to this sort of long-term struggle. In China, Vietnam, Nicaragua, Intifada I, the USSR-Afghan War, and Chechnya I, the losing side had superior technology but had no concept of how to apply it to this new generation of war. What really matters are well-trained, intelligent, creative people guided by a coherent long-term strategic approach tailored to 4GW.

Yet, within DOD, almost all our resources are focused on technology and hardware. Although the services repeat the mantra that "people are our most precious resource," their personnel policies make it perfectly clear that people are not considered a key part of the solution. In fact, the services tenaciously defend their antiquated personnel systems.

To ensure that we recruit, train, educate, and retain the personnel we need to fight in the 21st century, we have to fix two major problems. First, we have to reform our personnel system. Second, we need to drastically reduce the size of our bureaucracy. In particular, we must cut the number of field-grade officers. Our outdated manpower policies, combined with the excessive size of the service, joint, and DOD bureaucracies, ensure that we cannot effectively transition to 4GW. These are the most important reforms DOD can make—and the majority of this chapter will be dedicated to personnel reform.

Before suggesting what needs to be done to prepare our personnel to fight a 4GW conflict, it is important to understand why the current personnel system does not promote the type of free-thinking, aggressive, risk-taking officer needed to lead in such a conflict.

Consider the 1890s personnel system we currently use. This is not a typographical error. Our current military personnel system essentially flows from reforms instituted at the turn of the 19th century by Secretary of War Elihu Root. Using the theories of Frederick Taylor and Max Weber about bureaucratic personnel systems and requirements, Root fought to replace a personnel system that was virtually unchanged since the Revolutionary War.

Taylor and Weber's theories strove to refine the organization and personnel policies needed to run the emerging industrial giants of the late 1800s. They had to devise a method to coordinate the activities of large factories, based on decisions made centrally. As the nation moved from individual artisans to mass production, we needed to learn how to manage these new industrial companies. Taylor and Weber developed the personnel and organizational theories to guide that progress.

As the U.S. Army moved into the Industrial Age, Secretary of War Root used this industrial model to reform its personnel policies. This was necessary if the army were to evolve from a frontier constabulary to a modern industrial army. Secretary Root's reforms were absolutely right for their time. Unfortunately, they are now a hundred years old, but they still form the core of our personnel policies.

The most damaging aspect of our manpower system is its purely top-down evaluation system. This system grooms people to function well in a ponderous, hierarchical bureaucracy. Each service member's promotion is based purely on the evaluation of his boss and his boss's boss. Thus, the system relies on this single top-down view to choose its future leaders.

We loudly proclaim we want risk-taking networkers. What we actually do sharply contradicts that. Our day-to-day system is a hierarchical, risk-averse bureaucracy. For the majority of his career, an officer is working within a box in an organization chart and actively discouraged from "getting outside his lane." Somehow, an officer who has been groomed by this stovepipe system is supposed to suddenly thrive when put into a network in a tactical situation. This defies common sense. As VAdm. Herb Browne used to say, "What you do speaks so loudly, I cannot hear what you say."

Although there are numerous examples of officers who have succeeded in this system and are highly effective in a network, the odds are stacked heavily against them. Consider the problem. With our vastly inflated performance evaluation systems, a single report that uses faint praise rather than enthusiastic endorsement will finish an officer's career. Thus an innovative, risk-taking, outside-the-box officer needs to run into only one risk-averse, in-the-box, control-oriented boss to have his career terminated. To rise to the top, he has to be lucky enough not to run into such an individual in decades of service. Mathematically, this system has to result in an ever more risk-averse population that promotes people like themselves.

A second major problem is that we still use a manpower system designed to select and groom people to run an Industrial-Age bureaucratic organization. We somehow expect people selected by that system to excel in a networked world.

It may seem incredible that a hundred-year-old personnel system could survive, but it has. For a detailed discussion of how it evolved—and has sustained itself despite major efforts at reform—read Donald Vandergriff's *The Path to Victory: America's Army and the Revolution in Human Affairs.*

The basic weakness of our current personnel system is that it is a hundred years old and grooms people to run organizations based on concepts from another century. Unfortunately, that is not the only weakness. The bureaucratic model itself is a major problem. In this model, "career development" requires frequent moves and a wide variety of duties. The idea is to ensure that every person has the broad range of skills necessary to function at the top of the organization. It focuses on creating generalists rather than experts.

This model, combined with the huge growth in staffs and headquarters, means that a combat arms officer will spend less than twenty-five percent of his career training for combat. This is the inevitable outcome of our current manpower system and a military bureaucracy grown way beyond the needs of the combat forces. The majority of our jobs for field-grade officers are in high-level headquarters—most of them not part of our warfighting organizations. There are simply too few combat-related jobs compared to the number of officers on active duty.

Further exacerbating the problem is the typical officer's career pattern. It consists of series of short (one to three year) postings in a wide variety of jobs. These alternate between service in his specialty, joint service, and staff service. Although careers will vary somewhat, many ground combat-arms officers under this system arrive at the critical billet of battalion commander (about fifteen years of service) with fewer than six years in operational units—even counting their time as a staff officer in operational units. Their actual command time in operational units will often be limited to two or three years of the fifteen active duty. They are, in effect, amateurs by profession. They never spend enough time in any job to become an expert.

Think about that. Imagine being involved in a major lawsuit. Would you accept a lawyer who had spent only six of the last fifteen years practicing law, and only two or three of those in the first chair? I wouldn't. Yet our current personnel system places America's sons and daughters under the combat command of officers with that little time focused on learning war. Current career patterns ensure that they have a wide variety of amateur-level skills—but are truly expert at none. It is imperative that we rework career patterns so that our officers become professionals rather than today's amateurs. The U.S. Army has started a program to increase the time its combat arms field grade officers spend in operational units, the other services need to follow suit.

Unfortunately, our current manpower policies exacerbate the problem. They ensure that almost fifty percent of the officers in any unit leave every year. With this kind of turbulence as the norm, units cannot develop the trust needed for a networked organization.

In effect, we have combined the worst of bureaucratic manpower systems with top-down reporting and rapid personnel turnover. The result is that our people are always trying to get to know each other and learn how they will react in various situations. Thus, units never reach their full potential.

Short and infrequent tours in the operating forces mean the officers responsible for training, testing, and leading the units are essentially amateurs. This means units train harder, simply because the commander lacks the practical experience to train smarter. The resulting high personnel tempo, combined with the very high operational tempo of our units, drives people out. More damaging than even the high operations tempo is that organizations lacking experience are less confident and suffer more frustration; they don't have any fun. This results in both officers and enlisted leaving the service—further exacerbating our personnel problems.

The top-down reporting system, short tours, and high turnover of key personnel are not the end of the damage caused by our current manpower and training systems.

We also fail to test the units in realistic ways. The key to individual and unit growth comes from operating together under combat-like conditions. Short of war, the only way to truly create those conditions is through realistic, evaluated, free-play tactical exercises. Unfortunately, today, instead of realistic, free-play exercises, we use mostly scripted exercises with no chance of losing. These are supposed to prepare our leaders to succeed in the most complex, hostile environment known to man: conflict with other men. It is as if a team prepared for the Super Bowl by playing touch football against a junior varsity team.

In short, our current personnel system is antithetical to 4GW. Designed prior to World War I, it encourages the type of top-down, risk-averse leadership that led to the disasters of 1914–18. The end result of the last hundred years of our bureaucratic, egalitarian personnel system is career paths that cripple a force fighting a 4GW enemy. Units and individuals are always in turmoil. Career patterns emphasize exposure to a broad range of skills. Variety rather than mastery is the requirement for promotion. Today, we match our professional amateurs against a wide array of ever more adept enemies.

The manpower policies of all U.S. government agencies have similar problems. All have structures and policies rooted in the bureaucracies of the early 1900s. If they are to assist in defending America against the broad-spectrum threat of 4GW, each must change to function in a networked world.

### *Reforms*

To fix our personnel system, we need to reform how we evaluate, train, and educate our personnel. We must also extend tours of duty, so units can learn to function effectively. Given the urgency of the requirement to change our antiquated personnel system, we should start with reforms that can be accomplished most quickly.

First, we must replace the top-down fitness report system with a 360-degree system. Second, free-play exercises in chaotic, uncertain environments must become an integral part of our training program. Finally, we must greatly lengthen each tour of duty and make the majority of them with operating forces rather than with headquarters.

#### *Evaluation*

The first step is achieved by adopting a 360-degree performance evaluation. It is designed to provide a complete view of the officer evaluated. We have already discussed how the current top-down evaluation neither provides a comprehensive view of the officer nor rewards traits necessary to succeed in war. A 360-degree system would be a major step in overcoming those deficiencies in our evaluation system.

Under this system, each person is evaluated by his boss, peers, and subordinates. The overall grade is a compilation of input from these sources. Thus it provides a true 360-degree view of the officer evaluated. To do well, a leader not only has to please his boss but also gain the respect of his peers and genuinely lead, rather than drive, his subordinates.

In fact, in a truly networked organization, the relationships will change in a tactical situation. Sometimes a junior leader will have the knowledge and be in the key location and become, in effect, the person running the operation. This requires genuine trust among superiors, subordinates, and peers. A 360-degree report would evaluate those relationships essential in building an effective 4GW combat team.

Some will object that this will be a popularity contest, that we shouldn't trust an officer's career to one of his sergeants or junior officers. Yet if we trust the lives of our people to those same individuals, how can we possibly not trust our careers to them?

Overcoming a hundred years of ingrained bureaucratic hierarchy will be difficult. It will require aggressive, focused efforts from our top military leaders. In fact, given the demonstrated ability of DOD to resist change, it may take legislative action similar to the Nunn-Warner legislation.

However, once the decision is made, the administrative process of shifting to a 360-degree system should not be lengthy or expensive. Many civilian firms already use 360-degree reporting. As any search of the Internet will show, the software and processes already exist. Even better, they run on commercially available hardware. DOD will not have to invent anything. In fact, by drawing on our reservists, DOD will find many who already use or manage a 360-degree reporting system in their civilian jobs. We can draw on a wealth of experience to ease our transition to this more effective and equitable system.

Frankly, this is why performance evaluation is the challenge I would tackle it first. It can be accomplished relatively quickly, with relatively small expense—once we accept that our 19th-century personnel system simply cannot apply in the 21st century.

A 360-degree performance evaluation will largely eliminate the officer who is focused only on his career and insure that our forces are composed of men and women who seek what is best for the unit and the country rather than themselves. We all know you cannot fool your peers or subordinates. They can see when an individual is focused on his career rather than his mission. Just as important, they will know those officers who have genuine integrity, and that, too, will be reflected in the reports.

The 360-degree report will ensure that officers place the mission first and have the moral integrity we require. Unfortunately, it will not ensure that they can function effectively in the chaotic environment of combat—particularly the unstructured and uncertain environment of 4GW. This leads us to the second reform to our manpower policies: free-play exercises.

*Training*

This reform will be more expensive and will take more time than changing our performance evaluation system. It will require major investments in training facilities, trainers, and first-class opposition forces.

However, it is essential. Studies of military leaders and first responders show that the most effective tactical decision makers rely on recognitional decision making. Simply put, they have the experience to recognize the situation for what it is and make rapid, correct decisions to deal with the uncertainty. Just as important, they also know when rapid, decisive action is the wrong thing to do.

Only by making or observing decisions under pressure in realistic situations can an officer develop the *coup d'oeil* essential for recognitional decision making. Our current, methodical, systematic "staff planning process" works well in the scripted exercises we use in training but breaks down quickly in actual combat operations. Only frequent free-play exercises that match officers' decision-making skills and processes against a thinking enemy can develop the leaders we need.

Further, training at the tactical level will provide the basis for understanding chaos, uncertainty, and the complexity of 4GW. Only those who learn how to build and guide effective networks will thrive in such an environment. These are the people who will become senior officers who can deal with the operational and strategic issues of 4GW.

Although the trainers and opposing forces (OPFOR; the bad guys) for such a system must come out of active duty forces, these billets will provide superb training for 4GW warfare. In essence, the OPFOR will play the role of the enemy and, to be effective, must learn to think and act like him. They should be handpicked from among those who have proven themselves in previous exercises. These billets should be considered career enhancing. We need our best to further challenge the "good guys."

Then, to augment our best, we should hire some foreign nationals to ensure that we throw different cultural problems at the players. Finally, we should hire either police experts or reformed gang members to introduce the criminal element to our problems. The cost is worth it, because free play will enhance each individual's education in warfare rather than in the bureaucratic processes of a joint staff.

We have, in fact, taken some of these steps, particularly at the U.S. Army's Joint Readiness Training Center at Fort Polk, Louisiana. Unfortunately, despite the nearly $450-billion-dollar defense budget, the United States has built only one such free-play facility. Compounding the limited availability of these facilities, the units that do participate are often manned specifically to participate in this training, then broken up shortly after its completion to provide the bodies necessary for our highly "efficient" individual replacement system. Thus, although individual soldiers benefit greatly from the training, units often do not stay together long enough to maximize the benefits.

We need to create multiple facilities—perhaps not as elaborate as our current Joint Readiness Training Center—but they must be at every major training base. Then we have to design genuine 4GW free-play exercises, with three, four, five, or more sides involved in the exercise—so that it approximates the complexity of the situations in which our leaders will find themselves. Finally, once those units are trained we need to keep them together for much longer periods.

Such an exercise will be difficult to design, more costly to execute, and will require our best operators to run and evaluate it. Although these sound like reasons not to attempt such exercises, all but the increased cost are distinct advantages over our current systems. The challenge of designing, executing, and evaluating these more complex exercises will produce more professional forces. Unlike so many current costly DOD programs, this one would pay dividends immediately and keep paying dividends throughout the careers of those trained.

In addition to these known training methods, we must examine innovative approaches. One such approach is a platoon-level exercise conducted for the lieutenants at the Marine Corps' Basic School. In this exercise, the lieutenants move into a real town to assist the "local authorities" with security against an insurgent group. The town is the exercise site, and the townspeople are part of the play. Needless to say, the exercise is free play and presents lots of surprises to all involved.

Another promising possibility is the use of persistent, massive, multiplayer online games to provide genuine free-play environments. Such a system would provide the unique prospect of fighting against self-organizing, loosely allied networks. Although we will have to provide a core of trained OPFOR, we should also open the game to volunteer civilian game players who simply wish to claim bragging rights for defeating U.S. forces in a game. It will provide all the uncertainty, multiple sides, shifting alliances, and unpredictability we actually face in the streets of Iraq and countryside of Afghanistan.

Such games, although difficult to develop, will provide training at the tactical, operational, and strategic levels. Given their inherently distributive nature, they can involve all members of the interagency teams in the game play and, like all simulations, stimulate the team-building process.

These games would also be essential in training more senior officers, both as commanders and key staff officers. First, those officers will have to develop the commander's guidance and strategic/operational goals and measures going into the game. They will also have to develop the metrics to see how they are progressing—across the range of political, economic, social, and security areas. By conducting regular reviews of how the games unfold, they can begin to learn what works and what doesn't in building and using the friendly networks. By keeping the games truly free play, our leaders and staffs will also have to deal with the inevitable surprises presented by aggressive, thinking enemies.

Simply put, we have to be as creative in training as our 4GW enemies have been in their operations.

*Education*

The third major reform is to change how we educate our officers. Warfare draws more intensely on all human skills than any other activity. Yet, starting with our service academies, we focus on technical education for our officers. Although we obviously need some officers with advanced degrees in science and engineering, it is much more important to have officers with advanced degrees in history and foreign studies.

Dozens of authors have attempted to discern what characteristics great military leaders have had in common. In an American field as diverse as Grant, Lee, Sherman, Patton, Eisenhower, Nimitz, Halsey, and numerous others, one trait is consistent: all were serious students of military history. It is time to ensure that our officers value the study of history as highly as the study of technology. The only way to do so is to ensure it is valued by our personnel system.

*Longer Tours*

The fourth and most difficult reform is to lengthen all tours with operational organizations. The difficulty arises because the ratio of billets in operational forces to billets in non-operational forces is the exact reverse of what it should be. As our forces have shrunk, our headquarters have grown—almost exponentially. The result is that it is mathematically impossible for any significant percentage of our officers to spend the majority of their time with the operating forces.

Not only does this cripple our ability to prepare officers for 4GW, the sheer size of the bureaucracy is a major problem in itself. History has shown us that large bureaucracies are extremely slow to innovate. It has also shown that monopolies are inherently inefficient. Yet the DOD is a hierarchical, bureaucratic monopoly—essentially the world's largest since the fall of the Soviet Union. Almost by definition, bureaucracies strive to preserve the status quo. The larger the bureaucracy, the more effective it is at derailing change—particularly change that threatens its power. Why do we think such an organization can beat a network?

Although inertia is a major problem with a bureaucracy, the primary problem is its voracious appetite for field-grade officers. As the staffs within DOD have grown, particularly the joint staffs, the number of general and field-grade officers has swollen, while our forces have shrunk. The result is that officers are promoted more quickly and spend a great deal less time learning their basic combat fields.

Instead, they spend much more time on large joint staffs, where decision making is limited to key staff officers—and then only after hours of PowerPoint briefs. Many of the joint staff officers spend their time compiling the information and building the briefs—essentially, glorified clerks. Somehow this "joint" duty is supposed to prepare them for making decisions rapidly in a free-flowing tactical environment.

The only solution is to drastically reduce the number of field-grade and general officers on active duty. The goal should be a fifty percent reduction. We can do this in two ways. First, we must make deep cuts in the number and seniority of the staffs. Second, we should stop using unrestricted line officers to fill numerous jobs that can be done better by professional, focused, enlisted servicemen and warrant officers: in short, those jobs that require long-term focus, education, and expertise.

Give these servicemen opportunities for education and long-term stability, both in their jobs and their geographic locations. Also, raise their pay to reflect the exceptional professional expertise and education they bring to these billets. Their continuity and focus will be an improvement on the performance we currently get from rotating field-grade amateurs through the same billets. In addition, wherever feasible, we need to replace field-grade officers with civilians. The basic thrust should be to move field-grade officers out of those fields not related to warfighting.

More challenging will be major reductions in joint staffs. Many will claim that each and every staff is essential and must be preserved. In fact, under no less an authority than Gen. Colin Powell, the military was considering reducing the CINCdoms (now Combatant Commanders) to only three—PACOM, LANTCOM, and USACOM. These three CINCs would divide the world—and would do so without major increases in staff. Unfortunately, the Gulf War erupted before this idea could be thoroughly explored, and post–Gulf War, it was politically infeasible to do away with CENTCOM.

To cut those staffs, we will have to drastically reduce the amount of work each staff is doing. The people on the joint staffs are working hard—striving to accomplish the wide variety of tasks assigned in the hierarchical, bureaucratic system we employ. Clearly, we must move to the flatter, networked staffs of an Information-Age organization.

One start is to simply trust our people. We currently have "experts" on each staff whose sole task is to check the work of experts on the next lower staff. Plans or recommendations of junior commanders and staffs are checked by experts at half a dozen levels before they are acted on. The only solution is to trust our officers and decentralize decision making.

By cutting the number of staffs, replacing field-grade officers with highly professional senior enlisted, and pushing decision making down, we should be able to reduce the total number of field-grade officer billets by more than fifty percent. With the reduced demand for field grade, we can push back our promotion point to major or lieutenant commander a couple of years. Company-grade officers will spend more time in the operating forces and, once promoted to field grade, will spend a great deal more time in the operating forces than on high-level staffs.

Our primary task to prepare for 4GW warfare is to select and groom individuals who can function effectively in a free-flowing, networked environment characteristic of this type of war. Only aggressive, well-thought-out reforms focused on raising this type of officer will allow us to build effective 4GW organizations. We have to abandon our top-down, hierarchical 1890s personnel system and adopt a networked system focused on the demonstrated ability to thrive in realistic exercises.

Free-play exercises, 360-degree performance evaluations, and major cuts in officer strength will be opposed as risky. Historically, all attempts to change our personnel system have been opposed as "risky." In fact, they do present a major risk—to the status quo.

It is interesting that DOD is reluctant to incur risk by changing personnel policies yet never seems to fear risk when fielding advanced technology weapons. This is more puzzling given that history proves advanced technology does not ensure an organization can function in a new generation of war. All the technological progress in the world cannot drive an organization to move to the next generation of war—only its people can do that. The real risk lies in not changing our personnel system.

Fixing our manpower system is the most critical and most difficult task we face in reforming our military. However, by its nature, it is inwardly focused. We know war is a contest of wills—and requires two or more combatants. Therefore, at the same time we are modernizing our personnel policies, we must take a hard, honest look at our potential enemies.

# CHAPTER 16

# Evaluating the Threat

Given the collapse of the Soviet Union, one would think reevaluating the threat to the United States is an obvious requirement. Yet in none of our key documents has DOD provided a coherent view of the nations or entities that are threats to the United States. The new Office of Transformation has a number of documents that lay out vague discussions of what the enemy will look like, but nothing specific. Typical of them is the following: "Transformation is a process that shapes the changing nature of military competition and cooperation through new combinations of concepts, capabilities, people and organizations that exploit our nation's advantages and protect us against our asymmetric vulnerabilities to sustain our strategic position, which helps underpin peace and stability in the world."[1]

Transformation's predecessor, *JV 2020,* was slightly better. It provided a couple of paragraphs on what future threats look like but then failed to discuss how to address them. Finally, several draft DOD and joint staff documents acknowledge the fundamental changes to the types of enemies we face. Yet none attempts to conduct a systematic analysis of what our current and future enemies look like, so we can structure and train our forces accordingly.

Because we have failed to quantify the enemy, we are adopting a "capabilities-based" approach to defense. This seems to say that we are going to focus on the improving capabilities we have and assume they will suffice to defeat future threats. Unfortunately, this is a very inwardly focused effort—and more likely to support organizations that already possess a certain capability than to develop new capabilities for the types of enemies we actually face around the world.

Any honest threat evaluation, though a strategic imperative, faces a great deal of bureaucratic resistance. To the average citizen, the lack of an accurate estimate of the potential enemy would seem to make it impossible to determine how to spend a DOD budget of more than $450 billion a year. Unfortunately, that is not the case within DOD. This is true for a number of reasons.

First, and most mundane, is simple bureaucratic inertia. There is an old saying, "Bureaucracies do what bureaucracies do. When that doesn't work, they do more of it." In keeping with their industrial heritage, bureaucracies are designed to perform a certain function in a certain way—and not to deviate from that path. This is how industrial organizations achieved efficiency. Even without rapid communication, all the far-flung entities could continue to operate and produce quality products, because they knew the other entities would continue to produce their parts the way they were designed. There was no room for innovation.

This is certainly the case with DOD. The department was established to defend the nation against the armies, navies, and air forces of other nations. It is designed to fight a second- or third-generation enemy. Shifting to fight a completely different kind of enemy, using a way of war alien to the United States, is a tremendous demand to make of any bureaucracy. It is even more demanding for one that controls massive resources central to the political influence of many members of government.

This brings us to the second reason. There is a huge constituency not to change. Not only is this constituency huge, it is wide-ranging and influential. It includes entire organizations within DOD, major segments of the defense industry, and entire regions of the country that rely heavily on defense spending. Each represents major political constituencies and works hard through its congressional representatives to protect its purpose for existence or livelihood.

Third, segments within each service will be winners or losers depending on the outcome of any threat study. For instance, if we determine there is no viable new fighter program in the world, the air force air-superiority fighter budget could well be cut, and the influence of the fighter community will decrease.*

In short, our nation has a huge investment in weapons, training, production capability, intellectual property, and so on, focused on defeating a 2GW or 3GW conventional enemy. Obviously, many people have a great deal to lose to an honest study that points out that those generations of war have passed and that the fourth generation needs different skills and tools.

Finally, there is the normal and healthy disagreement about what the threat is. Depending on one's education, experience, and beliefs, one can argue that despite the lessons of recent history, the real threat is the conventional enemies envisioned by *JV 2020.* This allows those who make this argument to ignore the highly unconventional enemies that have succeeded in 4GW and are currently challenging us in Iraq, Afghanistan, and the worldwide war on terror.

Despite the conflicting views within the United States, any thinking enemy has realized that only 4GW has a chance of success against our overwhelming conventional power. They know that reliance on the tactics, techniques, and equipment of earlier generations of war will lead to their inevitable defeat. In fact, they have watched such forces suffer battlefield defeat in living color on TV—not once, but twice.

* In fact, the air force has renamed the F-22 fighter the F/A-22. Despite having sold and designed it purely as an air superiority fighter, they have seen that the utility of such a single-mission platform is virtually nonexistent. Although it will deliver little ordnance and the changes that allow it to do even that will not come along for years, the air force is now trumpeting the F-22 as a fighter attack aircraft—hence "F/A-22." Much like that other large bureaucracy, the Soviet Union, DOD has learned that naming something so can make it so—at least for bureaucratic and budgetary purposes.

Yet, for good reason, some of our potential enemies still retain large 2GW forces. They require those forces to maintain internal order, both by providing a politically reliable armed force to suppress their own citizens and by providing employment to many young men while focusing their frustrations against an external target rather than against the regime. In addition, the same bureaucratic inertia that affects the United States also afflicts our nation-state enemies.

Lacking a clearly articulated DOD position on present and future enemies and their capabilities, I am going to offer my own analysis of that enemy. This analysis is of course unclassified but is based on more than twenty-five years in operational and intelligence billets, where I focused on this range of enemies in preparing myself and my marines for potential conflict.

I will start my analysis of potential enemies with these 2GW opponents. They are not a genuine threat to our existence, but they still must be dealt with. Although we need to maintain forces to deal with them, we cannot let their presence drive our defense planning. They represent the past. We have to figure out how to fight future enemies.

### *Second- and Third-Generation Opponents*

*North Korea*

At the top of the usual post–Cold War list, North Korea is cited as a dangerous opponent with huge armed forces—and thus justifies large U.S. heavy forces. The North Korean army is, in fact, large. However, it has no supporting air force or navy to speak of, and limited training due to the desperate economic conditions in North Korea. North Korea is a nation with a marginally functioning Third World economy and a severely decayed infrastructure. It cannot feed its people, can barely feed its army, and is experiencing daily defections to the south and economic refugee movement to China.

Even if North Korea chooses to attack, it will have to attack through the most difficult terrain facing any major army in the world today. Attacking along the restrictive, mountainous routes between North and South Korea, the North Koreans will face numerous river and stream crossings.

If they make it across the rivers, they will face the incredible urban density of greater Seoul. Historically, urban terrain has severely restricted and slowed the movement of an army. Greater Seoul is more intensely built up than any urban area ever attacked. More than 10 million people are crammed into the narrow area between Inchon and the mountains to the east.

To understand the problem this presents to an enemy, consider the Seoul traffic on an average, peacetime holiday weekend. On those days, it can take ten hours to drive thirty miles across Seoul—simply because the roads are completely congested with civilian vehicles. Imagine the congestion that will result when millions of South Koreans try to flee an invasion amid thousand of rounds of impacting high-explosive and chemical rockets. Virtually all routes through the city will be completely blocked by abandoned vehicles. Those not blocked by wrecked vehicles can be easily blocked by defending forces, simply by positioning some of the thousands of buses and heavy trucks that are an integral part of Seoul's daily traffic problems. Obviously, attacking through one of the densest urban areas in the world against a first-class defending army will be incredibly difficult, if not impossible.

Thus, the enemy we use to justify large conventional forces faces virtually insurmountable obstacles to an invasion of the south. In addition to the incredible natural and manmade obstacles blocking the invasion routes, the inherent and growing weakness of the North's economy and government create even more problems for Northern aspirations.

In contrast, South Korea has an economy that dwarfs North Korea's, a military that is better trained and equipped, a First World infrastructure, and a population twice the size of North Korea's. Further, the south's population is healthy, educated, and has a vested interest in the country's success. In short, the strategic situation has completely reversed from 1950, when North Korea was the industrial half of the peninsula, with a large, robust, well-trained and -equipped army and South Korea was a poor, agrarian nation with a minimal constabulary for a military.

A final aspect often overlooked in considering Korea's defense is the impact South Korea's wealth will have on the soldiers and officers of the

North Korean army. Since birth, these men have been fed lies about the wonders of their "people's paradise" and how it is their obligation to "free" their oppressed brothers in the south. How will they react as they begin to move through the villages, then cities that lie north of Seoul? They will see the vast wealth of the south.

Although they may not recognize the VCRs, TVs, and computers (as it is unlikely that they have ever seen them), they will see that every home has cabinets stocked with food, warm clothing, soft bedding, even running water. They will know they are not "liberating" their southern brothers. Although we cannot gauge the impact on men from such a closed society, we can be certain it will create major discipline problems for the support troops moving up behind the forces in contact.

In early 2003, North Korea declared that they were restarting their nuclear program, and U.S. sources have since stated that they believe North Korea has nuclear weapons. Although this certainly changes the strategic situation on the Korean peninsula and in all of northwest Asia, it does not justify the retention of significant conventional forces. In fact, it makes our conventional forces less relevant than before.

Even before they developed nuclear weapons, North Korea could cause massive damage to South Korea in a surprise attack. They possess thousands of tube and rocket artillery pieces ready to rain tons of high-explosive and chemical munitions on Seoul. We can do nothing to stop this initial barrage.

However, even with their nuclear weapons, they cannot sustain an attack much beyond the initial spasm. The combination of terrain, congestion, a large, first-rate South Korean military, and the weakness of North Korean forces will stop the invasion long before they conquer the country. The threat North Korea poses can't honestly justify the maintenance of heavy forces in either our active or reserve organizations.

### *Iran*

A second potential enemy often used to justify the maintenance of large conventional forces is Iran. Yet Iran is not a reason to do so. First, the majority of young Iranians are disgusted with the current fundamentalist regime and yearn for greater contact with the outside world. The fundamentalist and progressive elements are engaged in an ongoing struggle. Demographics and technology are on the side of the progressives. The majority of Iranians are too young to remember the depredations of the Shah, but they are all acutely conscious of the daily deprivations they face due to the corruption and incompetence of the religious regime. They can access the Internet to see the vast differences between their freedoms and those of the West. Inevitably, the regime will have to moderate or fall.

In the meantime, Iran provides no reason for the United States to maintain large conventional forces. The only conventional threat Iran poses is to the flow of oil thorough the Straits of Hormuz and to the oil kingdoms of the Gulf. To prevent Iran from blocking the Straits requires only that we maintain the power projection capability to seize the islands in the Straits and deny Iran the use of the port of Bandar Abbas—at the curve in the Straits. From observing Iranian exercises, we know that they plan to use Bandar Abbas as a primary base to attack shipping with cruise missiles, missile boats, small craft, submarines, and even Ski-Doos.

If we maintain sufficient conventional naval forces to neutralize Bandar Abbas and defeat any attempts to close the Straits of Hormuz, we can prevail against Iran's 2GW and 3GW forces.

Iran's other threat is to the oil kingdoms of the Gulf. Protecting the oil kingdoms from a conventional Iranian invasion requires only that we maintain forces sufficient to protect the Gulf states from air attack or ground invasion via Kuwait.

### *China*

Unfortunately, the lack of genuine threat from Korea or Iran and the passing of the threat from Iraq has not discouraged those who envision a large, *JV 2020*, high-tech military. They will simply point to what they say is the real threat to the United States: the emerging peer competitor. Usually, this means China. Yet if we examine the problem, it is clear that, for now, China is focused on being a regional power. China is primarily a threat to Taiwan but also shows a distinct interest in controlling the seas and political entities around it. We must then ask ourselves two questions. One, what does China threaten that we are willing to fight for? Two, if we fight China, how do we do it?

The first has been answered by our treaty obligations and this administration. We will stand by our allies. Thus, we have to be prepared to prevent China from projecting power against Taiwan, Japan, the Philippines, and the vital shipping lanes of Southeast Asia.

The second question then becomes, How do we do so? First, we must heed President Eisenhower's warning and not engage in a land war on the mainland of Asia. This remains a sound caution. No nation since the Manchurians in the 1600s has fared well in a war on the mainland of China. If we accept Eisenhower's guidance, then the defense of our interests in Asia is primarily an air and sea defense problem. Our force structure for this theater should be based on denying China the ability to project power overseas rather than on defeating China on its mainland.

In fact, the Chinese are a genuine threat and are seeking to modernize. They are moving away from Mao's purely defensive concept based on the mass of the People's Liberation Army (PLA) to an armed force more capable of taking offensive action in support of external goals. They are modernizing their air, sea, missile, and ground forces.

Starting with ground forces, they are manning and equipping six mobile divisions for 3GW. Departing from their past reliance on massed manpower, these new formations will serve as "fist" divisions in what is clearly a 3GW concept. This is actually good news for us. As long as we refuse to fight on the mainland, these expensive new divisions have no effect on us. They simply consume Chinese resources purchasing and maintaining thousands of tanks, artillery pieces, and armored personnel carriers.

In contrast, modernizing their navy, air, and missile forces increases China's threat to the surrounding nations. But China will lack genuine power projection capability for the foreseeable future. Their current efforts appear more targeted at anti-access and area-denial efforts to keep U.S. forces at a distance. Obviously, powerful elements of the PLA remain wedded to 2GW and 3GW forces. At the same time, other elements of the PLA are exploring how to deal with the United States using 4GW techniques to overcome China's inferiority in high-technology conventional warfare.

For our part, we should never plan to fight her on the mainland, so we should not study China as a conventional enemy but as a 4GW enemy. We must understand how China plans to use 4GW to neutralize the power of the United States and ensure that we are prepared to defend against such attacks. This is the real key to defense against China. We will examine that in the next section, when we consider the entire range of potential 4GW enemies.

*Unforeseen Enemies*

The final conventional threat we must consider is the rise of an unforeseen enemy. The rise of just such an unforeseen enemy is often used to justify modernizing the forces we have today—without changing their basic nature. However, if history is any guide, new powers rise by employing the new generation of war rather than by attempting to overcome the current powers' huge lead in the older generation of war. After seeing the devastating effect of U.S. power in Desert Storm, Kosovo, Afghanistan, and Operation Iraqi Freedom, why would any new competitor decide to fight the United States on a conventional battlefield?

Further reinforcing the shift away from conventional war is our exceptionally poor record in unconventional conflicts, such as Vietnam, Lebanon, Somalia, Iraq, and Afghanistan. Although we must be prepared for the rise of a new power, we should be looking for a 4GW enemy, not one that uses older generations of war.

This analysis of the 2GW and 3GW capabilities of our potential enemies shows they are not a serious threat to U.S. interests. They can cause damage but will inevitably be defeated.

### *Fourth-Generation Opponents*

Obviously more challenging are potential 4GW enemies. Historically, it has been the emerging generation of war that has hurt the dominant power of the time. After all, it became dominant by mastering the previous generation of war.

Today, we face two types of 4GW enemies. The first is an insurgent movement using 4GW to seize control of a territory. The second is a nation that is using 4GW techniques and alliances to neutralize the power of the United States. Although the first, in the form of al-Qaeda, has drawn most of our attention and is a distinct threat to the well-being of American citizens around the world, it is not a genuine threat to the existence of our country. The second is. We will examine the threat presented by an insurgent first and then examine the more deadly threat presented by a nation-state using 4GW.

*Insurgents*

This book has described the evolution of insurgency over time to the form it currently takes: that of the transnational organization. One of the best summaries of this type of enemy is a recent description of al-Qaeda. This description could apply to a number of emerging insurgent enemies, from narco-traffickers to religious groups—and of course, still applies to today's insurgent groups:

> Al Qaeda's infrastructure has proved very hard to detect and combat, not least because law enforcement agencies lack the experience to respond effectively to the threat it poses or to counter its influence among Muslim communities. Al Qaeda is also characterized by a broad-based ideology, a novel structure, a robust capacity for regeneration and very diverse membership that cuts across ethnic, class and national boundaries. It is neither a single group nor a coalition of groups: it comprised a core base or bases in Afghanistan, satellite terrorist cells worldwide, a conglomerate of Islamist political parties, and other largely independent terrorist groups that it draws on for offensive actions and other responsibilities. Leaders of all of the above are co-opted as and when necessary to serve as an integral part of Al Qaeda's high command, which is run via a vertical leadership structure that provides strategic direction and tactical support to its horizontal network of compartmentalized cells and associate organizations.[2]

This is the insurgent enemy we must fight. It will be comprised of a network of groups—most with legitimate grievances. It will be idea-based rather than territorially based. The ideology will be clearly expressed as a vision by the senior leadership of the network. This vision will serve as the commander's intent for subordinate elements, guide the network's day-to-day operations, and provide the operational-level linkage to the various groups' tactical actions. The leaders will have to communicate only when they wish to designate specific targets or control specific operations.

As a result, the leaders will be difficult to target and, even when targeted, difficult to destroy. Although the destruction of al-Qaeda's Afghan bases and the capture of many of their senior leaders has hurt them badly, the organization is reestablishing itself in Afghanistan, Pakistan, Iraq, Sudan, and a half dozen other places in the world. It is highly unlikely they will make the mistake of creating distinctive, easily targeted military bases again. A 4GW enemy is resilient and resistant to the traditional concept of pure attrition.

Further, a 4GW enemy is difficult to decapitate—precisely because the leadership is a network. In Afghanistan, we saw it was virtually impossible to decapitate either the Taliban or al-Qaeda using our air power. Because the enemy always learns from each battle, we have to assume it will be even more difficult in the future to use air power to decapitate him. Instead, we must be prepared for the long-term, close in fight necessary to destroy a network.

In addition to networking its core leadership and primary operational forces, such an enemy will make extensive use of networked mass organizations—political, economic, social, and charitable. Mao set the standard for this and has been emulated by every successful insurgent since.

Although al-Qaeda is a prototype of the stateless insurgent enemy we will face, we should not think they will be the last. Many developing nations harbor great resentment toward America,particularly Arab-Islamic states. This resentment will remain as long as America is perceived to be supporting both oppressive Arab regimes and Israel. While we do this, we provide a perfect scapegoat for the failure of Islamic dreams, and we must accept that hatred will continue to spawn anti-American networks. We have already seen such groups in Indonesia, the Philippines, Thailand, and Pakistan.

It is also inevitable that diverse groups around the world will be left behind as the world progresses to an Information-Age economy. These groups will provide recruits for those who claim America is the cause of their failure and must be punished.

Thus, we can expect the rise of other networked enemies. We have seen that such an enemy can draw on significant resources, from legitimate businesses and charities to illegal activities ranging from petty theft to the international drug cartels. Given these resources and the hatred fueling these enemies, we know they will eventually obtain a weapon of mass destruction.

This first type of 4GW enemy, the insurgent, will be unpredictable and capable of causing great destruction and death—even within the United States. It will require great resources, effort, and time to protect ourselves from the worst of their attacks. It is essentially impossible to provide complete protection against this type of enemy. However, it cannot challenge America's existence or our leading position in the world.

*China*

The second type of 4GW enemy we will face is the nation that makes use of a wide network of alliances and 4GW techniques to neutralize the power of the United States. They, too, have been studying the results of the last fifty years of war. They know they cannot challenge U.S. conventional forces in a 3GW fight. They have seen what happens to those who try.

Just as certainly, they have seen the successes 4GW opponents have had against the United States and our allies. They will seek to apply those observations in any conflict with the United States. They can be dangerous to America's position—in particular, they can degrade our influence and economic power in various parts of the world.

China is clearly our most dangerous opponent in this arena. It has shown a remarkable, consistent, long-range strategy of making allies of our enemies. It has provided assistance with building long-range rockets and weapons of mass destruction to Iran, Iraq, and North Korea. Beyond supporting our enemies, China is also careful to support anyone who opposes its other potential enemies. For instance, it has supported India's primary enemy, Pakistan, in developing both a rocket program and a nuclear weapons program.

China has shown it is prepared to protect its interests in western China, both by suppressing internal opposition and by helping insurgents in surrounding nations. Finally, China takes a 4GW approach to the sanctity of international boundaries. It observes them only when this helps strategically but ignores them if they offer an impediment.

To deal with China, we must understand how China sees the future of warfare. Fortunately, the Chinese have published an unofficial strategy assessment by two colonels, Qiao Liang and Wang Xiangsui, which outlines how China could fight the United States. In their book, *Unrestricted Warfare,* they propose that China must use all means—military and non-military—to prevail in a war with the United States: according to the authors, unrestricted warfare will include such diverse tactics as employing computer hackers to attack military and government systems. It also features an increased emphasis on urban guerrilla warfare. Another new tactic is the use of financial terrorism.

Although this book is not official Chinese policy, its publication by senior officers in a nation where individual thought is not encouraged certainly indicates that the senior leadership is at least considering such an approach to war.

The pattern of China's alliances, combined with this book, reveals a nation that does not want a direct confrontation with the United States but seeks to have enough allies and 4GW weapons to discourage any use of U.S. power in what China considers its sphere of influence. It also shows that China does not envision a war with America as a second- or third-generation struggle. They do not seek conventional superiority. Rather, they seek ways to use a network of alliances and human ingenuity to overcome the U.S. lead in technology. They are considering not only information attacks but also purely economic attacks. These may take a wide variety of forms, all designed to avoid the conventional strength embodied in our armed forces.

Imagine the economic impact on the United States if a series of containers blew up in our ports, necessitating one hundred percent inspection of arriving container freight and the ships that carry it. We have seen that interruptions due to stevedore strikes on our West Coast can cost hundreds of millions, even billions of dollars per day in economic activity lost from America's seven trillion dollar economy. Whether China conducts a false flag operation or funds terrorists to conduct such an attack, the result is the same. We have no one to retaliate against militarily, despite suffering huge economic damage.

Or consider the major disruption to our economy and lifestyles if hoof-and-mouth or mad-cow disease were intentionally introduced into our livestock herds. Such an attack could be blamed on the Animal Liberation Front (ALF). Although it would involve killing many cattle, the statement "claiming" responsibility could rationalize that the end result would be a collapse of the U.S. cattle industry, which will save millions of other animals. Given the loose network that makes up ALF, even ALF itself might not be able to determine if its members conducted the attack. As Qiao and Wang state in *Unrestricted Warfare,* the Chinese see these as legitimate avenues of attack.

China can use a number of 4GW avenues to attack the United States—or, more likely, to neutralize our power in what they consider their sphere of influence by threatening such attacks. At the same time, they can limit our ability to concentrate power by ensuring that our enemies throughout the world obtain more advanced weapons that require us to maintain forces in those regions. This is a more sophisticated approach than the Soviet Union's use of proxies. The Soviets attempted to control the proxies. The Chinese simply provide them resources to use for whatever goals the proxies devise. China is engaging her allies in a fashion more resembling that of a venture capitalist than the vertical, bureaucratic approach the Soviet Union used.

Finally, the Chinese see the utility of attacks on our information systems. They know they don't have to destroy our forces—they have to destroy only the links between them. They will not restrict this to purely military attacks or on software only. They will seek out and attack the critical civilian infrastructure that carries a large portion of our logistic and administrative data. They are already analyzing our networks, to detect critical nodes that can cause the most disruption to both military and economic targets.

One additional concern is that much of the software that runs critical infrastructure in this country is starting to be written in China, India, and other foreign countries.

These, then, are the enemies we face. First are the 2GW and 3GW enemies. They are slowly learning to use 4GW techniques, but they still rely primarily on earlier-generation forces for war. They are essentially holdovers and are not serious threats to our security. In short, our current and potential 2GW and 3GW enemies are eminently containable—or, if not, defeatable.

Next are the two varieties of 4GW enemy: the insurgent/terrorist movement and the nation that is moving rapidly to 4GW. These 4GW players are the genuine threats to U.S. security and are the standard against which we must organize our forces. The key to defending against these enemies is to structure our forces for the fight we are likely to face rather than the one postulated in DOD documents.

Finally, we might have to face the 1GW and 2GW contestants involved in brutal civil wars over who will rule a given territory. The forces we restructure to deal with a 4GW enemy can easily defeat these enemies.

### *Reorganizing for the Future*

Our current forces, even with significant reduction in size, can deal with existing and projected 2GW and 3GW enemies and the minor warlords. However, although we have sufficient forces, they are not optimally configured even for such earlier-generation enemies.

Any 2GW or 3GW fight will be overseas, and we will want to win quickly. We know that early-arriving U.S. forces are the key to minimizing damage to our allies and to rapid defeat of the enemy. Unfortunately, we lack the sea- and airlift to rapidly deploy our current heavy forces overseas—and there is no indication future budgets will provide that lift. Both sea- and airlift are expensive, long-lead-time items.

Therefore, we need to make changes to our forces in several areas.

Currently the U.S. Army has ten divisions (six heavy, two light, one airborne, and one air assault). The Marine Corps has three divisions. The Army National Guard has eight divisions, plus fifteen enhanced separate brigades (more than five division equivalents) and three strategic brigades. We needed only nine U.S. divisions (five heavy, two Marine, one airborne, and one air assault) and one and a half European divisions to smash the Iraqi army in 1990. We needed only three U.S. divisions and one British to smash Iraq in 2002. One has to wonder why we need twenty-six divisions structured for conventional war today.

In fact, we don't. We have too many heavy ground forces and way too many heavy reserve forces for any foreseeable fight. Yet we are frequently short of the flexible, multi-mission-capable, medium-weight forces we need for forward presence, quick response, nation building, and peacekeeping or peace enforcement missions. In fact, we face a critical shortage of such forces today in Iraq and Afghanistan. Further, our current ground forces contribute little to homeland security functions.

Our air forces are also still organized to fight an enemy that no longer exists. They were planned, built, and organized to face a Soviet-style threat that has gone away. We now have too many air superiority fighters and too few transports, tankers, intelligence aircraft, bombers, and special-mission aircraft.

Given what has happened since the collapse of the Soviet Union and the current enemies we face, one could argue that all pure air-superiority aircraft are excess. In essence, the air force is a victim of its own success. Potential enemies have seen the incredible qualitative lead the United States has and simply do not fly against us. Yet the F-22, a single-mission aircraft, remains the air force's highest priority and biggest procurement project.

The navy has not only too few ships but a distinctly unbalanced fleet. Current and potential threats all emphasize anti-access weapons, such as mines, submarines, and anti-ship missiles. Yet the navy has virtually ignored the mine problem and long neglected anti-submarine warfare. The new "Transformation Planning Guidance" directs DOD to specifically address the anti-access issue, but that requirement has been emphasized in many previous documents. To date, the naval services have continued to neglect the issue.

We have to reorganize our forces both to face the few remaining 2GW and 3GW enemies and to more effectively fight the numerous 4GW enemies we are engaged with now.

First, I need to define what I mean by "medium-weight forces". Although this book is too short to get into the details, some characteristics can be defined. Organizationally, they must be capable of the following:

- engaging in not just joint but interagency operations. This makes lean headquarters a priority, to ensure clear coordination and prevent overwhelming the representatives from the other federal agencies essential in 4GW. The other agencies run with small staffs. In domestic operations, DOD simply overwhelms them with people. Our current joint staffs are huge—and inefficient. We must analyze what is really needed to fight a networked, mission-oriented force and get rid of the excess staff overhead.
- fighting a 2GW or 3GW enemy and winning. Accordingly, they must be able to fight a conventional enemy in any terrain as well as in urban areas. This does not require large numbers of tanks. It does require a balanced force capable of fighting on the mechanized battlefield.
- arriving in theater rapidly. Given the requirement for forces sufficient to defeat 3GW armor forces, the rapid deployment requirement probably means a prepositioned force. Maritime prepositioning has proven highly successful for the naval forces and allows the Marine Corps to put the equivalent of a heavy division ashore within two weeks of arriving at a port. However, we cannot simply preposition a heavy division on ships. Our current heavy divisions are perhaps the most fearsome organization ever created to fight a conventional fight in the open. Unfortunately, they are enormously expensive and provide little capability in a conventional fight in either urban or restrictive terrain. In a 4GW fight, their massive firepower is largely irrelevant. Army prepositioned forces must be similar to those of the Marine Corps.
- possessing the large infantry and military police units necessary, after the conventional fight is over, to secure and pacify both heavily populated areas and remote areas. These units must have protected mobility—vehicles that can survive roadside bombs and

mines—to move them from point to point. However, they will actually operate on foot.

• dealing with 4GW enemies. To do so, they must be intelligence-driven forces—with the emphasis on HUMINT and cultural intelligence rather than technical intelligence. These forces must be networked, flexible, and able to operate on mission orders with sound commander's guidance.

• including significant numbers of civil affairs personnel and be comfortable operating as part of an interagency task force, not just a joint one. They must be capable of operating in hostile environments and of dealing with a wide variety of cultures.

In short, we need a toolkit to build the forces for specific missions. A highly effective model, and the one I am most familiar with, is the Marine Air-Ground Task Force (MAGTF). Scalable from a few hundred to more than a hundred thousand men, the MAGTF is a combination of air, ground, logistics, and command and control elements that routinely train together for operations across the spectrum of war.

The largest MAGTF, the Marine Expeditionary Force, has succeeded in operations as varied as the high-tempo, large-scale Desert Storm and Operation Iraqi Freedom to humanitarian operations in Somalia, which involved stabilizing the security situation, stopping the hunger, and turning control over to the United Nations.

The intermediate-sized MAGTF, the Marine Expeditionary Brigade, has succeeded in operations as far-flung as those against the Taliban in Afghanistan to humanitarian operations in Bangladesh. The smallest, the Marine Expeditionary Unit, is routinely committed to non-combat as well as combat operations. At the time of this writing, a MEF is in Iraq and a MEU is in Afghanistan.

What makes these forces effective is a common ethos, common doctrine, integrated training, and flexible organization. For high-intensity war, the MEF fields hundreds of strike aircraft, battalions of tanks, and regiments of mechanized infantry and artillery supported by mobile, self-protecting logistics elements. For operations like Somalia, it can provide thousands of dismounted troops per regiment, to saturate the streets supported by engineering and logistics elements. These elements are capable of supporting the non-governmental organizations that provide relief to the population.

However, the MEF is not a complete or ideal force for 4GW. Although it is a good starting place, it is not the complete answer. Fourth-generation warfare forces will also require:

- staff members trained in interagency processes and procedures as well as liaison officers from the wide variety of federal and commercial organizations essential to running an effective government and society.
- robust, effective intelligence units—particularly HUMINT organizations that can coordinate with other federal agencies and the local authorities or organizations of the country they are in. These units should be trained to understand and analyze a wide range networks rather than build intelligence on military units.
- numerous military police units trained in the full spectrum of police operations, from community-type policing to full-scale combat military police operations.
- civil affairs units that can both teach and do. They must be able to deal with all the critical functions in a modern society. They have to be capable of establishing the functions of civil government and then transition to supporting the personnel from other government agencies who will conduct the complete reconstruction of the nation we are supporting.
- infantry units capable of operating as small units to patrol, outpost, and finally to live with and advise counterpart units of an indigenous force. This is along the model of the Marine Combined Action Platoons (CAPS) or the Army Military Advisory Teams (MATs). Both forces provided U.S. advisors to the Vietnamese local security forces. In both cases, the villagers, when properly led, successfully defended their villages against guerrilla forces. Even though the villagers' equipment was often inferior to that of the guerrillas, they succeeded by combining their local knowledge with

the superior tactical skill and firepower of the U.S. advisors. Although this is a primary mission for Special Forces A Teams, we cannot field sufficient numbers of A teams to cover an entire country. Our medium-weight forces must be capable of producing the much larger number of advisory teams or CAPs needed to defeat a 4GW enemy.

• significantly increasing the Special Operations Forces (Delta Force, SEALs, etc.) as well as the U.S. Army Special Forces (Green Berets).

Operationally, we need to understand 4GW networks. This will require a reorientation of our basic planning and execution concepts. We need to become intelligence driven. Even tougher, we have to focus on the human networks, cultural intelligence, and very long timelines characteristic of 4GW. Rather than focusing our technology on finding forces that look like us, we require major increases in HUMINT collection and analysis capability. We have the best information technology in the world, but unfortunately, we have focused it on finding conventional forces. We need to harness that same creativity and scientific prowess to understanding and defeating the human networks at the core of 4GW.

We must use old-fashioned HUMINT, supported by new, Information-Age tools and the science of network theory to develop an ability to recognize, analyze, and understand the networks arrayed against us. Only when we truly understand them can we know which nodes to attack and how to either destroy them or use them for our purposes.

Unfortunately, our HUMINT programs are currently broken. We need a complete reexamination of the requirements to grow effective HUMINT operators and how they build effective HUMINT systems. We must then ensure that their personnel systems are set up to reward those activities rather than remaining rooted in the bureaucratic policies of the past.

Once we fix the personnel policies that are crippling our HUMINT efforts, we need to make efforts to improve the technology we use in this field. Although not nearly as glamorous or expensive as space-based systems and common tactical picture systems, some simple computerized tools can improve our HUMINT analysis by orders of magnitude.

DOD has been employing a limited number of these systems in various operations around the world. They need to become part of every operational battalion that may find itself in a 4GW conflict. These systems are available and already in use by both DOD for overseas targets and civilian police agencies to track domestic gang activity. These are inexpensive, effective tools for analyzing and understanding the networks we must fight.

The technology emphasis must shift from speed of targeting to supplementing the human skills essential in understanding the 4GW enemy: language, area studies, social network analysis, history, and so on. Given the inherent robustness of a networked enemy, we know that only after we understand his network can we target it effectively. There will also be nodes we do not want to destroy but rather exploit.

We need to dramatically rethink our forces at the operational level. We need to ensure that they are relevant to the threat, expeditionary enough to get them there, and effective upon arrival. All these attributes are achievable with the current number of personnel, but we have to change the organization, equipment, and mindset of the forces. Although we will retain some heavy forces, they can no longer consume the majority, or even a major portion, of our resources.

Tactically, we know that a 4GW enemy relies heavily on a network of minds. Through personal contact and planning, they create a common view of the battlefield and common understanding of their mission and the commander's intent. As execution time closes in, they require only minimal communication to succeed. Therefore, we must rely heavily on HUMINT and Special Operations forces for offense and ensure that our fixed facilities and larger units are serious about force protection measures.

However, this should not mean hunkering down and restricting all our personnel to post. That concedes the fight to the insurgent. Instead, through education, training, longer tours together, and use of 4GW techniques, we must move away from our current hierarchical organization and bind our forces together in the same kind of mental network that has made the insurgents successful. These more professional forces, supported by effective HUMINT, will be able to move out into the society we are "protecting," coordinate and work with local personnel, and dominate the areas we need to control.

This was the situation during the first phase of our operations in Somalia. Aggressive U.S. leadership made highly effective use of HUMINT, saturation patrolling, targeted propaganda, and frequent contact with the people and the rebuilt Somali police forces to control the streets of Mogadishu. Using the same approach, the 101st Airborne Division and the 1st Marine Division effectively controlled their assigned sectors in Iraq. The 1st Marine Division sector was so quiet that it was turned over to a mixed division of international forces, and the division was sent home. The 101st made their sector by far the quietest of the U.S. Army sectors in Iraq.

At the time of this writing, insurgent activity is increasing in the old 101st section. However, this may be more the inevitable impact of cutting the U.S. force presence in the area by two-thirds and not having a clearly articulated plan for Iraqi sovereignty rather than a lessening effectiveness of the tactics. Neither U.S. nor Iraqi government forces have a clear idea what will happen after the return of sovereighty scheduled for July 1. Nor do the insurgents, but they are stepping up operations in an attempt to ensure that whatever turnover is attempted does not go smoothly.

Similarly, the 1st Marine Division is facing significant challenges as it takes over Fallujah from the 82nd Airborne Division. Vicious attacks on civilians in Fallujah immediately after the arrival of the division brought pressure for a major shift in the marines' approach to pacification. Time will tell if the marines have the patience and the operational autonomy to continue with their approach to restoring security. For, despite these challenges, in 4GW the most effective "force protection" tactics have consistently been saturation patrolling and personal contact with the people.

These are the basic concepts for organizational, operational, and tactical changes to ensure that our forces are capable of dealing with the enemies we actually face in the world today . . . and for the foreseeable future.

### *Homeland Security*

At least until the Department of Homeland Security (DHS) is fully functioning, the Department of Defense (DOD) is going to have to take an active role in homeland security. For the foreseeable future, DHS will most likely need support in two areas: armed security and consequence management.

The first mission, armed security, will most likely consist of protecting critical infrastructure, searching containers and ships, and performing post-disaster security. For each mission, the National Guard is better suited than regular forces, for a number of reasons. First, although operating under Title 32, they do not require a waiver of Posse Comitatus or federal mobilization orders. Second, they serve in or near their hometowns, which makes them more effective as backup to local law enforcement. They know the area and often know the police officers they back up. Finally, they tend to be older, and we want older, calmer soldiers dealing with our own citizenry.

Unfortunately, most National Guard forces are poorly trained and equipped for these security missions. Armor, artillery, air defense, and engineer and logistics units are not the right kind of units for this mission. Even traditional infantry units are a poor substitute for well-trained military police units.

Fortunately, the recent initiative by Gen. Peter Schoomaker to convert National Guard armor and artillery battalions to military police battalions will go a long way to fill this gap. This reorganization replaces the heavy units, which have not been used in combat since World War II, with versatile MP units that are in high demand overseas and provide genuinely effective backup to civil authority in this country. The key question is whether the change will be permanent or seen as a temporary requirement to meet current operational needs.

The second area in which DOD should provide major support is consequence management—the action taken after either a natural disaster or a successful enemy attack. It focuses initially on rescuing victims, mitigating damage, and initiating restoration operations. Under our Constitution, the lowest level of government has initial responsibility for any disaster—whether a natural disaster or the result of a weapon of mass destruction. This is both a matter of law and a matter of practicality.

When local and state authorities are overwhelmed, they call on federal resources. The response has been a traditional National Guard mission. The guard is routinely called out to deal with floods, fires, and storms. Again their local knowledge, relationships, and physical location in the community make them effective at this mission.

However, 4GW has created a much greater challenge in homeland defense. Unfortunately, an attack with a weapon of mass destruction is now a high-probability event. The Department of Homeland Security and the FBI have repeatedly provided warnings that terrorists are attempting to obtain nuclear, biological, or chemical weapons. We have captured al-Qaeda videotapes of their experiments using some form of poison gas to kill dogs. It is almost inevitable that a terrorist will use a weapon of mass destruction on U.S. soil. The U.S. government even released an official statement on June 10, 2003, predicting such an attack within two years.

When disaster does strike, people will call 911. They will not call the federal government. Thus, the first responders to a WMD event will be from local government. Depending on the size of the community and the resources available through mutual aid, they may be able to handle major disasters without federal help. However, if a major biological, chemical, radiological, nuclear, or high-yield explosive (CBRNE) attack is conducted against Americans on our soil, first responders will need help immediately to save lives and minimize property damage.

Aum Shinrikyo, a fringe Japanese cult, failed in their repeated attempts to disseminate large quantities of anthrax in Tokyo, but they succeeded in delivering a small quantity of sarin nerve gas into the Tokyo subway system. Even though the attack was not executed according to plan, the results still overwhelmed the Tokyo fire department—one of the largest and best equipped in the world.

DOD already recognizes that its resources will be needed in various disasters. DOD regulation 3025.1, "Military Support to Civil Authorities," states that any commander has authority to commit federal troops at the request of local authorities to save lives and reduce property damage. But unfortunately, other than the Marine Corps Chemical Biological Incident Response Force (CBIRF) and the National Guard Civil Support Teams (CST), the Department of Defense does not have any forces trained or equipped to operate in the hazardous environment a WMD attack will create.

Although the CST teams are either planned or active in every state, the teams have only twenty-two members, so they cannot function as much more than a sophisticated detection element. They can be on scene quickly but cannot save many victims. In contrast, CBIRF has four hundred marines and sailors but is a single, battalion-sized organization based just south of Washington, D.C. It can deploy by ground in less than one hour, so it can be a valuable asset in the capital region. However, for more distant locations it must either drive for a long period or deploy by air.

Either way, the most critical aspect of rescue in a contaminated environment is time. This means that CBIRF's effectiveness is inversely proportional to its distance from the target. Currently, DOD has no other units that can provide downrange assistance to first responders. It has many units that provide reconnaissance, advice, and communication links (Guardian Brigade, Chemical Biological Rapid Response Team, Technical Escort Unit, and numerous others). These, however, are mostly headquarters units and duplicate the capabilities of major city HAZMAT squads.

Thus, for the two critical areas where local and state authorities will need help—armed security and consequence management—the Department of Defense is poorly organized to provide that help. Although the Department of Homeland Security may eventually grow into those missions, the threat is here today. With a budget of $450 billion, Americans should be able to count on DOD to help protect them against 4GW enemies in this country, and if that fails, assist in mitigating the loss of life and property damage.

As stated earlier, General Schoomaker's initiative to reorganize numerous battalions is a positive first step. In a similar vein, Lt. Gen. Stephen Blum, chief of the National Guard Bureau, has initiated a program to develop ten chemical, biological, radiological, nuclear, high-yield explosive (CBRNE) response units. These units will be stationed around the country and be available to respond to CBRNE events in support of local authorities.

Although current worldwide commitments have stretched the active, reserve, and guard units, the guard should be able to provide dedicated CBRNE response forces out of its eight divisions and eighteen separate brigades. Given the fast response times needed in CBRNE response and the inherent transportation delays in getting overseas, it would make more sense to make the CBRNE the primary mission and organize and train accordingly. Then if the forces are needed overseas, the transportation delay will provide time for them to train before they deploy.

After the initial mitigation and rescue efforts, communities will need a massive amount of help in a WMD event. This is a traditional National Guard role and should remain so. In fact, given the drastically changed nature of the threat, perhaps security and recovery operations inside CONUS (the continental United States) should be the guard's primary wartime role. The heavy brigades essential to war plans against the Soviet Union have no mission against the enemies we now face. They cannot mobilize in time to have an impact, and no enemy looming on the horizon will revert to the second- and third-generation warfare for which these forces are most suited. The guard needs to take an honest look at its capabilities versus its possible commitments and reorganize to face 4GW attacks on American soil and provide support for 4GW operations overseas.

Under my proposal, selected units would be reorganized as CBRNE response forces. The conversion of others to MP units would continue. Finally, the rest of the guard would be organized into the medium-weight forces described earlier. These elements would be capable of augmenting regular forces in a conventional fight and would be well tailored to the much more likely missions of nation building, peace enforcement, and peacekeeping against 4GW enemies.

### *Funding*

One critical question is how to fund the reorganization and re-equipping of the regular, reserve, and guard forces. Americans are obviously reluctant to spend even more on defense in a time of record deficits.

The answer is reapportionment rather than increase. The U.S. Army has already canceled the Crusader artillery program and the Comanche helicopter. These weapons had been designed to fight the Soviets and could not be justified against the new threats. In the same way, the F-22 is an enormously expensive program that has no justification. Although the air force and the contractor are scrambling to give it a bombing capability, this effort merely creates an extremely expensive but barely effective attack aircraft.

In the same light, the billions we are spending on missile defense make no sense. Although missile defense is a logical goal, spending billions on an essentially untried and poorly tested system isn't. We should keep developing the technology but not waste precious funds rushing it into "operation." We can use these funds to support our shift to fighting 4GW.

Other funds will become available simply because medium-weight forces cost less to purchase and less to operate than heavy forces. Tank battalions, in particular, consume huge budgets. The medium-weight units will cost significantly less to operate. In the same way, deactivating the single-mission air superiority squadrons will free up a great deal of money.

In summary, our current armed forces have more than sufficient budget and manpower to deal with the current threat and 4GW threats. However, they must be reorganized to fight the enemy as he is rather than remaining organized to fight the enemy of the past. DOD's cyberwar literature focuses on fighting a major conventional enemy because that is the only enemy its proposed high-technology, very expensive systems are effective against. Because DOD has so completely bought into the concept of cyberwar, it maintains our current force structure to fight that same mythical enemy. Even worse, DOD is shaping its future forces to fight that same high-technology enemy.

The Cold War has been over for more than a decade. The real war got our attention dramatically on September 11—after seven decades of evolution. It's time our forces got on with the business of organizing, training, and equipping to fight the enemy attacking us now rather than the enemy we'd like to fight.

## CHAPTER 17

# The Future Is Flexibility

Once we have fixed our personnel system, then analyzed the enemies we face and organized our forces to deal with them, the third pillar of DOD's reorientation to 4GW must be flexibility. We must ensure that the forces we field can deal with the unexpected.

Although we have a good historical map of the evolution of 4GW, history also shows us that by the time one generation of warfare reaches maturity, the next is already developing. It cautions us that warfare is always full of surprises. Given the long interval since the inception of the fourth generation, we have to assume another generation is evolving and that 4GW still has surprises for us. We also have to accept that there is no turning back. The reigning powers have tried to stop change since nobility outlawed the longbow. It has never worked. War, like all human endeavors, is constantly changing. It is imperative that we anticipate change by building flexibility into our forces.

A further challenge is the accelerating rate of change. Although change is constant, the rate of change is not. It has been accelerating almost exponentially. We can see that acceleration in the rate of development and adoption of new thoughts, processes, and technologies in all areas of human endeavor. It took decades for electric power to penetrate to the far reaches of America but less than twenty years for the personal computer and less than ten years for the Internet to spread to the same regions. Instant messaging took less than five years.

In warfare, it took centuries to change from medieval warfare to 1GW but only decades to reach 2GW. Each new generation of war has developed and been disseminated in less time than the previous generation. We have to assume this trend will continue and prepare accordingly. We have to assume fifth-generation warfare is out there.

In fact, we may have seen the first of 5GW in the anthrax and ricin attacks on Capitol Hill. To date, neither has been solved. Apparently a small group, perhaps even an individual, decided to take on the power of the United States. They did so with an attack that was impossible to trace but that caused significant disruptions in the business of governing this country. No one, probably not even the perpetrators of the attack, could predict it would shut down multiple post offices and huge office buildings for months, but that has not gone unnoticed.

As stated in Chapter 15, the key to preparing for the future is to select and promote intelligent, innovative people and ensure that they are free to experiment and fail—provided they learn from those failures. We have seen that changes in warfare are evolutionary. They are driven by practical men seeking new ideas to solve operational and technical problems. They have never been top-down driven by "innovation cells." Nor have they been driven purely by technological superiority. The French proved conclusively that access to next-generation technology does not mean a nation is ready to fight in that generation.

All previous generations show that the key component to learning to fight in the next generation is practical operators who are also highly educated in warfare (not the same thing as technological education or simple tactical training). Further, these people must be provided an environment that encourages questioning dogma and rewards innovation. This reinforces the fact that the number one requirement to prepare U.S. forces for 4GW is reform of our personnel system. Only by creating a system that educates thoroughly, keeps people in operational billets, stimulates and rewards creativity, and rigorously tests competence can we develop the leaders needed not just to deal with the seventy-year-old phenomenon of 4GW but also to deal with 5GW as it evolves.

### *Networking*

Fortunately, the personnel and organization needed to create and man a 4GW force are inherently flexible. It is essential that we build such an organization, in which people are free to explore, experiment, and understand. Even more important, they must be free to share that understanding through the network rather than by passing everything through a vertical bureaucracy. This freedom to communicate via the Internet with minimal concern for organizational lines is essential to getting the most out of a 4GW organization.

When given solid commander's guidance and the freedom to use network tools, a creative member of a 4GW organization can literally tap the world for information, ideas, and techniques that apply to his or her mission. He or she can keep up with rapid changes—not just the technology but the ideas and the drive that make the technology effective.

All this can be done at minimal additional cost. Once we reform our personnel system and consistently train in a free-play environment, the marginal cost to develop a networked organization is insignificant. We have already paid for the personnel, their training and education, the hardware, the software, and the network. The only thing keeping us from reaping the tremendous benefits is our bureaucratic requirement that all contacts pass through vertical channels until they reach the "approved" level for moving across bureaucratic boundaries.

Freedom to communicate laterally based on commander's intent is the fundamental key to converting today's hierarchical organization into tomorrow's flexible, networked organization. Such freedom is antithetical to a vertical organization such as the Department of Defense (or to any other large bureaucracy). Yet when guided by commander's intent and a coherent vision of the organization goals, it is an incredibly powerful force multiplier.

This is not a new phenomenon. Nor is it a mystery how to build it. Many military units in the past have achieved it. Certain elements are essential: a forward-thinking commander who provides clear, understandable, actionable guidance; aggressive, well-trained subordinates who have a network of trust; freedom at all levels to take initiative (even to deviate from the plan) as long as it conforms with the commander's overall intent; hard, realistic unit training that ensures those who can thrive in the chaos of war are in leadership positions; and enough time together to learn how each member of the team will react in a crisis.

Units such as the 7th Panzer Division in France in 1940 and the 1st Marine Division at Chosin in 1950 established networked organizations—and did so with primitive radio systems. Often, only brief orders could be transmitted. In 7th Panzer's drive across France, complete changes in missions and objectives were transmitted in single sentences over weak and broken radio transmissions. Similarly, in 1st Marine Division's breakout, its battalions often had only tenuous communications, yet the division conducted a coordinated, effective fighting withdrawal that destroyed enemy formations many times its size.

This was possible through the mutual trust and understanding that came from living, training, and fighting together. This closeness meant that all understood the overall intent and worked toward that goal. The result was that when they faced entirely new situations—one an opportunity to exploit an exceptional success and the other to redeem a huge failure—both organizations had the inherent flexibility of mind and organization to immediately adapt to the new situation and continue the fight.

The Internet and its instantaneous, virtually free worldwide communications provides a much greater opportunity than the primitive radio systems of the 1940s and 1950s. These existing paths can allow our vertical organizations to maximize their networking potential while still maintaining the focus on the mission provided by commander's intent.

To understand how wide the reach of a networked organization is, consider what the Marine Corps Chemical Biological Incident Response Force (CBIRF) has accomplished. CBIRF is a single, battalion-sized organization with no special communications equipment and no special screening required to join the unit. It has marines and sailors assigned by the same system that mans infantry battalions, along with the normal email connectivity of a garrison unit. Yet by communicating with a network of contacts using connectivity provided by the Marine Corps network tied to the Internet, CBIRF has progressed way beyond where it could be if restrained to communicating only with other Marine Corps or DOD assets. It can serve as an example of how an organization that is fundamentally hierarchical in nature can take advantage of the power of networks to more effectively execute its mission.

It is not a coincidence that CBIRF is a truly 4GW organization. Its genesis was Aum Shinrikyo's 1996 attack on the Tokyo subway using nerve agent—a 4GW attack. After the attack, the commandant of the Marine Corps, Gen. Charles Krulak, saw that the Tokyo fire department was overwhelmed by the casualties from this primitive chemical attack. Recognizing that U.S. local emergency service organizations would also be overwhelmed and have to turn to the federal government, General Krulak formed CBIRF to provide immediate assistance to civil authorities in the event of a chemical or biological attack on the civilian population.

This unit is a recognition that 4GW opponents will use weapons of mass destruction against our civil population and that part of defending our country includes mitigating the effects of such an attack. CBIRF, by the nature of its mission, is focused on a 4GW enemy. It is not designed to respond to conventional military attacks on military targets but to the unconventional, WMD attacks that are an inevitable next step in 4GW.

Further, because it is the only unit in the Department of Defense with the mission of entering a contaminated environment to conduct rescue of personnel, CBIRF was forced to go outside normal DOD channels to learn what tactics, equipment, and techniques it required to succeed in this alien environment. Military units specialize in dealing with war chemicals and nuclear attacks. Yet a threat analysis showed that the most immediate threat to American civilians were toxic industrial chemicals and materials (TICs and TIMs). These are agents that only a select few DOD crash fire rescue personnel routinely deal with. As a result, CBIRF personnel had to make contact with a wide range of experts outside normal DOD channels.

Obviously, they needed to talk to the first responders (fire, EMS, and police) who routinely deal with hazardous material spills. They also needed to talk to the bomb squads who deal with improvised explosive devices and with heavy-rescue experts who deal with collapsed structures. At the same time, they had to develop and enhance their professional skills in their core areas of detection, decontamination, and emergency medicine. Finally, they had to devise entirely new techniques for their mission, such as controlling large numbers of rescuers working in small teams and making rapid entry and search of a contaminated area.

They developed contacts through professional associations, consequence management conferences, and military contacts. The use of email and the Internet allowed CBIRF personnel to build on those contacts. Through them, CBIRF could track a wide variety of advances in the diverse fields required to conduct rescues in a contaminated environment. Given the freedom to explore and learn as long as they took guidance from the commandant's mission statement and commander's guidance, CBIRF's area experts could share information daily through these networks.

The result is, CBIRF has become a node that connects military and civilian areas of expertise in response to chemical, biological, radiological nuclear, and high-yield explosive (CBRNE) events. The skills needed are widely varied, and each tends to be handled by a different part of the response community. CBIRF, a single unit, integrated and mastered a variety of skills, including civilian response to toxic industrial chemicals, medical treatment of CBRNE casualties, heavy rescue in a contaminated environment, neutralization of chemical and biological improvised explosive devices, military support for civil authorities, and elements of research, development, and manufacturing. All these skills are essential in preparing to respond to a WMD attack on a civilian population. CBIRF reached out worldwide to learn what it needed to become effective.

For instance, CBIRF's explosives technicians had to learn about improvised explosive devices, with a particular emphasis on those that can be used to disseminate a chemical or biological agent. To expand on their Marine Corps training, they reached out to civilian and other specialist military organizations to learn about improvised explosive devices the others were encountering. From this network of contacts, the CBIRF explosives team established a quarterly seminar on chemical and biological improvised explosive devices. It draws some of the top experts from local, state, and federal bomb squads to share their knowledge through lectures and hands-on training on firing ranges.

Further, because it is a seminar of professionals sharing, there is no requirement to hire instructors. The network has become self-reinforcing. Once they have attended the class, the students join the net of WMD explosives teams. They pass information directly to each other rather than via their painfully slow bureaucratic and disconnected hierarchies. Each professional has access to different knowledge by virtue of his geographic location and the organization he works for.

Traditionally, information availability has varied, based on a person's level in his organization. Now, the network established during the seminars moves the knowledge to all levels simultaneously. No one has to wait while the meetings/classes/discussions are approved by various layers of bureaucracy. The people who have to deal with the problem are in direct contact with each other. Yet each continues to operate within the guidelines provided by his supervisor. By focusing on the mission and required interaction rather than the bureaucratic process, they have achieved more than any individual bomb squad could possibly have achieved.

In a similar fashion, the medical team at CBIRF reaches out to both the civilian and military medical communities. On the military side, they can learn from the experts about the medical effects of military chemical, biological, and nuclear attacks. From their civilian first-responder contacts, they can learn how civilian agencies have responded and will respond to toxic industrial chemicals and radiological accidents. They have a unique view of the gaps between the military and civilian organizations that will hamper medical response to a WMD incident.

For instance, CBIRF's senior medical officer, while temporarily assigned in the Persian Gulf, used his free time and email to plan, coordinate, and establish a multi-nation study into the triage and treatment of patients in a chemically contaminated environment. No detailed study has been conducted on this subject since World War II, despite the fact that emergency medical protocols and drugs have changed completely since then. The study will also investigate the drug interactions among common emergency room drugs and chemical weapons.

The initial contacts and planning were all conducted using the email systems we have already paid for. The work continues in an ongoing exchange of information flowing through a network, irrespective of vertical hierarchy. Of particular importance is that unclassified treatment knowledge can be shared across international boundaries. As in all Internet discussion groups, key players are quickly identified, so the best people in various fields can meet in this neutral environment to exchange information on how to best save lives.

In addition to the exchange of information in a wide variety of fields, the contacts established by allowing cross-agency communications resulted in the establishment of a technology evaluation board. This allows manufacturers to meet users and buyers of equipment from a wide variety of federal, state, and local agencies, to determine their equipment needs and improve the manufacturers' designs.

From this and similar organizations, such as the InterAgency Board and the Technical Support Working Group*, a coalition of the willing has emerged that is driving improvements in first-responder equipment. Using email and lateral contacts, they have built a network that is bypassing much of the bureaucracy that delays action. CBIRF acts as only one node in a network of truly expert first responders and those who support them. This network is changing how America will respond to CBRNE attacks. In fact, for the first time, personal protective equipment is being tested against both military and toxic industrial chemicals.

These simple examples show how current, widely available tools can drastically change how a unit learns and develops. Yet most units do not use

*The InterAgency Board was developed by leading fire and emergency service organizations around the country to improve the quality of personal protective equipment available to first responders. The Technical Support Working Group is an organization run by the Department of State and Department of Defense to seek improvements in protection against WMD.

them well, due to the bureaucratic restrictions on communicating outside the command. Unfortunately, until we fix our current personnel selection and promotion system, such freedom will remain the exception rather than the norm. However, once we fix our personnel system and genuinely understand the function of commander's intent and guidance, we can free the incredible creativity of our people to attack their specific areas of expertise.

Of particular importance is the removal of barriers between military and civilian bureaucracies. Fourth-generation warfare does not function within clear bureaucratic boundaries—it thrives on the seams between the various governmental security organizations. Only by erasing those boundaries using human ingenuity and networking can we match the networked, creative enemies we face.

Each technical specialty in CBIRF is using the networked world to seek the best possible solutions to the real tactical problems they face in conducting rescue operations in a contaminated environment. I am convinced every marine, soldier, sailor, and airman would love to be free to communicate and innovate. Imagine the incentive to find the best possible solutions if all officers and NCOs knew they would be evaluated in free-play exercises. Rather than waiting for information to come to them through the stovepipes of our current bureaucracy, they would actively seek out information on tactics, techniques, and procedures that others had found effective in free-play exercises.

We have not begun to exploit the ability to discover, test, and disseminate the new ideas and techniques we need to win in 4GW. By introducing free play to stimulate the inherent competitive spirit of Americans and dropping artificial bureaucratic boundaries between our people, we can rapidly find and disseminate the techniques that work!

We might as well accept, encourage, and guide this activity. It is going on whether we like it or not. Trying to stop the adoption of cross-compartment communication is as hopeless as outlawing the longbow. Instead, let's encourage it and reward it. Confident, competent commanders focused on building units that can win will allow us to exploit the technology we have already paid a fortune for and that is currently producing at only a fraction of its potential.

### *Education*

A second critical step in maintaining the flexibility of our forces is to ensure that education of our officers goes beyond the technology of weapons systems and the "hard" sciences. In keeping with successful innovators of the past, our officers must immerse themselves in both history and the evolving sciences that seek to understand the shape of society in the future.

This does not mean the narrow study of a specific technical specialty. It means trying to understand complex human organizations and how they function. This is an entirely new area for DOD and will require aggressive, creative exploration of how to educate our people in these new scientific disciplines. Fortunately, DOD already knows what constitutes a well-rounded education in history—we simply have to start rewarding those who pursue that path rather than punishing them for missing time preparing PowerPoint briefs on a joint staff.

Historical study is an essential part of becoming an effective decision maker. It complements and reinforces force-on-force exercises, by building the experience base essential to effective combat decision making. Even more important, it provides a frame of reference to understand the complex, lengthy conflicts we are engaged in today. We should not punish those who pursue it as an advanced degree.

This is another critical reason for reducing the huge size of the joint combatant command and service staffs. Our people need time to pursue education. It must be made as important a criterion for promotion as a joint tour is now. Because a career has only so many years, the only place we can carve out the time for such education is by reducing the number of years spent on these high-level staffs. The only way to do this is to drastically reduce the number and size of those staffs.

There will still be plenty of staffs to provide officers with a single joint tour. They need that to understand how joint staffs work. However, they do not need multiple joint tours at the expense of developing professional expertise in their warfighting areas and obtaining true education in the complexities of modern society and systems.

The next aspect of developing flexibility is more challenging: identifying sciences that help us understand where the world may be moving. In the same way the science of the day supported each new generation of warfare, we must make today's science support our efforts to understand 4GW, its networks, and its successors. Two new areas of scientific exploration, chaos/complexity and network theory, seek to understand the complex systems and networks that characterize political, economic, social, and technical structures today. They can be of genuine help in understanding a 4GW enemy.

Unfortunately, our current thrust toward transformation is based on different sciences. Rather than studying complex systems as a whole, we stress the individual elements of each system. We think that by tracking those individual elements, we can build a common operational picture that allows us a godlike view of the fight. We have stated that the advances in networks and sensors mean our information will be so perfect that we can defy history and control centrally. It is based on the concept that we can gather information, pass it up the chain of command, process it, decide on a course of action, and transmit it to the forces—before the situation changes.

Although some of our literature claims we are pushing decision making down, the failure to change how we evaluate and promote personnel means the systems will simply be used to continue the centralization that is an inherent part of the Department of Defense. This is the antithesis of 3GW and is seventy years behind 4GW.

We must reject the concept of seeking certainty and instead focus on dealing with the uncertainty that is inevitable in the real world. Rather than seeking certainty, we must seek understanding of patterns and how expert decision makers use those patterns in recognitional decision making. Despite our current career paths and methodical approaches to decisions, warfare is an arena for experts, not amateurs. We must revise our personnel system to ensure that we develop those experts; then we need to turn to sciences that can help them deal with the uncertainty, complexity, and chaos they will face as an inherent part of human conflict.

### *Chaos*

The first new science we need to study is chaos theory, or complexity. It is a relatively new scientific concept—one that supports a Clausewitzean view of war. It flatly refutes *JV 2020*. Chaos theory states that complex systems are sensitive to input, particularly the initial conditions. Even minor changes in input can result in massive changes in the output of those systems. Popularly summarized as the "butterfly effect," it postulates that a butterfly flapping its wings in China (a minuscule input) may result in a thunderstorm in Washington, D.C., rather than the anticipated clear, dry weather (a huge change in output).

Some students of the theory hope that eventually we will develop the mathematical models to predict the outcomes of chaotic systems. Currently, the best we can do is predict the future for short intervals—and only in the simplest nonlinear systems. Certainly we cannot begin to model the complexity of war. The problem is that such a model will not work until we can identify and quantify all inputs. Given that any small input may make a huge change in output, it is highly unlikely we can measure every input to be sure of the output.

To realize the difficulty of such a task, consider our "butterfly" model. To predict the weather with absolute precision in Washington, we would have to monitor every butterfly, sparrow, hornet, and other winged creature in China. Further, we would also have to determine when to measure the "initial" conditions. Unfortunately, because time is continuous we cannot even be certain we have picked precisely the right time to measure initial conditions. Is it any wonder our meteorologists still get surprised?

Chaos theory recognizes Clausewitz's view of war as an incredibly complex system and therefore basically chaotic. Military professionals must understand and accept this. Although chaos may be a new science, history and common sense certainly make it intuitive. The entire concept of "for want of a nail a kingdom was lost" is based on the historical experience that minor occurrences (changes in initial conditions) can have a major impact on the outcome of a battle and even a war.

Many who favor technology as the solution to future war state that history no longer applies. They feel that recent scientific advances mean historical lessons are no longer valid. Because these people write off history, the only way to convince them of the fundamental chaotic nature of war and the impossibility of perfect knowledge is the new sciences. It is incredibly important that the unpredictable nature of war be the starting point for any discussion concerning the future of war. Yet as demonstrated by "Transformation Planning Guidance," *JV 2020,* and "Network-Centric Warfare," many honest people feel that war can be precisely controlled. They sound much like the proponents of the "dot-com economy," who were adamant that technology had fundamentally changed the economy. Thus we must use science, history, current events, and common sense to ensure that we understand war's true nature.

If we understand that warfare remains chaotic, we will know we can never achieve a "perfect" view of the battlefield. Warfare will always be filled with fog, friction, and uncertainty. Its complexity ensures that no one commander can clearly understand even the material he is seeing, much less the millions of interactions his information display represents.

By accepting the science behind chaos, we will understand that no single commander can possibly deal with the complexity and uncertainty inherent in war. No one person has the capability and will to overcome all the uncertainty inherent in a complex system. We will cease trying to centralize decision making. We will understand that in attempting to centralize control and decisions, we actually end up centralizing uncertainty and friction.

Instead of centralization, we should use the tremendous potential of networked systems to ensure a common understanding of the commander's intent and his concept of operations. We should emphasize a system that increases flexibility rather than centralization. We should leave the decisions and initiative to the correct level: the lowest possible.

If we do, the commander can use his networks to disseminate his vision of the battle. He will ensure that his subordinates understand what he sees as the strengths and weaknesses of each side, how he intends to use his strengths to attack enemy weaknesses, and what he sees as the end state of the fight. The commander provides his subordinates with what he wants done and why. He leaves the how up to them.

With this understanding of what the commander is attempting to achieve and why he seeks to achieve it, each subordinate leader will be free to use his initiative to execute that concept—and to deal with the inevitable friction, uncertainty, and surprises characteristic of all operations. He will do so with the assistance of the powerful networking tools developed specifically to decentralize decision making.

*JV 2020*'s attempts to centralize decisions, using state-of-the-art common operational pictures, will inevitably lengthen decision cycles—in the same way France's centralized system in World War II slowed decision making until those decisions were irrelevant. A system of distributed decision making based on understanding commander's intent will truly improve the decision cycle. By reducing the amount of friction and fog each commander has to deal with, it increases the speed with which he can make decisions. This is the system that made 3GW warfare so effective. Much more important for 4GW and its long timelines, it can be made even more effective by using high-technology networking capabilities to increase the situational awareness of all levels—without trying to increase the control exercised by each level.

The key is to seek a better understanding of the underlying dynamics that drive a 4GW struggle. It is a war of ideas. The ability to share information will improve each level of command's understanding of those dynamics.

Just as important, an understanding of the nature and timelines of 4GW and commander's intent will ensure that subordinate commanders understand when speed of decision is not as important as understanding the situation. The long timelines of 4GW reduce the premium on speed, except for immediate tactical actions, and place a much higher premium on understanding.

The information revolution notwithstanding, war will continue to be nasty, brutish, and not subject to "rational" analysis. As a country, we must recognize the fundamental nature of war, develop concepts for fighting in that environment, and then develop the systems to support concepts for fighting.

The sequence is critical. If we base our concept of war on complexity and uncertainty, we will train and equip to deal with the fog and friction. Then, if we are extraordinarily lucky and have perfect knowledge, we are simply more effective. However, if we base our concept of war on perfect knowledge and then cannot attain that perfection in every fight, we will lose.

This is not a new problem. Prior to World War II, the French based their national defense on the methodical-battle concept. This concept employed top-down planning with centralized control that severely restricted the freedom of action of subordinate commanders. The Germans based their operational concept on the fact that war is essentially chaotic. They built a great deal of flexibility into their doctrine and their command and control theory. Thus their subordinate commanders were free to pursue the fleeting opportunities presented in the disorder—as long as their actions conformed with the commander's overall intent.

When the Germans chose to flank the Maginot line in 1940, the French centralized system was simply too slow to react. By the time they gathered information, passed it up the line, decided what to do, and passed the orders back down, the situation had changed so drastically that the plan had become irrelevant.

Centralization does not work with an unpredictable enemy. We must accept this lesson of history and science. We must organize, train, educate, and equip our forces to deal with uncertainty. Thus, the study of chaos and complexity must be an essential subject in the education of military personnel.

*Networks*

The second evolving science that should be critical to our concept of fighting a 4GW enemy is network theory, which studies how networks emerge, evolve, organize, and operate. It ranges from formal, planned networks, such as traffic systems or company information networks, to naturally occurring, emerging networks such as those that allow ants to find food and neighborhoods to function properly.

Given that our enemies are now operating as networks, this new science will provide some interesting insights. For instance, almost all human-designed networks that have been mapped have distinct power nodes. These are nodes in the network that have many times the average number of connections. On the Internet, these are sites such as Amazon, Google, and Yahoo.

These power nodes exist in natural networks too and are essential to the smooth operation of any network. Although the elimination of a single power node will not decrease the network's efficiency a great deal, the simultaneous elimination of multiple power nodes will break the network into much smaller segments—each isolated from the other. Each segment will suffer greatly from that lack of connectivity, and some nodes will be disconnected entirely. Consider the effect if Yahoo, Google, Excite, 411, and several other major search engines were destroyed simultaneously. Many users of the network would no longer be able to find key goods and services they routinely need.

Given that these power nodes exist in almost all networks, it is logical to assume they exist in terror networks too. We should be able to break terror networks into much smaller and less effective elements. However, we should not fool ourselves into believing key terrorist leaders will be traceable to one of those nodes. They have learned over the years that the more contacts they have, the greater the possibility of being found by authorities. Therefore, they will set up cutouts—less important members who provide their links to the network.

Although the key leaders will not be major nodes in the network, they will communicate directly with one or more of those key nodes. The combination of HUMINT and the analysis of information flow through the network will lead to a much greater understanding of the enemy—and potentially to their key leaders. Most important, it allows us to attack the network in an intelligent manner, in a way that will cripple it rather than simply force it to reorganize.

This brief discussion just scratches the surface of the new sciences that are seeking to understand how our complex world fits together. Many of these sciences strive to understand how highly complex societies function together. This is essentially the same problem 4GW and 5GW warriors must understand too. Military leaders of the future, and the professionals who support them, must understand the world in a much broader context than the relatively simple target-servicing models of 2GW and 3GW. The world cannot be reduced to certainty through technology. It will continue to produce complex, unpredictable, innovative people who seek to hurt the United States and our citizens.

### *Summary: Into the Fourth Generation*

In designing our new personnel system and operational forces, flexibility must be a central tenet. Only a highly flexible organization can hope to succeed in 4GW and still be prepared to deal with emerging 5GW or variations on earlier forms of war.

The world is organizing into webs for political, economic, social, and even technical purposes. With this evolution comes both opportunity and hazard for individuals, groups, businesses, and nations. It has provided great opportunities for individuals and businesses who recognized the changes and adapted to them. Even those companies that produce only industrial goods benefit when they change their basic organizational structure to take advantage of Information-Age tools. Those who have failed to adapt have suffered accordingly.

It is unreasonable to assume that a hierarchical, ponderous, bureaucratically organized armed force based on an industrial model is the right force to operate in today's information environment. We have to change—and not superficially, overlaying high-technology systems on the existing structure. We must change our underlying organizational concepts.

Our choices are starkly different. We can continue to man 3GW organizations using an 1890s personnel system and hope that by applying ever more capable high technology we can maintain our superiority. Or we can accept that 4GW has arrived and that 5GW is evolving and organize ourselves accordingly.

We know that only people create change in an organization. Although political, economic, social, and technical conditions must either be present or be created before change can be effective, only people actually shift an organization—particularly a huge bureaucracy such as DOD. Therefore, our primary step in preparing for 4GW warfare is to reform our personnel system to one that selects and grooms those who can function effectively in the free-flowing, networked environment characteristic of this type of war.

The personnel we select must also be up to the challenge of confronting an organization reluctant to change and leading it to that change. We can successfully select such leaders only if we accept a need for 360-degree evaluation, free play, and extended time in operational units. Only personnel who thrive in such an environment will be the lifelong learners and adapters required to lead our forces through the inevitable and rapid changes facing us.

After we select such leaders, we must support them. Part of supporting this new generation of leaders is an honest examination of the potential enemies that threaten our nation. Once we have determined the enemies we are likely to fight rather than the enemies we wish to fight, we can reorganize our forces accordingly. We owe it to the new generation of leaders to cut 2GW forces that are excess to our defensive needs and restructure the rest of our forces to fight 4GW enemies. They have to have forces that can operate in the world as it exists.

Finally, we must genuinely be ready for the unexpected that is an inevitable part of our future. The unexpected is woven into every generation of war; it would be genuinely foolish to think we will be exempt. We have to build flexible organizations. The imperatives of running a centralized government mean we cannot totally abandon the hierarchical model, but we have to make it less bureaucratic. Personnel who thrive in a free-play environment will understand this. They will use the commander's intent as the coordinating guidance that frees their subordinates to use the networking tools we already provide. Such an organization, manned by properly selected personnel, will have the inherent flexibility to evolve as warfare evolves.

This is absolutely essential. Fourth-generation war has been around for more than seventy years; no doubt the fifth generation is evolving even as we attempt to deal with its predecessor. We may not recognize it as it evolves around us. Or we may look at several alternative futures and see each as fifth-generation war.

As mentioned earlier in this chapter, the anthrax and ricin attacks on Capitol Hill may be early examples of fifth-generation warfare. Although similar to fourth-generation attacks, they seem to have been conducted by an individual or, at most, a very small group. It is much too early to tell if these were fifth-generation attacks, but super-empowered individuals or small groups would be in keeping with several emerging global trends—the rise of biotechnology, the increased power of knowledge workers, and the changing nature of loyalties. Each of these trends increases the destructive potential of small groups and makes the Department of Defense's current structure less and less relevant. Previous generations of war have evolved from changes across the spectrum of society. It is essential that we remain alert to these changes and examine all aspects of them rather than the purely technological ones.

Super-empowered individuals are just one possible form of future war. Yet the very fact these new attacks took place reinforces the requirement to look at actual conflicts rather than remain wedded to our own high-technology cyberwar vision of the future. In short, America needs to understand that war evolves rather than transforms. If the United States can develop a proper force to fight fourth-generation war, that force is more likely than our current defense establishment to have the intellectual and physical flexibility to recognize and adapt to fifth-generation war as 5GW evolves.

In closing, one final point needs to be made. Fourth-generation warfare is about sending messages to decision makers—usually via the mass of people that support them. Once we recognize this, it becomes a tremendous advantage for the United States. An effective message requires that the basic theme be compelling and that the people who are crafting and disseminating the message be articulate and sincere.

The fundamental message of the United States is the most powerful message ever crafted by mankind: we treasure the individual and provide an environment where every person can strive for his or her own dreams. Here, each person knows he can make a better life for his children. The millions of people clamoring to come to America prove this is a widely accepted and valued message. By making this fundamental belief an integral part of the message, we take advantage of the exceptional strength our open society has in a 4GW conflict. No society has ever had a more powerful message to share with the world.

It is up to us to harness that message and use it to win.

# END NOTES

**Chapter 1**

1 Shalikashvili, *Joint Vision 2010,* 1.

2 Director, Office of Force Transformation, "Network-Centric Warfare."

3 Department of Defense, "Transformation Planning Guidance," 9.

4 van Crevald, "Through the Glass Darkly."

**Chapter 2**

1 *Economist,* "Like Herrings in a Barrel," 13.

2 *Economist,* "Road to Riches," 11.

3 Ibid.

4 Catton, *Civil War,* 551.

**Chapter 3**

1 Mellenthin, *Panzer Battles,* 4–6.

2 Dupuy, *A Genius for War,* 177.

3 Ibid., 147.

4 Gudmundsson, *Stormtroop Tactics,* 47.

5 Dupuy, *A Genius for War,* 212–213.

6 Murray and Millett, *Military Innovation,* 19.

7 Ibid., 34.

**Chapter 4**

1 Friedman, *Lexus,* 111.

2 Ibid., 113.

**Chapter 5**

1 Ebrey, *Cambridge Illustrated History of China,* 266.

2 Ibid., 55.

3 Short, *Mao,* 222.

4 Ibid., 246.

5 Asprey, *War in the Shadows,* vol. 1, 349.

6 Mao, *On Protracted War,* 137.

7 Ibid., 77.

8 Ibid., 49.

9 Mao, *Yu Chi Chan,* 55.

**Chapter 6**

1 Summers, *On Strategy,* 83.

2 Sharp, *Strategy for Defeat,* 3.

3 Davis, "Politics and War," 50.

4 Hayden, "Revolutionary Warfare" 50.

5 Fall, *Ho Chi Minh,* 316.

6 Fall, *Viet-Nam Witness,* 31.

7 Ibid., 33.

8 Ibid., 37.

9 Fall, *Ho Chi Minh,* 346.

10 Ibid., 348.

11 Mao, *On Protracted War,* 54.

12 Fall, *Ho Chi Minh,* 217.

13 Ibid., 355.

14 Ibid., 316.

15 Ibid., 366.

16 Laurence, *Cat from Hue,* 335.
17 Shy and Collier, "Revolutionary Warfare," 856.
18 Mao, *Yu Chi Chan,* 44.

**Chapter 7**
1 Christian, *Nicaragua,* 33.
2 Ibid., 35.
3 Ibid., 35.
4 Ibid., 41.
5 Ibid., 44.
6 Nolan, "From FOCO to Insurrection," 72.
7 Waghelstein, "A Latin American Insurgency Status Report," 44.
8 Ibid., 45.

**Chapter 8**
1 Schiff and Ya'ari, *Intifada,* 109.
2 Ibid., 125.
3 Hiltermann, *Behind the Intifada,* 13.
4 Schiff and Ya'ari, *Intifada,* 78.
5 Ibid., 192.
6 Ibid., 193.
7 Ibid., 54.
8 "American-Israeli Cooperative Enterprise," Myths & Facts Online.
9 Schiff and Ya'ari, *Intifada,* 50.

**Chapter 9**
1 Moore, "Grind of War," 1.
2 *Economist, The,* Editors of. *Pocket World in Figures: 2002 Edition.*
3 Palestinian Central Bureau of Statistics, "Census 1997,"
www.pcbs.org/inside/f_pophos.htm.
4 Perlmutter, "Israeli-PLO Accord Is Dead," 61.
5 Morris, "Is Peace Dead?" 41.
6 Economist, "Land to Give and Take Away," 46–47.

7 Morris, "Is Peace Dead?" 42.

8 Ibid., 44.

**Chapter 10**

1 Bergen, *Holy War,* 50.

2 Gunaratna, *Inside Al Qaeda,* 21.

3 Ibid., 35.

4 Corera, *"Inside the Terror Network,"* 69.

5 Yusufzai, *"Conversation with Terror,"* 38–39.

6 Gunaratna, *Inside Al Qaeda,* 49.

**Chapter 11**

1 Ignatieff, "Nation-Building Lite," 26.

2 Lowe, "How Provincial Reconstruction Teams."

3 Bearden and Risen, *The Main Enemy,* 532.

**Chapter 12**

1 Clausewitz, *On War,* 88.

2 Chandrasekaran, "Attacks Force Retreat," 1.

3 Tripp, *History of Iraq,* 44.

**Chapter 13**

1 Cebrowski and Garstka, "Network-Centric Warfare," 32.

2 Soloway et al., "Hiding (and Seeking) Messages on the Web," 8.

3 Ibid., 8.

4 Middle East Media Research Institute, "Bin Laden Lieutenant."

**Chapter 15**

1 Presidential Decision Directive 56, *Managing Complex Contingency Operations,* 1.

**Chapter 16**

1 Department of Defense, "Transformation Planning Guidance," 3.

2 Gunaratna, *Inside Al Qaeda,* 54.

# REFERENCES


**Books**

Asprey, R. *War in the Shadows: The Guerilla in History.* 2 vols. Doubleday, Garden City, NJ; 1975.

Baclagon, U. *Lessons from HUK Campaign.* M. Colcol, Manila; 1956.

Bain, D. *Sitting in Darkness: Americans in the Philippines.* Houghton Mifflin, Boston; 1984.

Barabasi, A. *Linked: The New Science of Networks*, Perseus Publishing, Cambridge, MA; 2002.

Bateman, R. *Digital War.* Presidio Press, Novato, CA; 1999.

Baxter, J., and Downing, M., eds. *The BBC Reports on America, Its Allies and Enemies and the Counterattack on Terrorism.* Overlook Press, New York; 2002.

Bearden, M. and Risen, J. *The Main Enemy: The Inside Story of the CIA's Final Showdown with the KGB.* Random House, New York; 2003.

Beckett, F., and Pimlott, J. *Armed Forces and Modern Insurgency.* St. Martin's Press, New York; 1985.

Bell, J. *On Revolt: Strategies of National Liberation.* Harvard University Press, Cambridge, MA; 1976.

———. *The Secret Army: The IRA 1919–1979.* MIT Press, Cambridge, MA; 1979.

Bergen, P. *Holy War Inc.: Inside the Secret World of Osama bin Laden.* Free Press, New York; 2001.

Biddle, T. *Rhetoric and Reality in Air Warfare.* Princeton University Press, Princeton, NJ; 2002.

Binkin, M., and Record, J. *Where Does the Marine Corps Go from Here?* Brookings Institution, Washington, DC; 1976.

Blaufarb, D. *The Counterinsurgency Era: U.S. Doctrine and Performance, 1950 to the Present.* Free Press, New York; 1970.

Bradsher, H. *Afghanistan and the Soviet Union.* Duke Press Policy Studies, Durham, NC; 1983.

Braestrup, P. *Big Story.* Yale University Press, New Haven, CT; 1977.

———. *Vietnam as History: Ten Years after the Paris Peace Accords.* University Press of America, Washington, DC; 1984.

Bridgeland, F. *Jonas Savimbi: A Key to Africa.* Paragon House, New York; 1986.

Browne, M. *A New Face of War.* Bantam Books, New York; 1968.

Cabezas, O. *Fire from the Mountain: The Making of a Sandinista.* Plum Books, New York; 1986.

Cable, L. *Conflicting Myths: The Development of American Counterinsurgency Doctrine and the Vietnam War.* New York University Press, New York; 1986.

Carey, R., ed. *The New Intifada: Resisting Israel's Apartheid.* Verso, New York; 2001.

Carr, C. *The Lessons of Terror.* Random House, New York; 2002.

Carver, M. *War since 1945.* G. P. Putnam's Sons, New York; 1981.

Cash, J., Albright, J., and Sanstrum, A. *Seven Firefights in Vietnam,* Bantam Books, New York; 1970.

Catton, B. *Civil War.* Fairfax Press, New York; 1984.

Chaliand, G. ed. *Guerrilla Strategies: An Historical Anthology from the Long March to Afghanistan.* University of California Press, Berkeley, CA; 1982.

Christian, S. *Nicaragua: Revolution in the Family.* Vintage Books, New York; 1986.

Clark, W. *Waging Modern War.* Public Affairs, New York; 2001.

Clausewitz, C. *On War.* Edited and translated by M. Howard and P. Paret. Princeton University Press, Princeton, NJ; 1976.

Cooper, M. *The German Army: 1933–1945.* Kensington Publishing, New York; 1978.

Corera, G. "Inside the Terror Network." In *The BBC Reports on America, Its Allies and Enemies, and the Counterattack on Terrorism.* Overlook Press, New York; 2002.

Corson, W. *The Betrayal.* W. W. Norton, New York; 1968.

Crawford, O. *The Door Marked Malaya.* Rupert Hart-Davis, London; 1958.

Czerwinski, T. *Coping with the Bounds: Speculations on Nonlinearity in Military Affairs.* National Defense University, Washington, DC; 1998.

Dean, D. *The Air Force Role in Low Intensity Conflict.* Air University Press, Maxwell Air Force Base, Alabama; 1986.

———. *Low Intensity Conflict and Modern Technology.* Air University Press, Maxwell Air Force Base, Alabama; 1986.

Dobson, C., and Payne, R. *Counterattack: The West's Battle against Terrorists.* Facts on File, New York; 1982.

———. *The Terrorists, Their Weapons, Leaders and Tactics.* Facts on File, New York; 1982.

Don, T. V. *Our Endless War: Inside Vietnam.* Presidio Press, San Rafael, CA; 1978.

Dragnich, A. *Serbs and Croats.* Harcourt Brace Jovanovich, New York; 1994.

Dupree, L. *Afghanistan.* Princeton University Press, Princeton, NJ; 1980.

Dupuy, T. N. *A Genius for War: The German Army and General Staff, 1807–1945.* Hero Books, Fairfax, VA; 1984.

Ebrey, P. B. *The Cambridge Illustrated History of China.* Cambridge University Press, London; 1996.

*Economist, The,* Editors of. *Pocket World in Figures: 2002 Edition.* Profile Books, London; 2001.

Fall, B. *Ho Chi Minh: On Revolution: Selected Writings 1920–66.* Westview Press, Boulder, CO; 1984.

———. *Street Without Joy.* Schocken, New York; 1961.

———. *Viet-Nam Witness 1953–66.* Praeger, New York; 1966.

Farwell, B. *The Great Anglo-Boer War.* W. W. Norton, New York; 1990.

Fauriol, G., ed. *Latin American Insurgencies.* National Defense University Press, Washington, DC; 1985.

Friedman, N. *Terrorism, Afghanistan and the American Way of War.* Naval Institute Press, Annapolis, MD; 2003.

Friedman, T. *From Beirut to Jerusalem.* Anchor Books, New York; 1990.

———. *The Lexus and the Olive Tree.* Farrar, Straus & Giroux, New York; 2000.

———. *Longitudes and Attitudes: Exploring the World after September 11.* Farrar, Straus & Giroux, New York; 2002.

Fuller, J. F. C. *Armored Warfare.* Greenwood Press, Westwood, CT; 1983.

Gabriel, R. *Operation Peace for Galilee: The Israeli-PLO War in Lebanon.* Hill and Wang, New York; 1984.

Gall, C., and de Wall, T. *Chechnya: A Small Victorious War.* Pan Original, London; 1997.

———. *Chechnya: Calamity in the Caucasus.* New York University Press, New York; 1998.

Gettleman, M., ed. *Vietnam: History, Documents and Opinions on a Major World Crisis.* Fawcett Books, Greenwich, CT; 1965.

Giap, V. N. *People's War, People's Army.* Bantam Books, New York; 1968.

Gleick, J. *Chaos: Making a New Science.* Penguin Books, New York; 1987.

Gregor, A. *Crisis in the Philippines.* Ethics and Public Policy Center, Washington, DC; 1984.

Gudmundsson, B. *On Artillery.* Praeger, Westport, CT; 1993.

———. *Stormtroop Tactics: Innovation in the German Army, 1914–1918.* Praeger, New York; 1989.

Gunaratna, R. *Inside Al Qaeda: Global Network of Terror.* Columbia University Press, New York; 2002.

Gurr, T. *Why Men Rebel.* Princeton Press, Princeton, NJ; 1970.

Halberstam, D. *War in a Time of Peace.* Scribners, New York; 2001.

Hammel, E. *The Root: The Marines in Beirut, August 1982–February 1984.* Harcourt Brace Jovanovich, New York; 1985.

Hammond, F., ed. *The Anatomy of Communist Takeovers.* Yale University Press, New Haven, CT; 1971.

Hamzeh, Muna. *Refugees in Our Own Land.* Pluto Press, Sterling, VA; 2001.

Henderson, C. *Marine Sniper.* Stein and Day, New York; 1986.

Henderson, W. *Why the Vietcong Fought: A Study of Motivation and Combat in a Modern Army in Combat.* Greenwood Press, Westport, CT; 1979.

Herrington, S. *Peace with Honor? An American Reports on Vietnam, 1973–75.* Presidio Press, Novato, CA; 1983.

———. *Silence Was a Weapon.* Presidio Press, Novato, CA; 1982.

Hiltermann, J. R. *Behind the Intifada: Labor and Women's Movements in the Occupied Territories.* Princeton University Press, Princeton, NJ; 1991.

Horne, A. *A Savage War of Peace: Algeria 1954–1962.* Penguin Books, New York; 1977.

———. *To Lose a Battle: France 1940.* Penguin Books, New York; 1969.

James, L. *The Savage Wars: British Campaigns in Africa 1870–1920.* St. Martin's Press, New York; 1985.

Johnson, S. *Emergence: The Connected Lives of Ants, Brains, Cities and Software.* Touchstone, New York; 2001.

Jones, G. *Red Revolution: Inside the Philippine Guerrilla Movement.* Westview Press, Boulder, CO; 1989.

Kaplan, R. *The Coming Anarchy.* Vintage Books, New York; 2000.

———. *Balkan Ghosts: A Journey through History.* Vintage Books, New York; 1994.

———. *Soldiers of God.* Vintage Books, New York; 2001.

Karnow, S. *In Our Image: America's Empire in the Philippines.* Ballantine Books, New York; 1989.

———. *Mao and China: Inside China's Cultural Revolution.* Penguin Books, New York; 1982

———. *Vietnam: A History.* Penguin Books, New York; 1983.

Kerkvliet, B. *The Huk Rebellion: A Study of Peasant Revolt in the Philippine Islands.* University of California Press, Berkeley, CA; 1977.

Kirk, D. *Wider War: The Struggle for Cambodia, Thailand and Laos.* Praeger, New York; 1971.

Kitson, F. *Low Intensity Operations: Subversion, Insurgency & Peacekeeping.* Shoe String Press, Hamden, CT; 1971.

Komer, R. *Bureaucracy at War.* Westview Press, Boulder, CO; 1986.

Krejci, J. *Great Revolutions Compared: The Search for a Theory.* Wheatshelf Books, Brighton, England; 1983.

Krepinevich, A. *The Army and Vietnam.* Johns Hopkins University Press, Baltimore, MD; 1986.

LaFeber, W. *Inevitable Revolutions: The United States in Central America.* W. W. Norton, New York; 1983.

Langley, L. *The Banana Wars: U.S. Intervention in the Caribbean, 1898–1934.* University Press of Kentucky, Lexington, KY; 1984.

Laurence, J. *The Cat from Hue.* Public Affairs, New York; 2002.

Leonhard, Robert R. *The Principles of War for the Information Age.* Presidio Press, Novato, CA; 2000.

Lewis, B. *What Went Wrong? Western Impact and Middle Eastern Response.* Oxford University Press, New York; 2002.

Liddell Hart, B. H. *The German Generals Talk.* Quill, New York; 1979.

Macdonald, L. *1915: The Death of Innocence.* Henry Holt and Company, New York; 1993.

Maclear, M. *The Ten Thousand Day War: Vietnam 1945–1975.* Avon Books, New York; 1981.

Mangold, T., and Penycate, J. *The Tunnels of Cu Chi.* Random House, New York; 1985.

Mao Tse-Tung. *On Protracted War.* People's Publishing House, Peking; 1954.

———. *Yu Chi Chan [Guerrilla Warfare].* Translated by S. B. Griffith. Praeger, New York; 1961.

Martin, M. *Afghanistan: Inside a Rebel Stronghold.* Blandford Press, Dorset, England; 1984.

Marshall, S. L. A. *World War I.* American Heritage Press, New York; 1985.

McCarthy, M. *Vietnam.* Harcourt, Brace & World, New York; 1967.

Mellenthin, F. *Panzer Battles.* Ballantine Books, New York; 1980.

Meyerson, H. *Vinh Long.* Houghton Mifflin, Boston; 1970.

Millett, A. *Semper Fidelis: The History of the United States Marine Corps.* Macmillan, New York; 1980.

———. ed. *A Short History of the Vietnam War.* Indiana University Press, Bloomington, IN; 1978.

Millett, A., and Murray, W. *Military Effectiveness: The Second World War.* Allen & Unwin, Boston; 1988.

———. *Military Innovation in the Interwar Period.* Cambridge University Press, Cambridge, England; 1996.

Morowitz, H. *The Emergence of Everything: How the World Became Complex.* Oxford University Press, New York; 2002.

Murray, W. *Luftwaffe.* Nautical and Aviation Publishing Company of America, Baltimore, MD; 1989.

Nivat, A. *Chienne de Guerre.* Public Affairs, New York; 2002.

Pakenham, T., *The Boer War,* Random House, New York; 1979.

Palmer, B. *The 25-Year War: America's Military Role in Vietnam,* University Press of Kentucky, Lexington, KY; 1984.

Palmer, D. *Summons of the Trumpet.* Ballantine Books, New York; 1978.

Paret, P. *French Revolutionary Warfare from Indochina to Algeria: An Analysis of a Political and Military Doctrine.* Praeger, New York; 1964.

Peters, R. *Beyond Terror.* Stackpole Books, Mechanicville, PA; 2002.

———. *Fighting for the Future.* Stackpole Books, Mechanicville, PA; 1999.

Petersen, J. *The Road to 2015: Profiles of the Future.* Waite Group Press, Corte Madre, CA; 1994.

Petit, M. *Peacekeepers at War: A Marine's Account of the Beirut Catastrophe.* Faber & Faber, Boston; 1986.

Pratt, J. *Vietnam Voices: Perspectives on the War Years, 1941–1982.* Penguin Books, New York; 1984.

Qiao, L., and Wang, X. *Unrestricted Warfare: China's Master Plan to Destroy America.* NewsMax.com, West Palm Beach, FL; 2002.

Race, J. *War Comes to Long An.* University of California Press, Berkeley, CA; 1972.

Randal, J. *Going All the Way: Christian Warlords, Israeli Adventurers and the War in Lebanon.* Viking Press, New York; 1983.

Rashid, A. *Jihad: The Rise of Militant Islam in Central Asia.* Yale University Press, New Haven, CT; 2002.

Rejai, M., ed. *Mao Tse-Tung on Revolution and War.* Peter Smith, Gloucester, MA; 1976.

Rheingold, H. *Smart Mobs: The Next Social Revolution.* Perseus Publishing, New York; 2002.

Rifkin, J. *The End of Work: The Decline of the Global Labor Force and the Dawn of the Post-Market Era.* G. P. Putnam's Sons, New York; 1995.

Roy, O. *Islam and Resistance in Afghanistan.* Cambridge University Press, New York; 1985.

Schell, J. *The Village of Ben Suc.* Vintage Books, New York; 1967.

Schemmer, B. *The Raid.* Harper & Row, New York; 1976.

Schiff, Z., and Ya'ari, E. *Intifada: The Palestinian Uprising—Israel's Third Front.* Simon and Schuster, New York; 1989.

———. *Israel's Lebanon War.* Simon and Schuster, New York; 1984.

Sharp, U. *Strategy for Defeat: Vietnam in Retrospect.* Presidio Press, San Rafael, CA; 1978.

Short, P. *Mao: A Life.* Henry Holt, New York; 1999.

Shy, J. and Collier, T. "Revolutionary Warfare." In *Makers of Modern Strategy,* edited by Peter Paret, Princeton University Press, Princeton, NJ; 1986.

Skidmore, T., and Smith, P. *Modern Latin America.* Oxford University Press, New York; 1984.

Snepp, F. *Decent Interval.* Vintage Books, New York; 1978.

Snow, E. *The Long Revolution.* Random House, New York; 1971.

———. *Thunder out of China.* William Sloane Associates, New York; 1946.

Stanton, S. *Green Berets at War: U.S. Army Special Forces in Southeast Asia 1956–1975.* Presidio Press, Novato, CA; 1985.

Stern, J. *The Ultimate Terrorists.* Harvard University Press, Cambridge, MA; 1999.

Stolfi, R. *A Bias for Action: The German 7th Panzer Division in France & Russia 1940–1941*, Marine Corps Association, Quantico, VA; 1991.

Sullivan, J., ed. *Embassies under Seige: Personal Accounts by Diplomats on the Front Lines.* Brassey's, Washington, DC; 1995.

Summers, H. *On Strategy: A Critical Analysis of the Vietnam War.* Presidio Press, Novato, CA; 1982.

Talbott, J. *The War without a Name: France in Algeria.* Faber & Faber, London; 1980.

Taruc, L. *Born of the People.* International Publishers, New York; 1953.

Thayer, C. *Guerrilla.* Harper and Row, New York; 1963.

Thayer, T. *War without Fronts: The American Experience in Vietnam.* Westview Press, Boulder, CO; 1985.

Thompson, R. *Defeating Communist Insurgency: The Lessons of Malaya and Vietnam.* Praeger, New York; 1966.

Thompson, W., and Frizzell, D., eds. *The Lessons of Vietnam.* Crane, Russak & Company, New York; 1977.

Toffler, A. and H. *War and Anti-War.* Little, Brown & Company, Boston; 1993.

Toolis, K. *Rebel Hearts: Journeys within the IRA's Soul.* St. Martin's Press, New York; 1995.

Tripp, C. *A History of Iraq.* Cambridge University Press, New York; 2000.

Troung, N. T. *A Vietcong Memoir.* Harcourt Brace Jovanovich, New York; 1985.

Tuchman, B. *Stillwell and the American Experience in China 1911–1945.* Macmillan, New York; 1971.

Tyler, P. *A Great Wall.* Public Affairs, New York; 1989.

Urban, M. *Big Boys' Rules: The SAS and the Secret Struggle Against the IRA.* Faber & Faber, London; 1992.

van Crevald, M. *The Transformation of War.* Free Press, New York; 1991.

Vandergriff, D. *The Path to Victory: America's Army and the Revolution in Human Affairs.* Presidio Press, Novato, CA; 2002.

Walt, L. *Strange War, Strange Strategy.* Funk and Wagnalls, New York; 1972.

West, F. *The Village.* Harper & Row, New York; 1972.

Westmoreland, W. *A Soldier Reports*, Dell, New York; 1980.

Williams, P. *Al Qaeda.* Alpha Books, Upper Saddle River, NJ; 2002.

Wolfert, I. *American Guerrilla in the Philippines.* Bantam Books, New York; 1980.

Wright, R. *Sacred Rage.* Simon and Schuster, New York; 1986.

**Papers**

BDM Corporation. "Counterinsurgency Questionnaire and Collection Guide." BDM Corporation; August 5, 1985.

Benningsen, A. "The Soviet Union and Muslim Guerrilla Wars, 1920–1981: Lessons for Afghanistan." Rand Corporation; August 1981.

Blaufarb, D., and Tanham, K. "Fourteen Points: A Framework for the Analysis of Counterinsurgency." BDM Corporation; July 1981.

Cushman, J. "External Support of the Viet Cong: An Analysis and a Proposal." National War College, Washington, DC; undated.

Drew, D. "Rolling Thunder 1965: Anatomy of a Failure." Air University Press, Maxwell Air Force Base, Alabama; 1986.

Drummond, R. "The British Counterinsurgency Campaign in Malaya, 1948–60." Unpublished private paper, undated.

———. "Oman—The Dhofar Campaign, 1965–75." Unpublished private paper, undated.

Fukuyama, F. "The Future of the Soviet Role in Afghanistan: A Trip Report." Rand Corporation; September 1980.

Heymann, H., Jr., and Whitson, W. "Can and Should the U.S. Preserve a Military Capability for Revolutionary Conflict?" Rand Corporation; January 1972.

Hosmer, T., and Tanham, G. "Countering Covert Aggression." Rand Corporation; January 1986.

Jenkins, B. "The Five Stages of Urban Guerrilla Warfare: Challenge of the 1970s." Rand Corporation; 1970.

———. "Future Trends in International Terrorism." Rand Corporation; 1985.

Klymann, R. "The CAP: An Alternative Not Taken." Unpublished paper; undated.

Lentner, H. "Recent and Extended History and Present Policy: Applying Vietnam and Central America to Central America." Unpublished paper; 1986.

Millett, A. "Vietnam in Retrospect and the Era of Détente." Unpublished paper; undated.

Razali, M. "The Communist Insurgency War in Malaya, 1948–1960." Air Force Defense College, Malaysia; 1986.

Rosenberg, D. "Revolution and Counter-revolution in the Philippine Islands." Unpublished paper; 1985.

Rylander, R. "The United States Marine Corps and Low Intensity Conflict," Unpublished paper; November 1986.

Spiller, R. "Not War but Like War: The American Intervention in Lebanon." Combat Studies Institute, USACGSC; January 1981.

Sunderland, R. "Antiguerrilla Intelligence in Malaya, 1948–1960." Memorandum RM-4172-ISA, Rand Corporation; September 1964.

Waghelstein, J. "El Salvador: Observations and Experiences in Counterinsurgency." U.S. Army War College; 1985.

Watts, B. "Unreported History and Unit Effectiveness." Unpublished paper; undated.

Wolf, C., Jr. "Insurgency and Counterinsurgency: New Myths and Old Realities." Rand Corporation; undated.

———. "Small Wars: Some Possible Lessons for the U.S. Air Force." Rand Corporation; February 1967.

**Periodicals and Government Publications**

Admire, J. "Understanding Limited War." *Marine Corps Gazette,* January 1983.

Arbuckle,T. "Same Hardware, Same Tactics and Same Conditions." *Armed Forces Journal International,* December 1985.

Arquilla, J., and Ronfeldt, D. "Cyberwar Is Coming." *Comparative Strategy* 12 (November 1, 1993), 141–165.

Ashby, T. "Bear in the Backyard." *USNI Proceedings;* 113:4 (April 1987), 110.

Bevechen, A. "Clausewitz, Nonlinearity and the Predictability of War." *International Security* 17:3 (winter 1992–93), 59–90.

Cancian, M. "Future Conflict and the Lessons of Vietnam." *Marine Corps Gazette,* January 1983.

Cannon, M. "The Development of the American Theory of Limited War, 1945–1963." *Armed Forces and Society* 19:1 (fall 1992), 71–104.

Cebrowski, A., and Garstka, J. "Network-Centric Warfare." *U.S. Naval Institute Proceedings,* January 1998, 28–35.

Chandrasekaran, R. "Attacks Force Retreat from Wide-Ranging Plans for Iraq." *Washington Post,* December 28, 2003, 1.

Davis, R. D. "Politics and War: Twelve Fatal Decisions That Rendered Defeat in Vietnam." *Marine Corps Gazette,* July 1990, 50.

Dean, D. "The USAF in LIC: The Special Air Warfare Center." *Air University Review,* January–February 1985.

Department of Defense. "Transformation Planning Guidance." April 2003.

Diehl, J. "Sharon's Stealth Plan." *Washington Post,* July 22, 2002, A15.

Diehl, P. "International Alternatives to Traditional U.N. Peacekeeping: An Assessment of Regional and Multinational Options." *Armed Forces and Society* 19:2 (winter 1993), 209–230.

Director, Office of Force Transformation, Office of Secretary of Defense, "Network-Centric Warfare: Creating a Decisive Warfighting Advantage," Washington, D.C., winter, 2003.

Dye, D. "Keeping the Peace in Lebanon." *Marine Corps Gazette,* August 1983.

*Economist, The.* "Israel Intransigent." June 28, 1997, 17–18.

———. "Land to Give and Take Away." November 28, 1998, 46–47.

———. "Like Herrings in a Barrel." Millennium special edition, January 1, 1000–December 31, 1999, 13–14.

———. "The Road to Riches." Millennium special edition, January 1, 1000–December 31, 1999, 10–12.

Elliott, M. "The Next Wave." *Time* 159:25 (June 24, 2002), 24–27.

Fallow, J. "Vietnam: The Class War." *National Observer,* February 21, 1976.

Farrell, W. "Responding to Terrorism: What, Why & When." *Naval War College Review* 34:1 (January–February 1986).

Friedman, T. "Listening to the Future?" *New York Times,* May 5, 2002.

Gavin, J. "Uncomfortable Wars: Toward a New Paradigm." *Parameters,* 16:4.

Gray, C. "Thinking Asymmetrically in Times of Terror." *Parameters,* 32:2 (spring 2002) , 5–14. Gidron, M. "Bombs, Bullets, Ballots." *Tikkun,* July/August 1996, 4.

Hamilton, J. "Coup de Grace." *Field Artillery Journal,* January–February 1984.

Hamilton, J., and Kaplan, L. "Le Roi des Batailles: The Decisive Role of Artillery at Dien Bien Phu." *Field Artillery Journal,* March–April 1983.

Harrison, S. "Afghanistan Stalemate: Self-Determination and Soviet Force Withdrawal." *Parameters,* 14:4.

Hashim, A. "The World According to Usama bin Laden." *Naval War College Review,* 54:4 (autumn 2001), 11–35.

Hawkins, W. "What Not to Learn from Afghanistan." *Parameters,* 32:2 (summer 2002), 24–33.

Hayden, H. "Revolutionary Warfare: El Salvador and Vietnam—A Comparison." *Marine Corps Gazette,* July 1991, 50–64.

Heinl, R. "The American Occupation of Haiti." "*Marine Corps Gazette* (3-part series), November 1978, December 1978, January 1979." It is in three parts.

Hoagland, J. "Resigned to Separation." *Washington Post,* June 9, 2002, B7.

Holmes, M. "With the Horse Marines in Nicaragua." *Marine Corps Gazette,* February 1984.

Homer-Dixon, T. "On the Threshold: Environmental Changes as Causes of Acute Conflict." *International Security,* fall 1991, 76–116.

Huntington, S. "The Clash of Civilizations?" *Foreign Affairs,* summer 1993, 22–49.

Ignatieff, Michael. "Nation-Building Lite." *New York Times Magazine,* July 28, 2002, 26.

Kaplan, R. "The Coming Anarchy." *Atlantic Monthly,* February 1994, 44–76.

Keller, B. "The Fighting Next Time." *New York Times Magazine,* March 10, 2000, 32.

Lind, W.; Nightengale, K.; Schmitt, J.; Sutton, J.; and Wilson, G. I. "The Changing Face of War: Into the Fourth Generation." *Marine Corps Gazette,* October 1989, 22–26.

Livingstone, N. "Mastering the Low Frontier of Conflict." *Defense and Foreign Affairs,* December 1984.

Lowe, C. "How Provincial Reconstruction Teams and the New Regional Development Zones May Change the Status Quo in Afghanistan This Spring." www.weeklystandard.com/Content/Public/Articles/000/000/003/779algoq.asp.

Lustick, I. "Writing the Intifada: Collective Action in the Occupied Territories." *Air University Review,* December 1982.

Malhuret, C. "Report from Afghanistan." *Foreign Affairs,* 62:2 (winter 1983–84).

Mendelson, J. "MAGTF TACAIR in Joint Sustained Land Operations: USAF vs USMC." Unpublished paper, February 1985.

Middle East Research Institute (MEMRI). Special Dispatch—Jihad and Terrorism Studies: "Bin Laden Lieutenant Admits to September 11 and Explains Al-Qa'ida's Combat Doctrine." February 10, 2000, no. 344. http://memri.org/bin/articles.cgi?Page=archives&Area=sd&ID=SP34402.

Moore, J. "Global Order, Low-Intensity Conflict and a Strategy of Deterrence." *Naval War College Review,* 34:1 (January–February 1986).

Moore, M. "Grind of War Giving Life to Opponents of Sharon." *Washington Post,* August 3, 2002, 1.

Morris, N., "Is Peace Dead?" *Maclean's*, October 7, 1996, 41.

Mrozek, D. "The Limits of Innovation: Aspects of Air Power in Vietnam." *Air University Review,* 36:6 (September–October 1986), 58–71.

Nan, L. "Unrestricted Warfare and Chinese Military Strategy." *Straits Times* (Singapore), October 24, 2002.

Nelson, D. "Soviet Air Power: Tactics and Weapons Used in Afghanistan." *Air University Review,* 36:2 (January–February 1985) 30–44. .

Nolan, D. "From FOCO to Insurrection: Sandinista Strategies of Revolution." *Air University Review,* 37:5 (July–August 1986), 72.

Omestad, T., et al. "The Spiral of War in Jerusalem: Ramallah." *U.S. News and World Report,* 129:16 (October 23, 2000), 24–31.

Paschall, R. "Low-Intensity Conflict Doctrine: Who Needs It?" *Parameters,* 15:3.

———. "Marxist Counterinsurgencies." *Parameters,* 16:2.

Peretz, D. "Intifadeh: The Palestinian Uprising." *Foreign Affairs,* summer 1988, 964–981.

Perlmutter, A. "The Israeli-PLO Accord Is Dead." *Foreign Affairs,* May 1995, 59.

Peterson, S. "Why Terrorist Attacks Are Not Inevitable, Say Saudis." *Christian Science Monitor,* May 23, 2002.

Petraeus, D. "Lessons of History and Lessons of Vietnam." *Parameters,* 16:3.

Pike, D. "American-Vietnamese Relations." *Parameters,* 14:3.

Presidential Decision Directive 56 (PDD 56). *Managing Complex Contingency Operations.* White House, 1997.

Raspberry, W. "Refusal to Negotiate Won't Lead Us to Peace." *Washington Post,* August 3, 2002.

Ridderhof, P. "Combined Action and U.S. Marine Experiences in Vietnam, 1965–1971." Unpublished paper, undated.

Sanders, S. "The Threat from Mexico." *Conflict,* 7:1.

Sarkesian, S. "LIC: Concepts, Principles and Policy Guidelines." *Air University Review,* January–February 1985.

Shalikashvili, J. *Joint Vision 2010.* U.S. Government Printing Office, June 1996.

Shelton, H. H. *Joint Vision 2020.* U.S. Government Printing Office, June 2000.

Simpson, H. "The Commando d'Indochine: The 'Pirates' of the Tonkin Delta," *Army*, December 1986.

Smith, P. "Transnational Terrorism and the Al Qaeda Model: Confronting New Realities." *Parameters*, 32:3 (summer 2002, 33–46).

Smooha, S., and Peretz, D. "Israel's 1992 Knesset Elections: Are They Critical?" *Middle East Journal*, summer 1993, 444–464.

Soloway, C., et al. "Hiding (and Seeking) Messages on the Web." *Newsweek*, 139:24 (June 17, 2002), 8.

Summers, H. "War: Deter, Fight, Terminate. The Purpose of War Is a Better Peace." *Naval War College Review*, 34:1 (January–February 1986).

Tanter, R., and Midlarsky, M. "A Theory of Revolution." *Journal of Conflict Resolution*, 11:3 (September 1967), 264–280.

*Time*. "South Vietnam: A New Kind of War." October 22, 1965.

Urban, M. "Grey's Scouts in Rhodesia's Counterinsurgency." *Armor*, January–February 1984.

*U.S. News & World Report*. "Not a Panacea for All Our Problems." 101:18 (November 3, 1986).

———. "Special Forces: Can They Do the Job?" 101:18 (November 3, 1986).

van Crevald, M. "New Face of War Confounds Modern Leaders, Technology." *Defense News*, January 17–23, 1994, 19.

———. "Through the Glass Darkly." *Naval War College Review*, autumn 2000,

Vlahos, M. "Our March Upcountry." *Marine Corps Gazette*, December 1993, 20–31.

Waghelstein, J. "El Salvador and the Press: A Personal Account." *Parameters*, 15:3.

———. "Latin American Insurgency." *Military Review*, November 1991, 42–47.

———. "A Latin American Insurgency Status Report." *Military Review* 67:2 (February 1987), 72.

———. "Post Vietnam Counterinsurgency Doctrine." *Military Review*, 65:5 (May 1985).

Walters, R. "The Marine Officer and a Little War." *Marine Corps Gazette*, December 1986.

Wasielewski, P. "Sea Power and Counterinsurgency." *USNI Proceedings*, 112:12 (December 1986), 1006."

Wilson, G., "Tit-for-Tat in Vietnam Is What the Brass Hated." *Parameters,* 16:2.

Williams, C., and Lind, J. "Can We Afford a Revolution in Military Affairs?" *Breakthroughs*, spring 1999, 3–8.

Wright, J. "Terrorism: A Mode of Warfare." *Military Review*, October 1984.

Wurmser, M. "Israel on the Road to Peace: Accepting the Unacceptable." *Middle East Journal,* 51:3 (summer 1997), 446.

Young, E. "El Salvador: Communist Blueprint for Insurgency in Central America." *Conflict,* 5:4.

Yusufzai, R. "Conversation with Terror." *Time,* 153:1 (January 11, 1999), 38–39.

Web Sites

American-Israeli Cooperative Enterprise. *Myths & Facts Online: The Palestinian Uprisings.* www.us-israel.org/jsource/myths/mf19.html.

*The Guardian.* www.guardianunlimited.co.uk.

MidEast Web Maps: The Wye Redeployment. www.mideastweb.org/mredeply1.htm.

Palestinian Central Bureau of Statistics. "Census 1997" (November 1998). www.pcbs.org/inside/f_pophos.htm.

The Wye River Memorandum. www.mideastweb.org/mewye.htm.

# INDEX